MAYORS IN ACTION

WILEY SERIES IN URBAN RESEARCH

TERRY N. CLARK, EDITOR

Resources for Social Change: Race in the United States
James S. Coleman

City Classification Handbook: Methods and Applications
Brian J. L. Berry, Editor

Bonds of Pluralism: The Form and Substance of Urban Social Networks
Edward O. Laumann

Nonpartisan Elections and the Case for Party Politics
Willis D. Hawley

Politics and Poverty: Modernization and Response in Five Poor Neighborhoods
Stanley B. Greenberg

Education, Opportunity, and Social Inequality: Changing Prospects in Western Society
Raymond Boudon

Guerrillas in the Bureaucracy: The Community Planning Experiment in the United States
Martin L. Needleman and Carolyn Emerson Needleman

The Roots of Urban Discontent: Public Policy, Municipal Institutions, and the Ghetto
Peter H. Rossi, Richard A. Berk, and Bettye K. Eidson

Human Activity Patterns in the City: Things People Do in Time and in Space
F. Stuart Chapin, Jr.

Ethnicity in the United States: A Preliminary Reconnaissance
Andrew M. Greeley

Mayors in Action: Five Approaches to Urban Governance
John P. Kotter and Paul R. Lawrence

Leadership and Power in the Bos-Wash Megalopolis: Environment, Ecology, and Urban Organization
Delbert C. Miller

MAYORS IN ACTION

FIVE APPROACHES TO URBAN GOVERNANCE

John P. Kotter
Paul R. Lawrence

A WILEY-INTERSCIENCE PUBLICATION

JOHN WILEY & SONS, New York • London • Sydney • Toronto

Library of Congress Cataloging in Publication Data

Kotter, John P 1947–
Mayors in action.

(Wiley series in urban research)
"A Wiley-Interscience publication."
Bibliography: p. 275
1. Mayors—United States. 2. Mayors—United States —Case studies. I. Lawrence, Paul R., joint author. II. Title.

JS141.K67 352'.0083'0973 74-10790
ISBN 0-471-50540-4

Printed in the United States of America

10 9 8 7 6 5 4 3 2 1

THE WILEY SERIES IN URBAN RESEARCH

Cities, especially American cities, are attracting more public attention and scholarly concern than at perhaps any other time in history. Traditional structures have been seriously questioned and sweeping changes proposed; simultaneously, efforts are being made to penetrate the fundamental processes by which cities operate. This effort calls for marshaling knowledge from a number of substantive areas. Sociologists, political scientists, economists, geographers, planners, historians, anthropologists, and others have turned to urban questions; interdisciplinary projects involving scholars and activists are groping with fundamental issues.

The Wiley Series in Urban Research has been created to encourage the publication of works bearing on urban questions. It seeks to publish studies from different fields that help to illuminate urban processes. It is addressed to scholars as well as to planners, administrators, and others concerned with a more analytical understanding of things urban.

TERRY N. CLARK

ACKNOWLEDGMENTS

The research described in this book was funded entirely by the Division of Research at the Harvard Business School under the direction of Richard Walton. Without such support, this study would not have been possible.

A number of people have significantly aided our work at various stages of the research process. John Collins was particularly helpful in getting us started with the Phase I field work, as were Louis Lyons and the Nieman Fellows office at Harvard with the Phase II field work. Eric Butler accompanied us in our field interviews in one city and helped us with the analysis and interpretation of those data. Ray Bauer, Max Hall, Eric Neilson, Chris Argyris, and Jay Lorsch read parts or all of this manuscript and offered us very useful suggestions. Ron Tagiuri's thoughtful and detailed comments have, in particular, had a real impact on this book.

We owe a very special thanks to the over 200 people who were generous enough to grant us extensive interviews, the nine urban experts who responded to our initial questionnaire, and in particular, the mayors we studied in Phase I: Ivan Allen, Jr. in Atlanta, H. Roe Bartle in Kansas City, Erik Jonsson in Dallas, Richard Lee in New Haven, Ralph Locher in Cleveland, and Victor Schiro in New Orleans. These six men were always courteous, responsive even to our most awkward questions, and very generous with their time. It is to them in particular, as well as to all of those who are brave enough to seek the job of Mayor, that we dedicate this book.

JOHN P. KOTTER
PAUL R. LAWRENCE

Graduate School of Business Administration
Harvard University
Cambridge, Massachusetts
March 1974

CONTENTS

MAYORS IN ACTION

Now as never before, the American city has need for the personal qualities of strong democratic leadership. Given the difficulties and delays involved in administrative reorganization and institutional change, the best hope for the city on the short run lies in this powerful instrument. For most cities the mayor will have primary responsibility.

REPORT OF THE NATIONAL ADVISORY COMMISSION ON CIVIL DISORDERS, 1968, P. 298.

CHAPTER 1

INTRODUCTION

During the 1960s a great deal of attention was focused on our urban areas. An often perplexed public and its leaders tried to identify the problems of our cities and to determine what could be done about them. As one would expect, the role of the mayor became the subject of more and more discussion and controversy.

Although there was nearly universal agreement that the nation would benefit if we had "good" mayors, the debate over what a good mayor was raised more questions than it answered:

- Do honesty, hard work, and intelligence alone make a good mayor?
- What is "strong leadership"? Does it mean advocating programs, creating a consensus, getting things done, or something else?
- Is there one approach to the job of mayor that works better than others?
- Should the mayor behave as a businessman? A statesman? An arbitrator and bargainer? A technical expert?
- Are some of the roles that mayors play (e.g. legislator, chief executive, chief of state, party head) more important to a city than others?

- Can a mayor have a significant impact on his city?
- Is one type of city charter best in helping mayors with their jobs?
- Can the mayor's job really be done, given current resource constraints?
- Is it possible to make any valid generalizations about mayors? Is every city and situation unique?

When looking for answers to these questions and hundreds more, people generally found that outside of individual speculation little more than a vacuum existed. Despite a great deal of casual rhetoric to the contrary, our civilization still knows very little about most classes of large scale social system phenomena.

THE RESEARCH

This book is the result of an exploratory, interdisciplinary, comparative examination of the behavior of 20 mayors and of their administrations during the 1960s (see Table 1-1). Our purpose was to try to improve current understanding of twentieth-century mayors in large and moderate-sized United States cities and to expand our knowledge of the processes by which they attempt to govern our urban areas.

This study was initiated in the spring of 1971. As is undoubtedly the usual case, the personal and professional motives that led to the project were complex. Both researchers were applied social scientists who had been associated with a professional (business) school. They were interested in large-scale purposive action, human behavior in organizational settings, organizational and interorganizational phenomena, and social change—among other areas. Paul Lawrence had been involved in a few projects relating to urban issues in 1968 and since then had been considering a research effort that focused on cities. A series of coincidences brought the authors together in 1970. Their common interests in interorganizational phenomena in particular led Paul Lawrence to initiate the joint research effort.

The work did not begin with a crystal clear focus or research question to be answered. Instead, we specified only the general parameters of our effort. It would focus on cities. It would promote understanding of the role mayors play in solving and creating urban problems. It would conceptualize some of the phenomena as

Table 1-1 The Mayors Studied

Mayors[a]	City	1960 Population	Charter[b]	Term of Mayor
Ivan Allen, Jr.	Atlanta, Georgia	487,455	W	1962–1970
Chester Kowal	Buffalo, New York	532,759	S	1961–1965
Walton H. Bachrach	Cincinnati, Ohio	502,550	CM	1963–1967
Ralph Locher	Cleveland, Ohio	876,050	S	1962–1967
W. Ralston Westlake	Columbus, Ohio	471,316	S	1960–1964
Erik Jonsson	Dallas, Texas	679,684	CM	1964–1971
Thomas A. McCann	Fort Worth, Texas	356,268	CM	1957–1961
Louis Welch	Houston, Texas	938,219	S	1963–1973
Charles H. Boswell	Indianapolis, Indiana	476,258	S	1959–1963
Thomas J. Whelan	Jersey City, New Jersey	276,101	S	1965–1971
H. Roe Bartle	Kansas City, Missouri	475,539	CM	1955–1963
William O. Cowger	Louisville, Kentucky	390,639	S	1961–1965
Arthur Naftalin	Minneapolis, Minnesota	482,872	W	1961–1969
Richard Lee	New Haven, Connecticut	152,048	S	1953–1969
Victor H. Schiro	New Orleans, Louisiana	627,525	W	1961–1970
Hugh Addonizio	Newark, New Jersey	405,220	S	1963–1970
Roy B. Martin, Jr.	Norfolk, Virginia	304,869	CM	1962–1974
Frank T. Lamb	Rochester, New York	318,611	CM	1963–1969
Frank E. Curran	San Diego, California	573,224	CM	1965–1971
George Christopher	San Francisco, California	740,316	W	1956–1964

[a]Other mayors more casually observed included 1 in Atlanta, 4 in Cincinnati, 1 in Cleveland, 1 in Columbus, 3 in Fort Worth, 1 in Jersey City, 1 in Louisville, 1 in New Orleans, 1 in Norfolk, and 1 in San Francisco.

[b]W = weak mayor charter, S = strong mayor charter, CM = city manager charter. Generally in a city with a strong mayor charter, the mayor appoints the principal administrative officers, prepares the budget, supervises expenditures, and manages the city bureaucracy. In a city with a weak mayor charter, the city council has much of that authority. The mayor presides over the council, recommends legislation, exercises a veto, and shares responsibility for managing the city bureaucracy. With a city manager charter, the mayor has still less formal authority. A city manager, appointed by the council, names principal administrative officers and manages the bureaucracy. Often the mayor is authorized only to preside over council meetings and attend ceremonial functions.

"interorganizational." It would try to utilize and test some of the models and frameworks recently created by organization theorists

The basic approach to the research was modeled after a design that had been very effective in some of Lawrence's prior work.[1] That is, we initially agreed to a two-phased comparative study. In the first phase, we would try to understand the differences and similarities among a

[1]As in Lawrence and Lorsch (1967).

small number of mayors. In the second phase we would then try to test the conclusions drawn in the first phase on a larger number of mayors.

During the late spring and early summer of 1971, we read the available material on mayors, talked to a variety of people about the subject, and designed the initial phase of the study. The data collection design that evolved by midsummer called for six former mayors to be studied by interviewing a limited number of carefully chosen people in each mayor's city. To fully understand why this design evolved, as opposed to any of a thousand variations, one needs to be aware of the dilemmas we encountered and the tradeoff decisions we made.

One of our first discoveries was that there was a relative scarcity of prior work on the subject of mayors. Chapter 2 describes the models of mayoral behavior that currently exist and explains why none appears to be very satisfactory for our purposes. During the initial period, we found it rather engaging to translate models of administration developed by organization theorists into mayoral models. Although these conceptions sometimes led to very interesting insights, it became apparent that they too were lacking. Practitioners often found them to be limited and "naïve."

Nevertheless, even though we could not find a model or framework in which we could place much faith, we could have chosen or constructed what appeared to be the best available model, and proceeding in a rather strict methodological sequence, generated researchable hypotheses and identified data collection tools that can persuasively gather information to test the hypotheses by using established statistical or other methods. We did not choose to follow this sequence, however, primarily because of our particular values and interests.

As a result of our own histories and socialization patterns, we tend to place a higher value on the "usefulness" and "innovativeness" of our research and a lower value on its methodological "cleanness" (how well it follows existing standards), than do many of our academic colleagues. We are quite aware of the consequences of research guided by those values. Such research often obscures the incremental orderly development of knowledge in some areas, and it wastes resources. On the other hand, it also leads to innovation and significant increases in applicable insights.[2]

[2]Kuhn's (1970) discussion of the structure of scientific revolution is relevant to this point.

Therefore, we decided to use a fairly flexible clinical approach for the first phase of the research. That is, we would be sure to collect some data on the variables that past research suggested to be important, but in addition we would try to be sensitive to a broad range of variables and a wide variety of stimuli. We would collect more data instead of fewer and we would focus on exploration instead of mechanical data collection. Our chief tools would be observation and the interview.

Our second important design choice was not to study current administrations. The mayor who is in office today is a very busy person, and he has little reason to be candid with a researcher. Indeed, anyone of any stature in a city would be inclined to weigh the information he supplies a researcher against its possible impact on the incumbent administration, regardless of whether he likes or dislikes that administration. If it were possible to collect data without speaking to the mayor or others in a city, this circumstance would not be important; since we had chosen a clinical approach, however, it clearly was a problem.

We therefore chose to study only former mayors in the first phase. Of course, this path has its drawbacks also. First of all, it meant that we had to rely on the imperfect memories of others. Second, it did not allow us to observe the administrations firsthand. Both these problems can be (and ultimately were) partially overcome by other elements of a design, but not completely.

Having decided on clinical-interview tools to study former mayors, we next faced the usual questions of scope and practicality. In a city of 500,000 people, it is possible to spend years collecting data (some have done just that). The problem, then, was how to collect enough data to gain a reasonable understanding of what had happened during a particular administration, as well as some insight into the city, the people, and the mayor, all in a minimum amount of time.

We decided to interview in each city a limited number of people who, for the purposes of the study, would be information centers. We would identify about a dozen people in each city who, because of their respective role during the years in question, could be prime sources of information about the mayor and his actions. These people might include the mayor, a few of his closest aides, and leaders from the major sections of the community: the president of the Chamber of Commerce, the head of the Council of Churches, and so on. Obviously the group would include people who liked the mayor and people who did not.

We designed interview schedules (see Appendix A, Exhibits I, II, and III) that called for 90-minute interviews with everyone except the mayor, who would be interviewed for 4 hours. Each person would be asked a number of specific questions, along with open-ended questions about the mayor, the city, and the mayor's impact on the city. To provide some assurance that we were getting relatively accurate information, all questions were to be asked of at least two people. If informants disagreed, we planned to study more closely the area that had produced the discrepancy.

Selecting exactly who to interview would be dependent on a number of factors.

1. The structure of the town (types of groups that were important).
2. Who the leaders were while the mayor was in office.
3. Who was available and would cooperate.

Our choice of the number of mayors to study was guided primarily by practical considerations. We would always prefer more to less. Given the design as we have articulated it to this point, we decided that we could study about six mayors within our time and resource constraints.

Our choice of mayors was influenced by our previous success with comparative studies. Specifically, selecting extreme situations (very "successful" and very "unsuccessful") enables one to more easily identify differences in variables and relationships that may be responsible for a large difference in outcome. We decided to find three "conspicuously successful" and three "conspicuously unsuccessful" mayors to study in the first phase.

In narrowing the list of all American cities and mayors down to a manageable group from which six subjects could be chosen, the following criteria were applied:

1. Size: large, but not atypically large. We decided to eliminate cities that might be so large that they were unique. Most data on mayors today come from New York and Chicago. Cities of 250,000 to 2,000,000 population in the 1960 census were accepted (with one exception, New Haven).
2. Time: the period between 1960 and 1970. Although the historical approach was required, it seemed foolish to go back in time any further than was necessary, because of the memory problem.

3. Mayor in office at least 4 years. We feared that unless a mayor had been in office for some minimum amount of time, it would be difficult to judge his impact on a city.

Table 1-2 lists 48 mayors in 43 cities meeting the foregoing criteria.

To select six cities from this list, we identified a number of national "experts" on the subject of cities and mayors. From this group, a dozen names were chosen, including three university sociologists, three men from the U.S. Conference of Mayors–National League of Cities, one independent consultant, three university political scientists, one urban expert working at a foundation, and one state government employee.

Table 1-2 Mayors Who Met Study Criteria

City	Population (1960)	Predominant Mayor in 1960s	Term	City Manager
Akron, Ohio	290,351	Edward Erickson	1961–1965	No
Atlanta, Georgia	487,455	Ivan Allen, Jr.	1961–1970	No
Baltimore, Maryland	939,024	J. Harold Grady	1959–1963	No
		Theodore McKeldin	1963–1967	
Birmingham, Alabama	340,887	Albert Boutwell	1963–1967	No
Boston, Massachusetts	697,197	John Collins	1960–1968	No
Buffalo, New York	532,759	Chester Kowal	1961–1965	No
Cincinnati, Ohio	502,550	Walton H. Bachrach	1963–1967	Yes
Cleveland, Ohio	876,050	Ralph Locher	1962–1967	No
Columbus, Ohio	471,316	W. Ralston Westlake	1960–1964	No
Dallas, Texas	679,684	Erik Jonsson	1965–1971	No
Dayton, Ohio	262,332	R. William Patterson	1959–1962	Yes
		Frank R. Somers	1963–1966	
		Dave Hall	1967–1970	
Denver, Colorado	493,887	Thomas G. Currigan	1963–1969	No
Detroit, Michigan	1,670,144	Jerome P. Cavanagh	1962–1970	No
Fort Worth, Texas	356,268	Thomas A. McCann	1958–1961	Yes
El Paso, Texas	276,687	Judson F. Williams	1963–1969	No
Honolulu, Hawaii	294,194	Neil S. Blaisdell	1960–1960	No
Houston, Texas	938,219	Louis Welch	1963–1973	No
Indianapolis, Indiana	476,258	Charles H. Boswell	1959–1963	No
Jersey City, New Jersey	276,101	Thomas J. Whelan	1965–1973	No
Kansas City, Missouri	475,539	H. Roe Bartle	1958–1963	Yes
Louisville, Kentucky	390,639	William O. Cowger	1961–1966	No
Memphis, Tennessee	497,524	William B. Ingram, Jr.	1959–1968	Yes

Table 1-2 (Continued)

City	Population (1960)	Predominant Mayor in 1960s	Term	City Manager
Minneapolis, Minnesota	482,872	Arthur Naftalin	1961–1969	No
New Haven, Connecticut	152,048	Richard Lee	1953–1969	No
New Orleans, Louisiana	627,525	Victor H. Schiro	1962–1970	No
Newark, New Jersey	405,220	Hugh Addonizio	1963–1970	No
Norfolk, Virginia	304,869	Roy B. Martin, Jr.	1962–1974	Yes
Oakland, California	367,548	John C. Houlihan	1963–1967	Yes
Oklahoma City, Oklahoma	324,523	James Norick	1960–1963	Yes
			1968–1971	
Omaha, Nebraska	301,598	J. Rosenblatt	1958–1961	No
		James Dworak	1962–1965	
		A. V. Sorenson	1966–1969	
Phoenix, Arizona	439,170	Milton Graham	1965–1970	Yes
Pittsburgh, Pennsylvania	604,332	Joseph Barr	1959–1970	No
Rochester, New York	318,611	Peter Barry	1957–1962	Yes
		Frank T. Lamb	1963–1969	
St. Louis, Missouri	750,026	Raymond R. Tucker	1953–1965	No
St. Paul, Minnesota	313,411	George J. Vavoulis	1961–1966	No
San Antonio, Texas	587,718	Walter W. McAllister	1963–1971	No
San Diego, California	573,224	Frank E. Curran	1963–1971	Yes
San Francisco, California	740,316	George Christopher	1956–1964	No
Seattle, Washington	557,087	Gordon S. Clinton	1956–1964	No
Tampa, Florida	274,970	Nick Nuccio	1966–1969	No
Toledo, Ohio	318,003	John W. Potter	1963–1968	Yes
Tulsa, Oklahoma	261,685	James M. Hewgley	1967–1970	No

We sent a letter to each man asking him to put each of the 48 mayors named in Table 1-2 into one of four categories:

Category 1. During this administration many of the city's short-run problems were solved and the health of the city was improved. The outlook for the future was more optimistic at the end of the administration.

Category 2. This category is reserved for all cities and administrations that fall between categories 1 and 3.

Category 3. During this administration the situation in the city worsened. The short-run problems were not solved, and the city's health declined. The outlook for the future was bad or worse at the end.

Don't Know. The final category is reserved for the situations in which one does not have enough information to make a judgment. (The instrument sent to the judges is reproduced in Appendix A, Exhibit IV.)

Of the 12 inquiries sent out, 8 brought replies as requested. One person responded that he felt too uninformed to be of use, one declined saying he was too busy, and two declined because they felt the task as defined was impossible.

As a protective maneuver, all the opinions from the experts were handled by a colleague who gave us the names of six mayors without indicating which three the experts had agreed were very successful and which three they had agreed were quite unsuccessful.

Gaining cooperation from the six mayors turned out to be relatively easy. Only one mayor politely refused to be studied. Former Boston mayor John Collins wrote to four mayors, introducing the research and describing the research team in very complimentary terms; this helped a great deal.

The six cities and mayors we eventually studied in phase 1 were

Atlanta:	Ivan Allen, Jr.
Cleveland:	Ralph Locher
Dallas:	Erik Jonsson
Kansas City:	H. Roe Bartle
New Haven:	Richard Lee
New Orleans:	Victor H. Schiro

By September 1971 we were ready to start the field work. The task of securing the cooperation of the people in the communities, although time-consuming, went relatively smoothly. A total of 70 people were interviewed—about 12 per city. The roles occupied by these people are shown in Table 1-3. This list does not represent an attempt at a random sampling of people or leaders in the towns involved; rather, it indicates the critical information sources as we had defined them earlier.

Most of the interviewing was done by John Kotter. While interviewing, he spent about 5 hours with each mayor and about 1 to 1.5 hours apiece with the others. After interviewing 10 to 20 people, he became familiar with the questions and no longer had to follow the guides mechanically; this acquired facility gave the interviewee more leeway to talk about matters that he felt to be important. At the end of an interview, if the respondent had not touched on some areas of importance in the guide, the researcher asked appropriate questions. This procedure worked quite well.

Table 1-3 Phase 1 Interviewees

Categories[a]	Number	Total
Mayor and staffs		22
Mayors	6	
Aides	5	
City government officials	11	
Business leaders		18
Bank chairmen	4	
Bank presidents	3	
Chamber of Commerce president	1	
Chamber of Commerce Executive Director	1	
Major department store presidents	2	
Other business presidents	7	
Newspapermen		11
Publishers	2	
Editors	6	
Reporters	3	
City councilors		4
Labor leaders		4
Teamster presidents	2	
Local AFL–CIO president	1	
Local labor council president	1	
Ministers and religious leaders		4
Educators		5
School board president	1	
School board member	1	
Superintendent of schools	1	
University president	1	
University dean	1	
Airport director		1
Former mayoral candidate		1

[a]Included in the list are: 9 black leaders and 7 ethnic group leaders.

The researcher also developed the technique of reviewing twice daily what he thought he had learned, for two reasons. First, this procedure identified gaps in his knowledge, which could be actively dealt with in subsequent interviews. Second, it helped him become more sensitive to contradictory data. When he could identify discrepant data on the spot, he could ask probing questions to determine the exact nature of the contradiction. Often the interviewee had simply made a verbal mistake, which he retracted. When the responses offered a real contradiction, it often revealed an area of importance of which the researcher had previously been unaware.

By mid-November 1971, the field work was completed. The rather large amounts of handwritten interview data were then analyzed in two steps. First, case studies of all six cities were written in a format based on the data collected in the field. The primary concern in this phase was to create a well-organized, clear presentation of the data.

In the second part of the analysis we divided the six mayors into two groups based on three measures of the "effectiveness": the experts' ratings, the mayor's record at the polls, and the interviewees' responses to a question about the mayor's "successes" and "failures." In all six cases, these three measures tended to rate each mayor similarly. Generally the three mayors we labeled "effective" were rated highly by the "experts," were easily reelected, and were praised by those interviewed. The three mayors we labeled "ineffective" tended to be rated very low by the "experts"; in addition, they were voted out of the office and criticized by those interviewed.

From January to April 1972 we sifted through the case data, looking for patterns that differentiated the three "effective" mayors from the three "ineffective" ones. The two sets of cases were clearly different, however we looked at them. Our task was to arrive at the most useful way of conceptualizing these differences.

We began by stating some 50 "hypotheses" about the differences between the two sets of cases. The hypotheses tended to be somewhat trite, however, and their form was quite unesthetic (to us). While searching for alternative forms, we came on the macroconceptualization approach, which we eventually adopted. Instead of talking about 50 relationships between this minor variable and that minor variable, we formulated nine pattern statements that seemed to capture the differences between the two sets of cases. These statements tended to deal with the entire phenomenon or a large part of it, not with a few small pieces. These pattern statements all took the form: "The more effective mayor is/has/does. . . ." Starting with an unspecified (large) number of variables, we finished with a small number of concepts —mayor, agenda, office, city, network, agenda setting process, network building process, and task accomplishing process.

The process that resulted in the final formulation was a complex, interactive one; certainly it did not follow any simple, reproducible rules. An insight here led to a reexamination there, which led to a new idea in another area. We completely reexamined all the literature on mayors, and this review eventually produced the insights presented in Chapters 2 and 3, which in turn significantly influenced our conceptualization of the field work data.

By May 1972 our analysis was complete. We were convinced not only that the previous "models" of mayors were very weak but that we understood why they were weak. Each one made key assumptions about contingencies and constraints in the situation which sometimes were true and sometimes were not. We felt we were on the right tract, although we also recognized that we had much to learn. Even as we wrote our analysis, we recognized that it was lacking.[3]

As a result, we set three objectives for the second phase of the research. The first was to test out the conclusion we had already drawn—namely, that nine specific patterns were associated with "effective" mayors. The second was to examine a range of mayors broader than we had focused on in the first phase (not just the extreme types the "experts" had defined). The third was to learn more about why certain patterns emerged in some situations and others emerged under different conditions. In the first phase we wanted to identify the patterns that existed, not how or why they developed or emerged.

During the summer of 1972 we designed the second phase of the field work. We decided that our time and resource constraints would allow us to look at another 14 mayors, bringing the total to 20. We again utilized the "expert" ratings in selecting administrations to study. Since we had already examined three mayors who had received a category 1 rating from the experts (positive impact) and three who had received a category 3 rating (negative impact), we chose four more category 1 mayors, seven category 2 mayors, and three category 3 mayors. We assumed that regardless of the validity of the expert ratings, this procedure would assure us of a fairly rich variety of mayors.

We also decided that the clinical interviewing approach had worked well enough in phase 1 to justify using it in phase 2 to achieve our third objective—learning more about pattern development and emergence. Designing a procedure to test our conclusions from phase 1 proved to be much more difficult. We considered a number of alternative methodologies and finally settled on a "pattern recognition" idea.

[3]Kotter and Lawrence (1972).

Each of the patterns that we found in phase 1 to be associated with either "effective" or "ineffective" mayors could be described in a paragraph. We designed a questionnaire that included these descriptions and asked a respondent to identify the patterns that were associated with the mayor he knew. The choices we offered him varied, but always included at least three descriptions for any one pattern (two from the first phase of the research and one other). When the patterns found in phase 1 could be described as points along a continuum, we simply described that continuum on the questionnaire and asked the respondent to note where the mayor in question fit. Recognizing that our choices might not be exhaustive, in each case we allowed the respondent to say "none of the above" and describe something else. We also used more than one continuum, when necessary.

We considered mailing the questionnaire to people but decided that because of its size, our response rate would be much too low. Again, the most practical alternative seemed to be to hold interviews, allowing for one-half the session to be spent on the questionnaire itself.

Given this decision, it was immediately clear that our procedure for locating interviewees had to differ from that used in phase 1. To answer our questionnaire we needed well-informed and relatively unbiased people. Our interviewee selection procedure in phase 1 often put us in contact with rather passionately biased individuals. Given our clinical methodology, such people provided interpretable and very useful data. However, this type of person would not be particularly helpful as a questionnaire respondent.

We designed a procedure for locating well-informed people who would not tend to distort their memories of past events (see Table 1-4). The procedure was time-consuming, but it allowed us to be satisfied with 10 interviews per city instead of 20 or 30.

In August we tested our phase 2 design in one of the six cities from phase 1. We followed the interviewee selection procedure and interviewed 10 people. In general the process worked as we expected. The information we obtained was consistent with what we knew about the city and mayor. We even learned a number of new things, especially concerning how and why the patterns developed.

In September we began the phase 2 field work in Jersey City. The other phase 2 cities were Buffalo, Newark, Columbus, Cincinnati, Houston, Fort Worth, San Diego, San Francisco, Minneapolis, Rochester, Norfolk, Louisville, and Indianapolis. We immediately ran

Table 1-4 Interviewee Selection Procedure, Phase 2

1. Call a local newspaper reporter or editor who had once been a Nieman Fellow at Harvard and ask him to name the principal leaders from the various parts of the city when the mayor in question was in office.
2. Call each of the community leaders and ask for a list of "articulate, well-informed, unbaised" people in the city. Also ask the community leader his opinion of all the possible interviewees whom he did not mention, although they had been mentioned by other community leaders.
3. After talking to all the community leaders, eliminate all possible interviewees who were mentioned by only one or two people. Eliminate all interviewees who were "blackballed" by someone.
4. From the remaining list of interviewees, choose the 10 to 12 who were mentioned by the most people and who received the most favorable comments (on the dimensions of "articulate, well-informed, unbiased").

into problems because the pattern questionnaire was too time-consuming and prevented us from getting all the information we wanted from the interviews. Respondents preferred to talk to us, not respond to a questionnaire. As a result it took time and effort to induce them to answer our pattern questions. Because our pattern questions did not include an exhaustive list of possibilities, people found it difficult and annoying to formulate their answers. Many could recognize a correct pattern if we had it written down, but if there seemed to be no appropriate response, they were reluctant to check the "none of the above" category. Unlike the mayor of the city in which we tested the questionnaire, the mayor in Jersey City was different from anyone we had seen in phase 1. Therefore, we left the first city we studied in phase 2 with very little understanding of what really happened when Mayor Whelan was in office.

At this point we confronted a difficult issue and question. If we continued according to plan, we would be able to accomplish only one of our three goals: testing our conclusions from phase 1. It was already apparent that on a simple yes–no test, many of these conclusions would be given a no because of small but important points. If, on the other hand, we decided to try to focus on the other two goals also, we would be forced to abandon the strict pattern recognition test methodology, which was so time-consuming. If we followed the latter course, we would of course be stepping back toward the clinical methodology with all its associated benefits and drawbacks.

We chose to abandon the strict pattern recognition test, basing our decision on the same values that had guided us previously. We modified the pattern recognition questionnaire and combined it with all our other questions into one interview guide (see Appendix A, Exhibit V). We continued to try to persuade people to respond to pattern questions as before, but we placed *top* priority on achieving a personal understanding of each situation.

With the second design, the field work was carried out in the fall of 1972. The interviewee selection procedure worked well. Some of the same types of people who were interviewed in phase 1 were selected in phase 2 also, along with more newsmen and academics in particular. Table 1-5 gives a final listing of those interviewed in phases 1 and 2. In all 14 cities the researcher was able to get satisfactory agreement on all the information called for in the interview guide with just 10 interviews of approximately 1.5 hours apiece. The clinical techniques developed in phase 1 were used and elaborated in phase 2.

A number of important issues surfaced during this field work. It became apparent that there were not just two types of mayor, or even three. There were at least four or five different types. It also became more and more apparent that our use of the terms "effective" and "ineffective" was not at all precise. Whereas almost all data in the

Table 1-5 People Interviewed

Category	Number
Newsmen (publishers, editors, reporters)	40
Businessmen (primarily bank heads and Chamber of Commerce executives)	32
Mayor's staff and other local government officials	28
Educators and academics (primarily political scientists)	22
Elected officials (city councilors primarily)	17
Former mayors (those studied and others)	14
Lawyers	12
Union officials	10
Political party officials	10
Clergy	10
Leaders in civic and charitable organizations	10
Other	5

phase 1 study agreed with respect to how the six mayors should be rated, the data on many of the 14 in the second study were far less clear and consistent. Chapter 12 contains a detailed discussion of the problems we encountered and the forces causing them.

Data analysis for the second phase of the field work was accomplished in the spring of 1973. As in phase 1, this was a fluid process using both induction and deduction, going from interview data to tentative models to past research to interview data, and so on. The bulk of this book, of course, represents the results of that analysis. In Chapters 4 to 12 we describe our empirically derived model of mayoral behavior. A number of fascinating theoretical issues came to light during our final data analysis, and these issues are treated in Chapter 14.

THE RESEARCH EFFORT IN PERSPECTIVE

It is important to recognize exactly what this report represents and what it does not. The reader should be aware that this was an *exploratory* study. We did not test certain propositions: when we began the research, we could not find (or create with any confidence) any general model from which to deduce testable hypotheses. We tended to probe the unexplored much more than the explored. For example, we spent little time and effort investigating the one aspect of urban government that seems to have been studied most—the election process.

This work is *interdisciplinary*. This is not a political science essay. The research examines a wide range of variables at numerous levels of analysis, although it does emphasize some variables and levels more than others.[4]

Its primary focus is *behavior*. Our concerns are: What does the mayor do? Why does he do that? What impact does such behavior have on his city?

Because of the behavioral focus, this research effort represents to those interested in the problems of local government and urban affairs an approach that differs slightly from most others. Other work has

[4]Personality variables, for example, receive very limited attention. See Appendix A.

focused on new technologies and tools,[5] governmental reorganization,[6] and new institutional forms.[7] We hope that our approach will complement and supplement previous efforts.

For social scientists, this effort is a modest attempt to add to our understanding of action in large-scale human systems. The researchers are particularly interested in interorganizational and organizational analysis and in administration. It is hoped that this research will provide some useful insights in those areas.

[5]Rosenbloom and Russell (1971).
[6]Committee for Economic Development (1967) and (1970).
[7]Rosenbloom and Marris (1969).

CHAPTER 2

CURRENT CONCEPTIONS OF THE MAYOR

It is probably safe to assume that enough newspaper copy has been devoted to the description and analysis of mayors and their actions in the past 50 years to fill a moderate-sized library. At the same time, however, the number of books and research reports on this subject could not fill a moderate-sized bookcase. Furthermore, nearly all the literature on the behavior of mayors is in the form of case studies.[1]

[1]Between 1906 and 1963, not a one of the 2614 articles in the *American Political Science Review* mentioned "mayor" in its title. The bulk of the literature on mayors today is in the form of case studies, biographies, and autobiographies. These include such items as:

Allen's account of his years in Atlanta (1971)
Bean's study of Ruef in San Francisco (1932)
Buckley's comments of Lindsay in New York (1966)
Carter's study of Lindsay (1967)
Curley's autobiography (Boston) (1957)
Dorsey's description of Christopher in San Francisco (1962)
Fowler's biography of Walker in New York (1949)
Garrett's study of La Guardia in New York (1961)
Gottfried's work on Cermak in Chicago (1962)
Lindsay's observations about his own job (1967)
Mann's study of La Guardia's 1933 election (1965)
McKean's description of the Hague machine in Jersey City (1940)
Pilat's study of Lindsay's campaign (1968)

There currently exists no general purpose model of mayoral behavior capable of: describing the different ways in which mayors behave, explaining why a particular behavioral pattern emerges in a specific situation, and predicting the impact of a mayor's behavior on his city. There are, however, literally hundreds of popular conceptions of what a mayor does, why he does those things, and the effect of his actions on a city. Most of these notions are fairly naïve and have never been the subject of serious thought or investigation.

Nevertheless, it appears to us that at least 10 distinctly different and important models of mayoral behavior can be found today in the more serious literature. The majority are somewhat implicit. That is, they are not stated or written as a model of mayors' behavior per se.[2]

THE POWER BROKER MODEL

Our first model of mayoral behavior, derived from Edward C. Banfield's *Political Influence*,[3] focuses primarily on *power*, defined as "the ability to establish control over another person." Such control can be based on material inducement, verbal persuasion, or a number of other factors.[4]

In the Power Broker model, the mayor behaves much like the capitalist, with one key difference. Instead of money or a product or commodity, the mayor deals in power. That is, he uses power as a capitalist uses capital. He invests to get more power, or at least to maintain what he has.

More specifically,

1. A mayor "seeks to maintain or increase his stock of power. That is, capital is always 'invested,' never 'consumed.' A [mayor] exercises

---

Talbot's descriptions of Lee in New Haven (1967)
Wendt's study of Thompson in Chicago (1953)

This type of literature is interesting, but it tends to be limited by its focus on one case, its anecdotal style, and its emphasis on only a few cities (especially New York).

[2]We recognize the danger, inherent in this approach, of unconsciously creating "straw men" to serve some purpose we have in mind. We have discussed our conceptions at length with others, however, and are satisfied that they represent what we have stated.

[3]Banfield (1961). We say "derived" because Banfield does not formally offer this as a model of mayoral behavior.

[4]Banfield does not clearly state all the sources of power or control.

power only when he thinks doing so will improve his net power position. When there are alternative investment opportunities, he always chooses the one he thinks will be most profitable."

2. "In making his choice of [power] investments, [the mayor] takes into account the uncertainty of the return as well as its probable value." Thus mayors, like capital investors, sometimes make unprofitable investments and lose. For example, "power may be wasted by establishing controls over actors who, it turns out, do not control requisite actions."

3. "The terms upon which control may be required (assuming it may be acquired at all) are established through a process of bargaining."

4. Occasionally a mayor will "maintain control of a structure" on a continuous basis, but he requires "repeated investments of power" to do so.[5] (Mayor Daley, for instance, was able to maintain control of Chicago's city council only by continual outlays of patronage to ward committeemen).

The picture of a mayor that emerges from this model is one of a cigar-chomping power broker. Like the capitalist, he is highly skilled at bargaining and establishing deals. His concern is with maintaining and increasing his supply of power, not with keeping the streets clean or helping the city per se. Yet like the capitalist, in pursuing his own selfish ends, the mayor (usually) does what is good for the public. The outcomes of the major decisions that Banfield studied indeed seem to be "public serving." Why is this true?

The urban environment in Banfield's model is characterized by highly decentralized powers. The mayor, acting as a power broker pursuing his own goals, centralizes enough power to allow things to happen. That is, in the process of maintaining and increasing his own power, the mayor enables decisions to be made, conflicts to be resolved, and projects to be undertaken. Without this centralization, the city could grind to a halt. "If [Mayor Daley's] machine were dismantled without there occurring any compensating centralization of authority, the city government would be paralyzed."[6]

[5]All quotations from E. C. Banfield, *Political Influence* (New York: Macmillan, 1961), pp. 312, 313. Copyright © 1961 by The Free Press. A Division of MacMillan Company and reproduced by permission. In the text Banfield is talking about all "actors," not just mayors.

[6]*Ibid.*, page 318.

Furthermore, since power is distributed widely among the population, the "power market" is relatively free, and the ultimate results of the process usually appear to be "public serving." Although both the capitalist and the mayor may behave in self-serving ways, "invisible hands" in the capital and power markets see to it that the end results usually benefit society. This model implies that the good or effective mayor is the successful power broker (but Banfield never explicitly confirms this assumption. Mayor Daley, for one, is reputed to be a very successful power broker.

THE PUBLIC ENTREPRENEUR MODEL

In one of the few existing comparative studies of mayors, James V. Cunningham measured four administrations on a scale of "public entrepreneurship."[7] The mayor with the highest rating displayed behavior dominated by "originality, risk-taking, initiative, energy, openness, organizational ability, and promotional ingenuity." The mayor with the lowest rating, a nonentrepreneur or trustee-manager, had dominant qualities of "caution, inflexibility, bureaucratic authoritarianism, physical inertia, heavy-handedness, and organizational confusion."[8]

The "good" mayor in this conception is very active—a bold problem solver. His two most important characteristics are originality and the willingness to take risks.

> A mayor may go to the state capital to ask legislative leaders to allow him to tax suburbanites who work in the city. He risks a public rebuff and the loss of prestige such a rebuff would mean. But if he is successful, he gains increased stature as an effective bargainer, and revenue to put forward his program. Nearly any bold thrust of a mayor initiating an urban renewal project, promoting jobs for blacks, intervening with the Board

[7]James V. Cunningham, *Urban Leadership in the Sixties* (Cambridge, Mass.: Schenkman, 1970).
[8]*Ibid.*, p. 15.

> of Education for curriculum reform, setting up an elite tactical police unit—risks the loss of the votes of certain groups whose interests may be harmed, while it chances the gain of the votes of many whose interests may be advanced or who may at any rate judge that their interests are being advanced.[9]

Cunningham's logic, which stems from J. A. Schumpeter's original development of the entrepreneurial concept,[10] is very straightforward. In the private sector, the behavior he has defined as entrepreneurial has been associated with successful action and profits. Cunningham indicates that similar behavior can be effective in the public sector, and he asks, "What can urban leadership do to maximize the benefits from the limited resources that are available to a city?"[11] His answer —behave like an entrepreneur.

There is one important difference between this model and the first one we presented. Whereas Banfield simply tries to describe what was happening in certain cities, Cunningham constructs a model and tries to test it. That is, Cunningham begins by suggesting that the "name of the game" is problem solving and benefit creating, given limited resources. Therefore, he deduces (and tries to confirm) that the effective mayor is the one who behaves like an entrepreneur.[12] Another important difference between the two models can be seen in their application to the mayor of Chicago. Daley ranks high as a power broker, but, according to Cunningham, relatively low as a public entrepreneur.[13]

THE PUBLIC EXECUTIVE AND POLICY EXPERT MODELS

Two additional models of mayoral behavior are outgrowths of a "reform" movement that began in the United States near the turn of the

[9] *Ibid.*, p. 15.

[10] Schumpeter (1947) and (1965).

[11] Cunningham (1970), p. 11.

[12] One can, of course, argue that Banfield's research design "assumes" that the name of the game is decision making. Nevertheless, this distinction between Banfield's approach and Cunningham's is useful.

[13] Cunningham studied the administrations of Richard Lee (New Haven), Ralph Locher

century.[14] Like the first two, these models are related to behavior in the private sector and, like Cunningham's model, they were developed as a prescription or hypothesis, not as the result of exploratory descriptive field research.

Banfield and Wilson have described these models as follows:

> The reformers assumed that there existed an interest ("the public interest") that pertained to the city "as a whole" and that should always prevail over competing, partial (and usually private) interests. Local government entailed simply the businesslike management of essential public services. The task of discovering the content of the public interest was therefore a technical rather than a political one. What was necessary was to put the affair entirely into the hands of the few who were "best qualified"; persons whose training, experience, natural ability, and devotion to public service equipped them best to manage the public business. The best qualified men would decide "policy" and leave its execution ("administration") to professionals ("experts") who would work under the direction of an executive (mayor or manager).[15]

The distinction between policy and execution is responsible for the presence of two different models here. In the first (the Public Executive), the council or some group of staff professionals decides public policy, while the mayor behaves like an executive in a large corporation—he plans, controls, organizes, directs, delegates, evaluates, communicates, and so on. He manages the "public business." His

---

(Cleveland), Richard Daley (Chicago), and Joseph Barr (Pittsburgh). On his public entrepreneurial scale, Lee ranked first with 30.5 points and Daley ranked third with 16.5 points.

[14]Hofstadter (1959).

[15]E. C. Banfield and J. Q. Wilson, *City Politics* (Cambridge, Mass.: Harvard University Press and M.I.T. Press, 1963), p. 139. Copyright ©1963 by the President and Fellows of Harvard College and the Massachusetts Institute of Technology and reproduced by permission.

two predominant concerns are efficiency and effectiveness. That is, he attempts to manage the city bureaucracy in a way that will lead to the achievement of given policy objectives (effectiveness) with the least expenditure of given resources (efficiency).

In the second model (the Policy Expert), a city manager handles the job of execution while the mayor, in conjunction with the council or his own staff, sets policy. In a sense he behaves like a chairman of the board, charting the future course of the body he nominally heads. Using his expert knowledge of the city and local government, he establishes direction, goals, policies, and priorities for the city and for the city manager.

The reformers explicitly stated that this is the way a mayor *should* behave. Under a city manager charter, he should be a policy expert. Under a weak or strong mayor charter, he should be a public executive. When a mayor's behavior falls outside the appropriate model, we can expect to find inefficiency, waste, corruption, and ineffective local government.

COALITION BUILDING MODEL

Still another model of mayoral behavior has resulted from Robert Dahl's study of New Haven.[16] The predominant focus of this model is on a coalition that is created and maintained by the mayor. Unlike the four previous models, this one does not make an analogy with economic or corporate behavior. Instead, it is rooted in the pluralistic notions of political science, according to which society is made up of many groups with different interests. The essence of the mayor's role (and political leadership in general) in this type of society is to create a workable coalition of interest groups. The successful mayor is the one who finds a program or approach to his job which can integrate a variety of community interests.

A typical coalition in recent years, according to Robert H. Salisbury, includes

> . . . two principal groups, locally oriented economic interests and the professional worker in technical

[16]Dahl (1961).

> city-related programs. Both these groupings are sources of initiative for programs that involve major allocation of resources, both public and private. Associated with the coalition also are whatever groups constitute the popular vote-base of the mayor's electoral success.[17]

In creating such a coalition the mayor uses a wide variety of resources, the most important of which is an appeal to common purposes or interests. A mayor of this type during the last decade

> . . . is relatively articulate on local television, and his campaigns are likely to stress his competence at communal problem solving rather than the particular group benefits that may accrue following his election. Nor is this mere campaign talk. His administration concentrates on solving or alleviating particular problems rather than building memorials or dramatizing the city's commercial prospects. Again, this posture requires collaboration with those possessing the relevant resources, the experts and the businessmen.[18]

This model has received wide attention from political scientists recently. It has many variations in which the processes used by the mayor in coalition building vary and the mayor is more or less active in determining the direction of the coalition.[19] Nevertheless, the core conceptions are similar in all cases, and it is always implied that the good or effective mayor is the expert builder and maintainer of coalitions.

Although this formulation resembles the Public Entrepreneur and Power Broker models, there are important differences. A mayor could

[17]Robert H. Salisbury, "Urban Politics: The New Convergence of Power," *Journal of Politics*, **26**, November 1964, p. 782. Reprinted by permission.
[18]*Ibid.*, p. 785; reprinted by permission.
[19]For example, Dahl originally saw the mayor as doing little actual leading, whereas others have perceived him as the chief "policy setting" leader.

be entrepreneurial without ever creating a stable coalition. The entrepreneur focuses on problem solving, the coalition builder on building his coalition. The power broker, on the other hand, is very much like the coalition builder except that he tends to be less concerned with group interests. He builds his power by making discrete exchanges (I give you, you give me), whereas the coalition builder tends to increase his power by appealing to the common interests of different groups.

"MUDDLING THROUGH" MODEL

David Braybrooke and Charles E. Lindblom's *A Strategy of Decision,* an analysis of the policy evaluation process, is certainly one of the better products of social research in the 1960s.[20] They argue that the rational process of policy evaluation (the synoptic ideal), which is so often prescribed in academic literature and in everyday life—indeed, it is implicit in the Policy Expert model—is inappropriate for the real situations in which people must judge public policies.

> Many people, social scientists among them, are inclined to think that the most rational and satisfactory procedures for evaluating policies would be something like that described in the following instructions, assuming that they could be carried out: Let ultimate values be expressed in general principles satisfactory to everybody who is ready to attend to the arguments identifying them—or, if there is no hope of that, satisfactory at least to those who are now undertaking a specific job of evaluation. Let these principles, which may embody notions of happiness, welfare, justice, or intuitive notions of goodness, be stated so exactly that they may be arranged intelligibly in an order of priority that indicates precisely which principles govern the application of others and when. Then derive within the limits of such a system intermediate principles that are

[20]David Braybrooke and Charles E. Lindblom, *A Strategy of Decision* (New York: Free Press, 1963). Copyright © 1970, 1963 by The Free Press.

> suitable for application in particular cases, and that—allowing for rare cases of equality in net benefits—will indicate unambiguously which of alternative policies is to be chosen, according to the values they would promote.
>
> The intermediate principles of such a system would specify the sort of information that would be decisive for rating any policy above or below its alternatives. If these principles are formulated as hypothetical propositions (which is the most convenient way to formulate them), they take something like the following form:
>
> In conditions C, D, E, etc. (themselves derived from the ultimate principles), if such-and-such are the facts about Policy P and such-and-such are the facts about Policy Q, then P is better than Q.
>
> For example, given that due process is observed and compensation is paid and (perhaps certain other conditions), if Policy P would remove certain dangers to the health and safety of the community caused by an existing use of private property, while Policy Q, although it would improve certain recreational facilities would leave those dangers (and the existing use of private property) untouched, then P is better than Q.[21]

The authors point out in detail that the process just described does not adapt itself to the following conditions:

1. Man's limited intellectual capacities.
2. His limited knowledge.
3. The costliness of analysis.
4. The analyst's inevitable failure to construct a complete rational-deductive system or welfare function.
5. Interdependencies between fact and value.

[21]*Ibid.*, pp. 9, 10. Copyright © 1970, 1963 by The Free Press and reproduced by permission.

> 6. The openness of the systems to be analyzed.
> 7. The analyst's need for strategic sequences to guide analysis and evaluation.
> 8. The diversity of forms in which policy problems actually arise.[22]

Because of these elements of reality, the rational-deductive ideal strategy is impracticable and impossible. As the authors note, policy evaluation in Washington does not take this form at all, even though many people think it should, and even though there is pressure to adopt such strategy.

Instead, an adaptive alternative that is often used, for good reason, is the "disjointed-incremental" process:

> It is decision making through small or incremental moves on particular problems rather than through a comprehensive reform program. It is also endless; it takes on the form of an indefinite sequence of policy moves. Moreover, it is exploratory in that the goals of policy-making continue to change as new experience with policy throws new light on what is possible and desirable. In this sense, it is also better described as moving away from known social ills rather than moving toward a known and relatively stable goal.[23]

This is a process of men with limited information and thinking capacity muddling along and making small improvements here and there. Unlike the synoptic ideal, it is not a holistic and rational-analytic process.

Although the "muddling" process has not been formally translated into a model of mayoral behavior, we include it here because such a translation is implicit in the statements made to us by a number of important local leaders and politicians. That is, many people appear to

[22] *Ibid.*, p. 113.
[23] *Ibid.*, p. 107.

conceive of a mayor's behavior in terms very similar to those of Braybrooke and Lindblom's disjointed-incremental process. As one of our respondents said:

> A good mayor, and an effective one, is a pragmatic guy who takes things as they come and does the best he can under the circumstances. He doesn't run off in some direction half-cocked. He faces the issues which come up and takes small, sure, steady steps to deal with them based on the best information he can get and the difficult realities of the situation.
>
> This type of guy will be criticized by some for not having some type of ridiculous master plan, by others for not acting more like an executive is supposed to act, and by others for not being more of a statesman. They say he shouldn't just muddle along the way he does. That's a laugh. If he behaved in any of their great ideal ways, he'd really screw up the city.

MULTIHAT ROLE MODEL

A mayor's behavior is often characterized in terms of the various "roles" he performs. These include his role as chief executive, as legislative leader, as party chief, as "chief of state," and so on. As the chief executive, the mayor is an administrator of the public bureaucracy. As legislative leader, he behaves more like a congressman as he proposes legislation and judges the proposals of others. As party chief he heads a political organization—partly as executive, partly as hustler. As chief of state he assumes ceremonial roles, giving speeches, cutting ribbons, and conducting himself in the way his constituency expects the chief to behave in public.

Big City Mayors, one of the few books available on mayors (not just *one* case study), is organized according to the Multihat model.[24] The book is divided into eight sections: Mayors—What Manner of Men?, Electoral Pathways to City Hall, The Mayor as Chief Executive, The Mayor as Chief Legislator, The Mayor as Chief of Party, The Mayor

[24]Ruchleman (1969).

and the Public—His Ceremonial Role, The Mayor Speaks on Questions of Policy and Resources, and Conclusions. For the editor's purposes, this organization seems to be very useful.

The Multihat model assumes that a mayor must work in a certain specified number of settings, addressing a specified set of tasks in each setting. There are, of course, better and worse ways to perform in each role. Indeed, executive, legislative, and other types of behavior have been studied independently, and people have drawn conclusions about effective role performance in each case. Thus the model suggests that an effective mayor is one who can perform each of the mayoral roles well, one who has the capacity to shift from role to role as he changes settings and tasks. That is, an effective mayor has an appropriate role repertoire, as well as role flexibility.

This model is different from the preceding ones in an important way. It says explicitly that the mayor's behavior is a function of the roles that are a part of the mayor's job and as such does not focus directly on behavior alone. A number of other mayoral models also emphasize causal elements, attributing almost all the mayor's behavior, and its effect on a city, to some factor which is the focus of the model. There were three well-known models of this type. One focuses on formal governmental structure, another on personality, and a third on informal community structure.

FORMAL STRUCTURE MODEL

In nearly half the cities we studied, we saw active public debate over the type of charter the city *should* have—strong mayor, weak mayor, city manager, or some hybrid. More of our respondents tended voluntarily to initiate a discussion of the formal structure of the city government than of any other single issue. Typical arguments are as follows:

- A strong mayor charter is best for a city. With power spread out as much as it is these days, a mayor cannot do his job without a strong mayor charter. People expect him to be able to do things he has no control over. No sane businessman would expect a person who is not in charge of Division X to be responsible for the health and well-being of that division. Yet that is exactly what we demand of our mayor.
- A city manager charter is best for a city by far. Such an

organization puts the city bureaucracy in the
competent professional. It eliminates graft, waste, pa
inefficiency. The mayor under this plan takes care
business, helps set policy, and serves as "chief of
breaking an unmanageable job into two parts and givi to
competent men, the city is best served.

- The weak mayor charter we now have is the best. It was designed over the years by some pretty smart people and it incorporates many lessons that they learned the hard way. It is a delicate system of checks and balances. Like the strong mayor charter, it offers the advantage of having one focal executive, not two. Like the city manager charter, it contains checks against corruption and demogoguery. It has served us well.

No well-known academic has developed a descriptive or prescriptive Formal Structure model. Instead, local organizations (the "Citizens' Association") and active individuals tend to have developed these conceptions. Many firmly believe that one form of charter is best and that it is the key to "good" mayoral behavior. (Of the three types of charters, the weak mayor charter has by far the smallest number of supporters.)

PERSONALITY MODEL

Another model of the causal type focuses on the mayor's personality and its development. Implicit in this formulation is the belief that the mayor's behavior and its effect on a city are primarily a function of his "personality." A number of the case studies of mayors have been written from this perspective. Alex Gottfried's study of Anton J. Cermak in Chicago is one of the best.[25] Great man theories and their variations are based on this type of model.[26]

This model is impossible to state briefly, and therein lies its basic weakness. One can choose from among numerous widely divergent personality theories, and each is quite complex by itself. We will not take time here to articulate any of these theories.[27] All, however, imply that a "good" mayor is one who has a proper personality—healthy,

[25]Gottfried (1962).
[26]Bullock (1962); and George (1964).
[27]For a description of personality models, see Maddi (1968); or Hall and Lindzey (1970).

strong, perceptive, skilled, or whatever. "Bad" mayors, on the other hand, are people with psychological problems left over from their youth which seriously hinder them from exhibiting consistently rational behavior.

COMMUNITY POWER STRUCTURE MODEL

In his study of Atlanta around 1950, Floyd Hunter reported finding a very clear "power structure" in that community. The elite on top tended to make all the major decisions affecting the community.[28] In a sense, the mayor was an employee of the group on top. His behavior was guided by their decisions.

One of our respondents aptly summarized the popular form of the Community Power Structure model: "You shouldn't be studying mayors. They're not the key. It's the power structure. If the elite in a city are a capable, public-spirited group, the city will do well. If, on the other hand, they are self-serving and untalented, God help the city."

People usually assume that the top of the urban power structure consists of the heads of the banks, the newspaper publishers, the local industrial giants, and the "first families" who are still wealthy and active.

EVALUATION OF EXISTING MODELS

Each of the foregoing models dealing with a mayor's behavior is logically consistent within itself and is based on assumptions that are difficult to disprove. They are not naive models. But they are not always consistent with one another—recall the case of Mayor Daley. Which models are right and which are wrong? Are some more useful than others? Is any one good enough to use as a framework for our study? Can some combination of models provide a basis for a new general purpose model?

In Table 2-1 we present a rough evaluation of each model in each of the 20 situations studied in this inquiry. These data are judgments made by the authors; they are not offered as "proof" of anything but simply to help the reader follow our conceptual development. For each situation and each model we asked three questions:

[28]Hunter (1953).

- How well does the model describe the mayor's behavior?
- How well does it predict the mayor's impact on his city?
- How well does it account for why the mayor behaved as he did?

We used four ratings: E (excellent), G (good), F (fair), and P (poor). An ideal general purpose model of mayoral behavior, as we have defined it, should rate G or E on all three questions in all 20 situations.

One example should help clarify Table 2-1. In the upper left-hand corner of the chart are the ratings for the Power Broker model in Atlanta during Ivan Allen's administration. The P standing alone means that overall, the model does a poor job of describing, predicting, and explaining this situation (see diagram accompanying table). The F above it and to the left indicates that the model does a fair job of describing Ivan Allen's behavior as a mayor; that is, his behavior included some power brokerage aspects. The P to the right of the F means that the Power Broker model is poor at predicting the impact of Allen's administration on Atlanta. According to the model, because Allen spent relatively little time at power brokering, he should have amassed little power as mayor and should have had a relatively small impact on his city. Such was not the case, however. The P on the far right shows that the Power Broker model does a poor job of explaining why Allen's behavior had a small Power Broker element in it, instead of more or less.

As the far left column in Table 2-1 indicates, the Power Broker model receives an overall rating of E in no situation; it rates G in two situations, F in nine, and P in nine. It does a good or fair job of describing a mayor's behavior in 75% of the cases. It receives an F or better rating for predicting the impact a mayor would have in 10% of the cases. In 35% of the situations it receives an F or better for helping us to understand why the mayor behaved as he did.

The Public Entrepreneur model does well (G) in three situations. Ivan Allen (Atlanta), Richard Lee (New Haven), and Erik Jonsson (Dallas) all behaved very much like Cunningham's public entrepreneur, and their behavior does seem to be associated with large changes in their cities, as predicted. Unfortunately, this model does not help us to understand why a few mayors behaved in this way while most did not. One senses from the data that some mayors would have liked to be public entrepreneurs but were unable to.

Three of the mayors in this study behaved much like the Public Executive (Christopher in San Francisco, Cowger in Louisville, and

Table 2-1 Rating the 10 Mayoral Models in 20 Situations

City, Mayor	Model									
	Power Broker	Public Entre-preneur	Public Exec-utive	Policy Expert	Coali-tion Builder	Mud-dler	Multi-hat Role	Formal Struc-ture	Person-ality	Community Power Struc-ture
Atlanta, Allen	FPP P	EEF G	PPP P	X	GFP F	PPP P	PPP P	PPP P	PEF F	PGG F
Buffalo, Kowal	GGF G	PGF F	PGP F	X	FGP F	GPP F	PPP P	PPP P	PPF P	PPP P
Cleveland, Locher	GFF F	PGF F	PGF F	X	PGP F	GPP F	FPF F	PPP P	FPG F	PPP P
Cincinnati, Bachrach	PPP P	PPP P	X	PPF P	PPP P	EEP G	FPF F	FEE G	FPG F	PFF F
Columbus, Westlake	FPP P	PGP F	PGF F	X	PGP F	EPP F	PPF F	PPF P	PPP P	PPG F
Dallas, Jonsson	FPP P	EEF G	X	GGG G	GFP F	PPP P	PPP P	FEF F	FPF F	PGG F
Fort Worth, McCann	FFP F	PGF F	X	PEF F	FFP F	GPF F	PPP P	FPG F	PPP P	PPP P
Houston, Welch	GGF G	GGP F	FFP F	X	FFP F	PPP P	PPF P	FFF F	PPF P	PFF F
Indianapolis, Boswell	FPP P	PPP P	GFG G	X	PPP P	PPP P	FPF F	PPF P	PPF P	PEF F
Jersey City, Whelan	FPP P	PFP P	FGP F	X	FFP F	PPP P	PPF P	PPP P	PPP P	PPP P
Kansas City, Bartle	PGF F	PFF F	X	GPF F	GPP F	PFP P	FPF F	PPF P	PFG F	PPF P

Louisville, Cowger	FFP F	FFF P	EEF G	X	GGP F	PPP P	FPP P	PPF P	PPF P	PPP P
Minneapolis, Naftalin	PGF F	PFF F	PFF F	X	EPP F	PFP P	PPP P	PPF P	PFG F	PPP P
New Haven, Lee	FFP F	EEF G	PPP P	X	EEF G	PPP P	PPP P	PPP P	FPF F	PPP P
New Orleans, Schiro	FPP P	PFP P	PFF F	X	PGP F	GPP F	FPF F	PPF P	FPF F	PPP P
Newark, Addonizio	GFP F	PFP P	PFF F	X	FFP F	GFP F	FPP P	PPP P	PPF P	PPP P
Norfolk, Martin	PPP P	FFF F	X	PPF P	FFF F	PPP P	PPP P	FPF F	PPP P	PGG F
Rochester, Lamb	PFF F	PPF P	X	PFF F	PGP F	GPP F	FPF F	FPF F	PPP P	PPP P
San Diego, Curran	PFF F	PPP P	X	PFF F	PFP P	GPP F	FFF F	FFG F	PPG F	PPF P
San Francisco, Christopher	FPP P	FFF F	EGG G	X	GGP F	PPP P	FPP P	PFF F	PPG F	PFF P

Key: E = excellent
G = good
F = fair
P = poor
X = not applicable

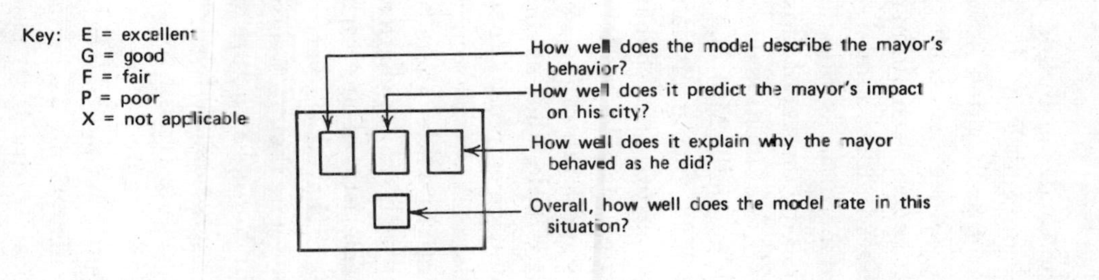

Boswell in Indianapolis). However, the model does not adequately explain why most did not, nor does it explain why New Haven and Atlanta, for example, were *not* plagued by ineffectiveness and inefficiency (as the model predicts).

The Policy Expert model receives an overall rating of good (G) in only 14% of the applicable cases. It seems to suffer from the same types of problems as the Public Executive model. In particular, it fails to help us understand why the administrations of Bachrach (Cincinnati) and Curran (San Diego) were not rife with inefficiency, waste, and ineffectiveness.

The Coalition Builder model receives an overall rating of G in one situation and F in 16. It completely fails to explain why mayors behaved as they did. At best, our efforts to rate mayors in various ways with respect to their positive impact on their city and their effectiveness as coalition builders show a very weak relationship.

The Muddler model receives a G or E in describing mayoral behavior in nine situations. It fares much worse in its attempts to predict the impact of those mayors or to explain why they "muddled." In only one situation does this model receive an overall G.

Although the Multihat Role model rates very poorly, it is useful, to a degree, in sorting out the data we have gathered in this study. Indeed, most mayors often behave as one would expect from the multirole descriptions. The model receives a poor overall rating in 60% of the cases and a fair rating in 40% because it leaves so much unexplained. For example, the mayors in this study varied considerably in the amount of emphasis they appear to have placed on one role versus another. Why do some spend most of their time behaving like executives while others typically behave like chiefs of state? (Even in cities with similar charters!) Some occasionally displayed behavior not characteristic of any of the roles we talked about previously. Why? Some behaved in very similar ways and yet the impact of such behavior on their respective cities appears to be very different. Why?

The Formal Structure model fares only slightly better. The data from this study most certainly do not support the proposition that one form of structure is best for cities (almost regardless of how one defines "best"). Figure 2-1 presents the ratings made by a group of eight urban "experts" we polled (see Chapter 1 for the procedure) on each of our 20 administrations. We include these data simply because the people who advocate a structural model will in general see the opinions of our "experts" as a legitimate measure of an administration's effectiveness.

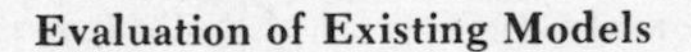

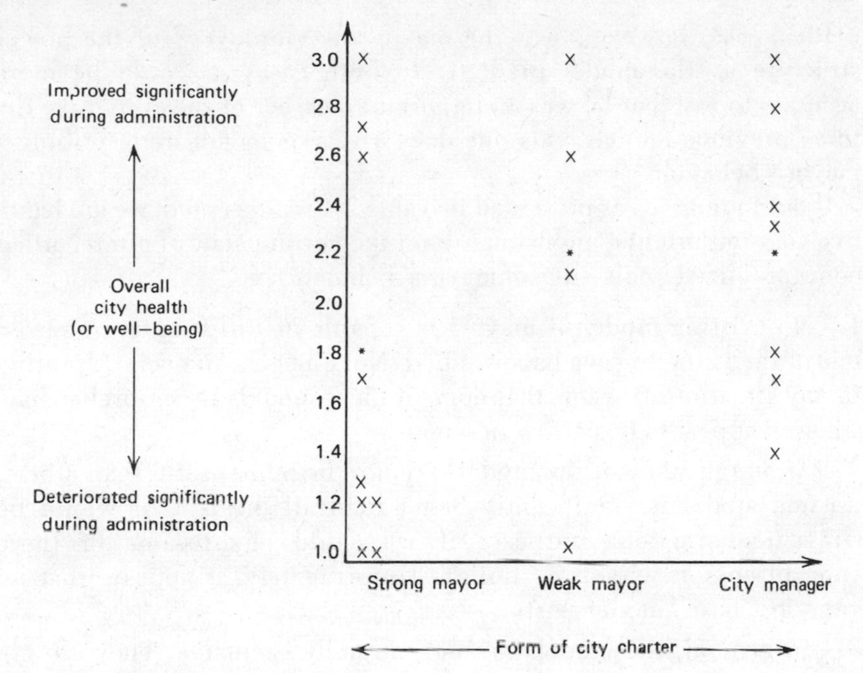

Figure 2-1 Ratings of changes in city health during the 20 administrations studied as made by eight urban "experts." Asterisk indicates mean rating for each charter.

As the figure indicates, no one type of charter does significantly better than the others. Although the model also is poor at describing behavior, it seems to be very useful in some cases in providing an explanation of why the mayor behaved as he did.

The Personality model does not rate well overall, but in 30% of the situations it furnishes a good explanation of why a mayor behaved as he did. It is particularly difficult to rate this model, however, because we did not attempt the systematic gathering of a great deal of data at the personality level of analysis.

Finally, only two of the cities in this study bear a reasonable resemblance to the community Hunter originally reported (one of the two was the city he studied). Three or four others seem to have something like a "power structure" in the broadest definition of the concept. At the other extreme, three or four of the cities bear no obvious resemblance to Hunter's community. In the two cities that had a somewhat clear power structure (Atlanta and Dallas), the elite were talented and public serving as most people would define those terms, and the cities did "well" as many people would define that word. In neither case, however, was the mayor an "employee" of the power structure as the model predicts. In both cases it would be more accurate to say that he was an important member of the elite. Like the three previous models, this one does a very poor job in describing a mayor's behavior.

If our judgments as presented in Table 2-1 are accepted, we are led to five very important conclusions about the current state of our recorded conceptualized knowledge of mayors' behavior.

1. No existing model of mayors is capable of fully explaining even *one* of the situations we have studied. Not one gets an overall E rating in any situation. It seems that none of these models is comprehensive. They all appear to be narrow in scope.
2. Although some of the models seem to be more useful than others, no one model is significantly better than all the rest. It would be convenient for our purposes if we could choose one of these conceptions on which to "build." Unfortunately, it appears that no superior "base" model exists.
3. In general, the models are not mutually exclusive. They are not constructed so that if one does well, all the others will do poorly (e.g., P P P F P E P P P P). Instead, in a typical situation, some rate good, some rate fair, and some rate poor (e.g., P F G P F P P F F F). In many ways the models supplement one another.
4. The models are somewhat exhaustive. Not a single case in this study receives a poor explanation from all ten. No situations exist in Table 2-1 in which all or even most of the models receive an overall rating of P. Taken as a lot, they seem to be covering most matters of importance.
5. Finally, the models tend to do better in different situations. The Power Broker model receives an overall G in cases 2 and 8; the Public Entrepreneur in cases 1, 6, and 14; the Public Executive in cases 9, 12, and 20, and so on. In a way, the models are mutually complementary.

Thus it appears that each model has a certain limited usefulness. None is entirely satisfactory at this point, however, and none is significantly better than all the rest. Among them all, they do not seem to be ignoring any key elements in the situations we have studied. Perhaps our most important observation is that the models often complement and supplement one another.

CHAPTER 3

A NEW FRAMEWORK

Given our analysis in Chapter 2, it is tempting to build a new framework by somehow combining some or all of the current models. Unfortunately, this task is not a simple one. Lumping the models together produces a very cumbersome theory that is inconsistent internally. It would suffer from the same problems of the weakest of the 10 current models (the Multihat Role model).

To produce a useful synthesis we need to understand more precisely how the current models are similar and how they are different, where they overlap and where they diverge, where they are consistent and where they are not. In Table 3-1 we have specified the focus of attention of each of the 10 models, as well as the important assumptions that each model makes. The material is mainly a summary of our previous discussion.

As we noted before, six of the models focus on the behavior of the mayor, and four treat the context in which the behavior occurs. Of the six, two models focus on setting policy (the Policy Expert and the Muddler), although they describe and prescribe very different ways of behaving. In one, policy setting is perceived as the rational-deductive behavior of an expert; the other sees it as the disjointed-incremental behavior of a muddler. One source of these differences is in the polar opposite assumptions made by the models about the mayor's domain.[1]

[1]As we use the word, "domain" refers to that subpart of the total city in which the mayor consciously tries to have an impact.

Table 3-1 Comparison of the Focus and Assumptions Made by 10 Important Models of Mayoral Behavior

Model	Focus of Model	Important Assumptions about Dependencies (Contingencies, Constraints)
1. Power Broker	Behavior Maintaining and gaining power—organization and resource management	Assumes extreme decentralization of power in city and fairly free "power market."
2. Public Entrepreneur	Behavior Problem solving—getting things done	Assumes problems are defined; or at least macro goals are set.
3. Public Executive	Behavior Task management—getting things done	Assumes policy setting and authority over an organization are not issues of importance.
4. Policy Expert	Behavior Establishing policy; deciding what to do	Assumes that mayor's domain is well understood.
5. Coalition Builder	Behavior Building and maintaining a coalition—organization and resource management	Assumes distribution of power in city is structured in a pluralist environment.
6. Muddler	Behavior Establishing policy; deciding what to do	Assumes that mayor's domain is not well understood.
7. Multihat Role	Context Different roles that charter defines for mayor	Assumes roles are defined (to some degree) and determine mayor's behavior.
8. Formal Structure	Context Formal structure of city government	Assumes formal structure is primary determinant of mayor's behavior.
9. Personality	Context Personality of mayor	Assumes personality is prime determinant of behavior.
10. Community Power Structure	Context Distribution of power in community	Assumes power is centralized in hierarchical manner and that it determines the mayor's behavior.

The Policy Expert model assumes that this domain is well understood and that man has developed technical expertise in the areas in which the mayor must perform. The Muddler model, on the other hand, assumes that the domain is not well understood and the mayor has little or no technical expertise at his disposal in those areas.

Two of the other models that focus on behavior tend to assume that policy setting is a given, that the problems are already defined, or that the policy setting process is unimportant or not difficult. These models concentrate on execution, or getting things done. The Public Entrepreneur model describes aggressive, innovative problem-solving behavior, whereas the Public Executive model describes more reserved task management behavior. Nevertheless both are concerned primarily with the achievement of given objectives. One possible source of these different prescriptions and descriptions is in the assumptions they make about formal authority. The Public Executive model seems to assume that the mayor has formal authority over the resources he needs to do his job. The Public Entrepreneur model seems to assume that this is not necessarily the case.

The last two of the six behavior-oriented models appear to treat the question of resources directly. The Power Broker model talks about gaining and maintaining power, and the Coalition Building model focuses on building and maintaining a coalition. Both deal with what one might call organization and resource management. Their descriptions of the mayor's behavior are somewhat different, although there are many similarities. In some ways the Power Broker model emphasizes discrete exchanges (I give you, you give me), whereas the Coalition model stresses appeals to common group interests and superordinate goals. Again, one source of these differences may lie in the slightly different assumptions these models make—in this case, concerning the distribution of power in the community. The Power Broker model assumes extreme decentralization of power to individuals, but the Coalition model assumes decentralization of power to numerous groups (a pluralist setting). In addition, both models appear to assume that as a result of coalition building or power brokering, policy setting and execution happen automatically—they are taken to be a natural consequence of the primary activities of coalition building or power brokerage.

The concept of "distribution of power in the community," which is implicitly important in the resource management models, is the explicit focus of the Community Power Structure model. That model, however, assumes that power in the community is fairly centralized in a hierarchical arrangement. It assumes further that the elite of this hierarchy determine the mayor's behavior.

The Community Power Structure model and three others differ from the first six in that they do not describe aspects of the mayor's behavior at all. Instead, they describe an element that surrounds the mayor, which they assume to be the primary determinant of his behavior. Specifically, the Personality model assumes that the mayor's behavior is primarily determined by his personality. The Multihat Role model assumes that some formal definition of the mayor's role is the primary determinant. The Formal Structure model makes the city charter the primary determinant.

Of course if we ignore the word primary, these four contextual models are not inconsistent or in conflict. No doubt it seems intuitively obvious to many readers that the power distribution in the community, the mayor's personality, the formal government structure, and the formal definition of his role will *all* influence and shape the mayor's behavior. Exactly how they will influence the mayor's behavior is not clear, but it seems reasonable to suppose that such influence exists.

The three aspects of the mayor's behavior on which the other six models focus are not necessarily conflicting, either. Indeed it seems to make sense to break down an actor's behavior in terms of three processes: one in which he decides what to do, another in which he gets and manages the necessary resources, and another in which he carries out specific tasks he has decided on.

No doubt it has been clear to some readers from the beginning that the six behavioral models and the four contextual models are not necessarily inconsistent or contradictory. The behavior emphasized in the first type could be influenced or shaped by the contextual variables emphasized in the second type (or vice versa). Indeed, we can easily enlarge the general framework that is emerging here to include three key behavioral processes occurring *within* some context that influences the shape of the processes, and vice versa. This abstract model is depicted graphically in Figure 3-1.

The framework in Figure 3-1 by itself looks somewhat trite. Its strength comes from its capacity to put the 10 current models of mayoral behavior in a useful perspective. In a sense, it shows how the 10 models "fit together." We have done just that in Figure 3-2—with a few exceptions, this figure is a graphical organization of our previous discussion. There are several minor differences, however. We have put

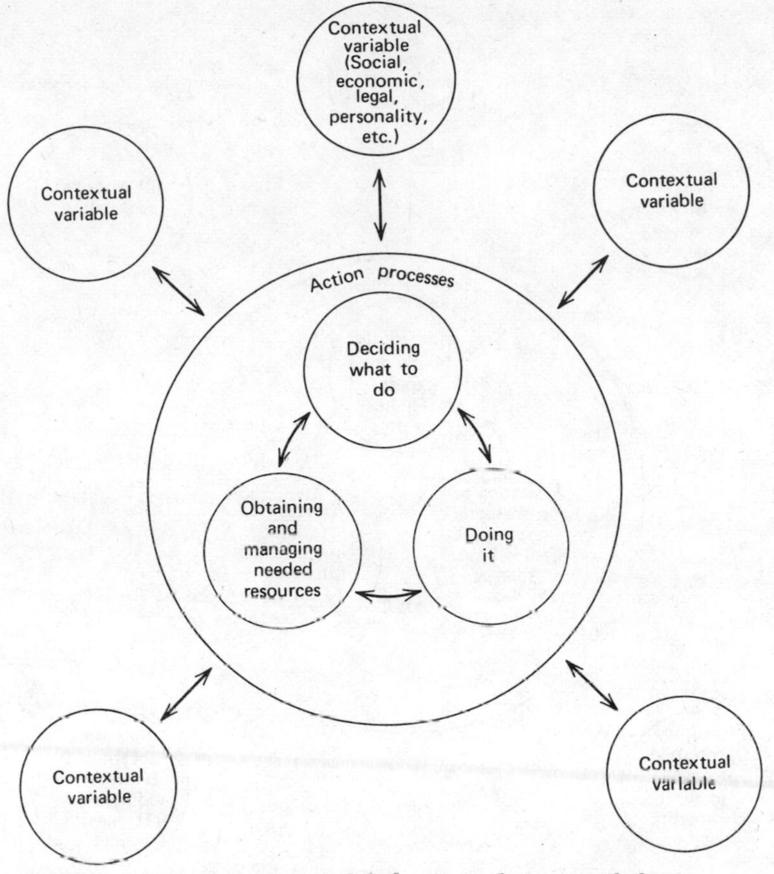

Figure 3-1 An abstract model of action and purposive behavior.

together two of the contextual variables, formal structure and role definition, since they are closely related. For example, both are defined in the city charter. We have added the one contextual variable that was implicit in the Policy Expert and Muddler models: the urban environment that defines the mayor's potential domain. The contextual variables that were implicit in the other four behavioral models are automatically included, since they were the focus of the other contextual models (the Personality model, the Formal Structure model, etc.)

We can discuss the framework developed in Figure 3-2 as follows: A mayor's behavior can be seen as occurring in three different but somehow interrelated processes. In one he decides what to do—he sets his agenda. In another he builds and maintains a network of

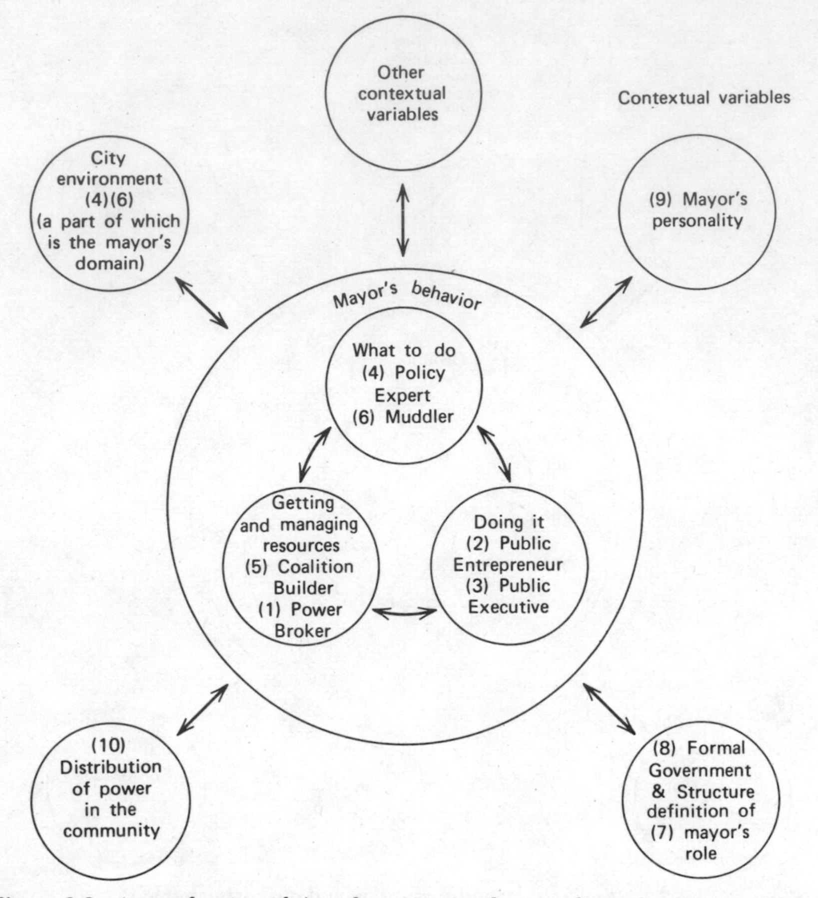

Figure 3-2 A new framework (numbers in parentheses refer to the 10 major models of mayoral behavior; see Table 3-1).

relationships to resources he needs or may need to pursue his agenda. In a third he accomplishes tasks that are on his agenda.

This behavior—the *processes* of agenda setting, network building, and task accomplishment—occurs in a context that affects the behavior and in turn is affected by it. This context includes at least four parts: the mayor's own personality, the formal structure of the city government and the mayor's role in it, the distribution of power in the community, and the city itself.

The mayor's personality affects his behavior because it influences his preferred ways of doing things, the set of skills which allow him to do some things well and others poorly, and his orientation to the world (which helps him see and understand some things better than others). The formal structure of the government affects the mayor's behavior by giving him formal powers in some areas and not in others, and by explicitly stating some responsibilities and not others. The distribution of power in the community determines who had the resources the mayor might need to pursue his agenda. These resources could be controlled by a few people who are like or unlike the mayor, or they could be distributed among many people who are like or unlike the mayor. The city itself, in a sense, presents the mayor with a continuous stream of problems and opportunities on which he might act. It provides him with potential agenda items.

A mayor has a variety of behavioral options in all three key processes. For example, in some cases we would expect him to establish his agenda with the rational-deductive process of the policy expert; whereas under other circumstances he would probably set his agenda with the disjointed-incremental behavior of a muddler. Among other things, we would expect that the degree to which the mayor's domain, the city, is understood will influence which of these two processes emerges. That is, the greater the understanding, the more we would expect to see rational-deduction behavior; the less the understanding, the more we would expect disjointed-incremental behavior.

Furthermore, in some cases we would expect mayors to obtain and maintain resources by coalition building, in other cases by power brokerage, and in still other cases by a combination of these. For example, we would expect that the distribution of power in the community would influence which of these or other behaviors actually emerge in a situation.

Finally, we would expect that some of the mayor's actual accomplishments would be due to executive-type behavior, others to entrepreneurial actions. Among other things, we would expect the amount of formal authority given to the mayor by the formal government structure to influence the emergence of the behaviors observed.

This framework is intriguing because it seems to do a reasonably good job of integrating the current models of mayors; in addition, however, it offers logical clues to how and why these 10 models emerged in the first place. For example, it suggests that in a very large and heterogeneous city in which power is largely decentralized among the population, we would expect to find the mayor handling resource management with a power brokerage process. It is interesting to note that the Power Broker model was developed in a study of Chicago. On the other hand, if power is decentralized into a number of identifiable subgroups, the mayor would probably handle resource management by coalition building. Significantly, the Coalition Building model was developed in New Haven, Connecticut. Likewise, this framework suggests that the more a mayor understands his domain, the more likely he is to behave like a policy expert, and the less he understands it, the more probable it is that he will muddle. Thus the framework suggests that these two models were developed in very different settings. Again, it is not surprising to learn that the Muddler model is a product of studies of national or federal policy making, and the Policy Expert model was originally advocated by people in fairly small and homogeneous cities.

HIGHER ORDER ABSTRACTIONS AND EMPIRICAL DATA

The new framework is appealing for a number of reasons. We indicated at length that it makes a great deal of sense in light of all the conclusions we have drawn from the existing models of mayoral behavior.

The framework also seems to be a strong one because its basic form is consistent with some threads that run through a great many of the abstractions created by social scientists to describe large-scale social action, purposive behavior, and administration. Breaking large-scale social action into policy setting, resource management, and execution is not new by any means. Parsons has described social systems in terms of four key processes.[2] One deals with determination of goals, one with getting things done, and two with resource management and system maintenance. Chester Barnard, who has perhaps contributed more to our understanding of administration than any single individual, talks of three executive functions.[3] He cites "the formulation of purpose and objectives" (policy setting), "the securing of essential services" (getting and managing resources), and "the maintenance of organization communication," which he defines in a way that is consistent with our execution process. Others who have written about large-scale purposive action have proposed other variations on the same theme. On the surface some look quite different and some remarkably similar (see, e.g., Figure 3-3).

[2]Parsons (1957).
[3]Barnard (1938).

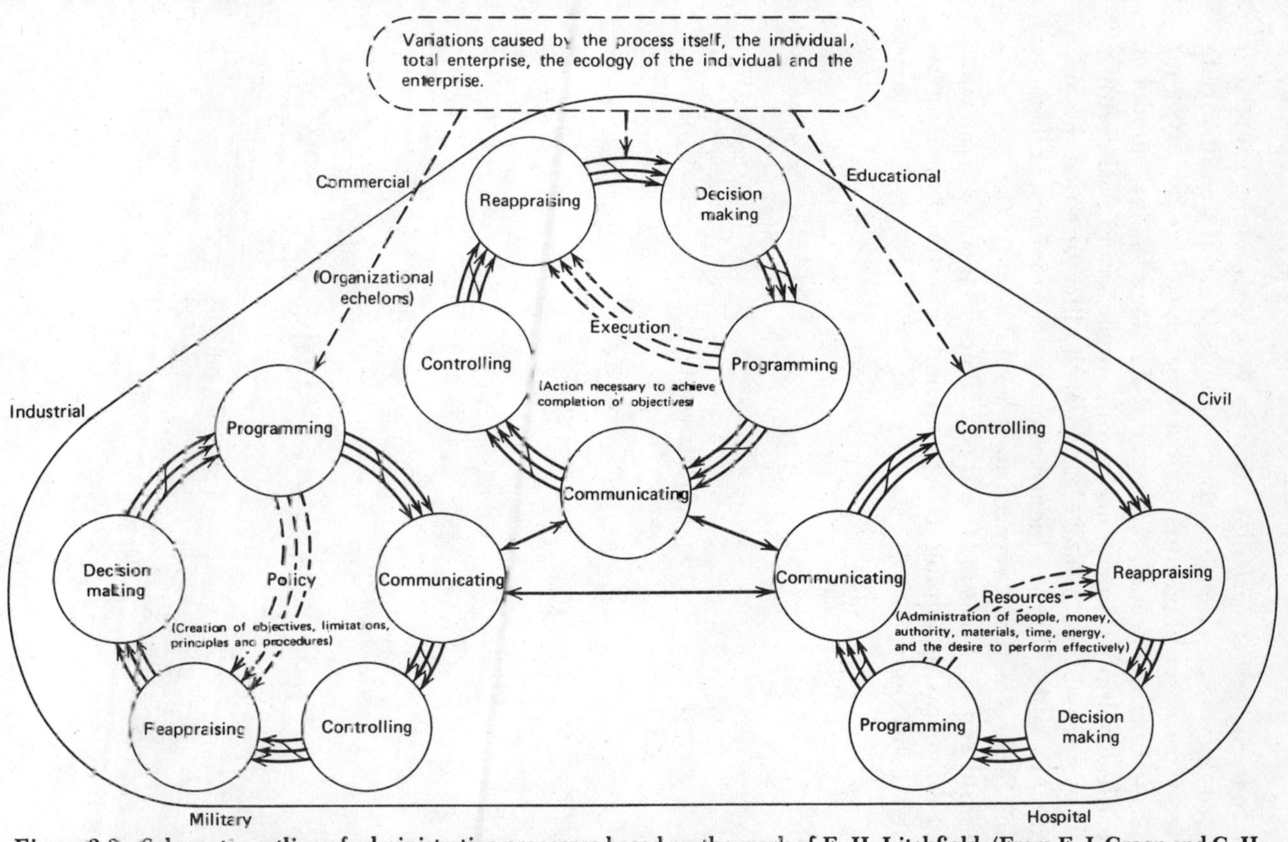

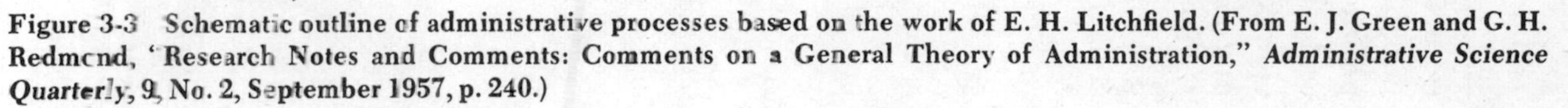

Figure 3-3 **Schematic outline of administrative processes based on the work of E. H. Litchfield. (From E. J. Green and G. H. Redmond, "Research Notes and Comments: Comments on a General Theory of Administration,"** ***Administrative Science Quarterly*****, 9, No. 2, September 1957, p. 240.)**

Our four contextual variables are also very commonly articulated and used by social scientists. For example, Leavitt's multivariate framework for describing intraorganizational dynamics employs four variables—structure, people, tasks, and technology.[4] Paige's model of political leadership uses personality, role, organization, task, setting, and values.[5] It is by no means clear from the literature that the four contextual variables we have identified are the correct ones, or the only ones, but they seem to be a very reasonable set.

The third and final reason for our confidence in the new framework is its effectiveness in helping us sort out and understand the data we collected in this study.

[4]Leavitt (1964).
[5]Paige (1972).

CHAPTER 4

AGENDA SETTING

Agenda setting is simply the process by which a mayor decides what he is going to do. It is the setting of long-run goals and objectives as well as deciding what to do after lunch.

It is common knowledge that different mayors often have very different agendas. Most people also recognize that mayors go about creating their agendas in very different ways. For example, one mayor might do very little agenda setting because his city charter clearly states what he is to do. Another might have considerable latitude to establish an agenda based on his ideology or his "expert" assessment of the situation. A mayor may have his agenda dictated to him by someone else—his staff or his political party, for example. Or, a mayor may simply choose items from a continuous stream of requests and ideas and projects that come to him daily. This process could be rational-deductive as in the Policy Expert model or disjointed-incremental as in the Muddler model.

One of our more interesting findings is that the different agenda setting behaviors used by our 20 mayors seem to be variations along *one* continuum (Figure 4-1). At one end of this continuum the agenda setting process is reactive, short-run oriented, individual or part-oriented, continuous, and sometimes "irrationally" unconnected. This process resembles what Charles Lindblom has labeled "muddling through."[1] At the other extreme the process is proactive, middle- to

[1]See Braybrooke and Lindblom (1963).

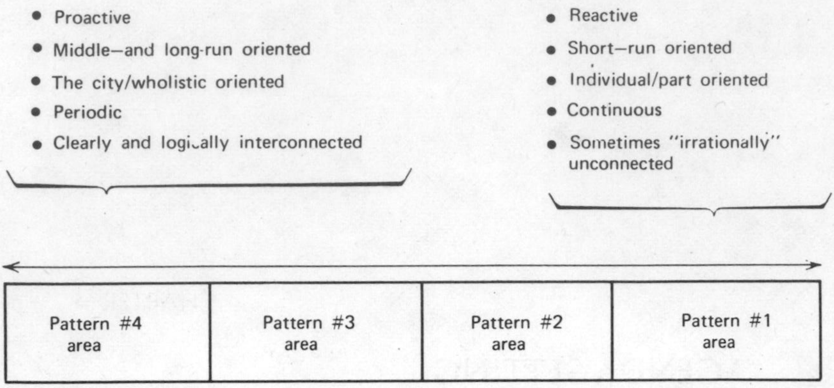

Figure 4-1 Description of the extreme agenda setting behaviors along a continuum, arbitrarily divided into four areas for discussion purposes.

long-range oriented, city-wide or holistic oriented, periodic, and logically interconnected. The latter process, which is one of "rational-deductive" planning, is said to be used by leaders in the military and in large corporations.[2]

The agendas created by these different processes are of course quite different themselves (see Figure 4-2). The mayor who uses the "muddling through" (pattern #1 area) process tends to have few if any items on his longer-run agenda. In a sense, his daily agenda is set for him by people who wish to see him, by "crises" reported in the paper, and so on. He has some control over what he puts on his agenda—that is, over whom he sees and what he reacts to. A mayor who uses the pattern #1 process usually chooses items that appear to be most important in the short run and focus on discrete issues. The connection between items on his daily agenda is not terribly "rational" in the sense that the word is used by planners. The logical connection between his daily agenda and his longer-run agenda—perhaps "to make the city a better place"—is usually fairly loose also.

The agendas created by the mayor using a "rational planning" (pattern #4) process tend to have a great deal of detail in their longer-run versions. To a large degree, the daily agenda is simply a statement of what logically needs to be done to move toward the monthly agenda, which is a logical statement of what must be done to achieve the yearly agenda, and so on out to perhaps 25 years. The

[2] *Ibid.*

agendas are created and modified, not continuously but in cycles. The daily agenda may be normally created once a day (in the morning), the monthly agenda once a month, the yearly agenda once a year, and so on. These agendas are established as the result of an analytic, problem-solving thought process that focuses on the entire city as the "client system."

The agendas that lie between the extremes just discussed (pattern #3, pattern #2 areas) represent a blending of the #1 and #4 agendas. The reader should carefully examine Figure 4-2 for all four patterns, especially #2 and #3 (those between the extremes).

Figure 4-3 reveals where agenda setting processes used by each of the 20 mayors in the study fit on our continuum. About the same number of mayors used agenda setting processes in pattern #1 and #2 areas. A much smaller number fell into the pattern #3 area, and the pattern #4 area had *none.*

That is, not one of the 20 mayors in this study set his agenda with the rational planning process that is the ideal of the Policy Expert model. About 45% of the mayors behaved in a manner similar to the Muddling model. Even more interesting, perhaps, is that 55% of our mayors behaved in neither way. They set their agendas with what we have called a #2 or #2 process, and neither process is explicitly identified in the models we explored in Chapter 2.

Mayors who use similar agenda setting processes, of course, look alike in a number of ways. With a few examples, the reader can gain a better sense of what that behavior looks like operationally.

THE #1 AGENDA SETTING PROCESS

Exemplifying the mayors who used a pattern #1 agenda setting process is Victor H. Schiro in New Orleans. Schiro has described his "typical day" as mayor in the following manner:

> My driver would come by at a specified time depending on my appointments. We'd probably stop on the way downtown and have a cup of coffee, and then go to my first appointment. Occasionally there were openings of new businesses, new stores, etcetera, and they invited the mayor to cut the ribbon.

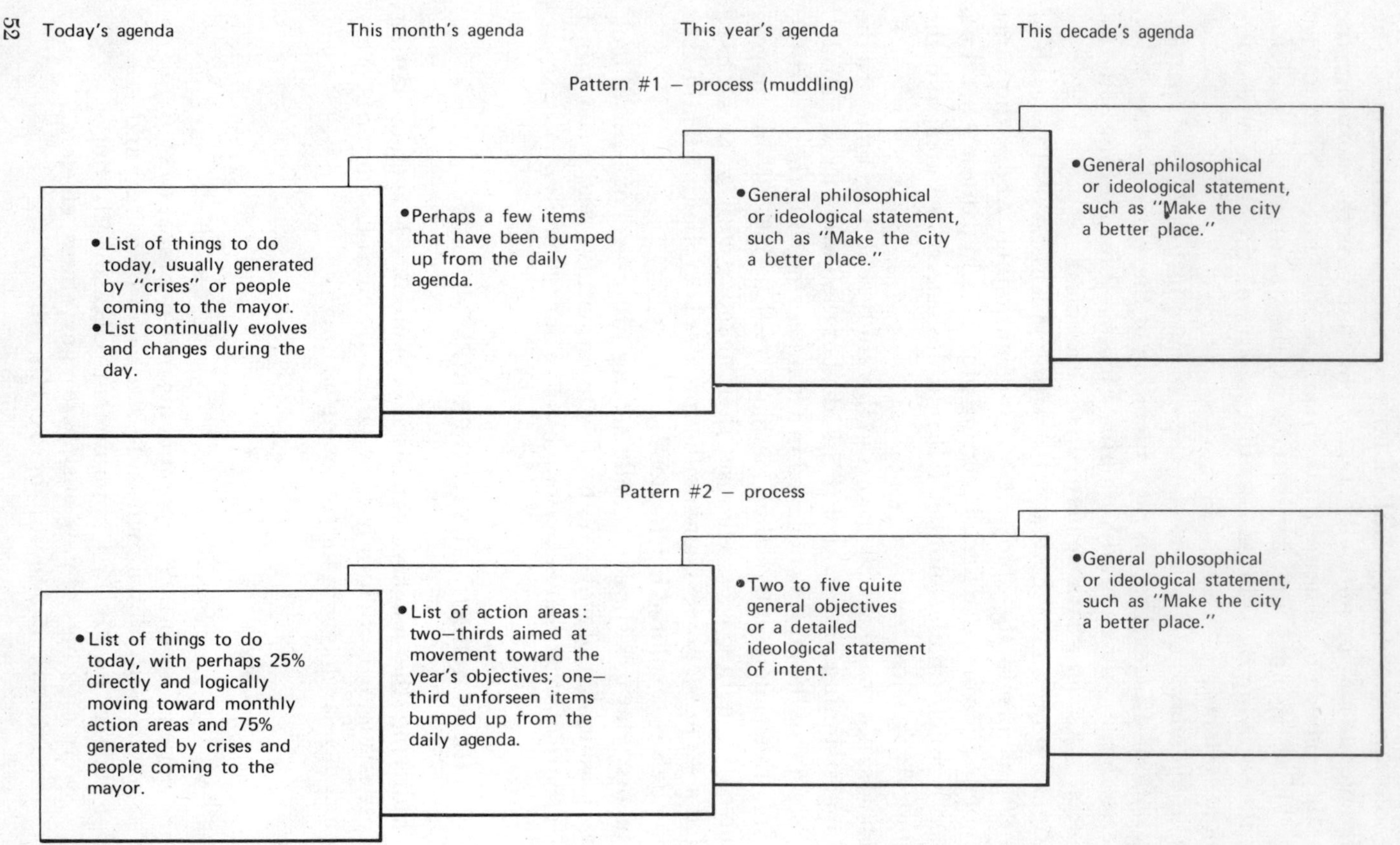

Figure 4-2 Agendas.

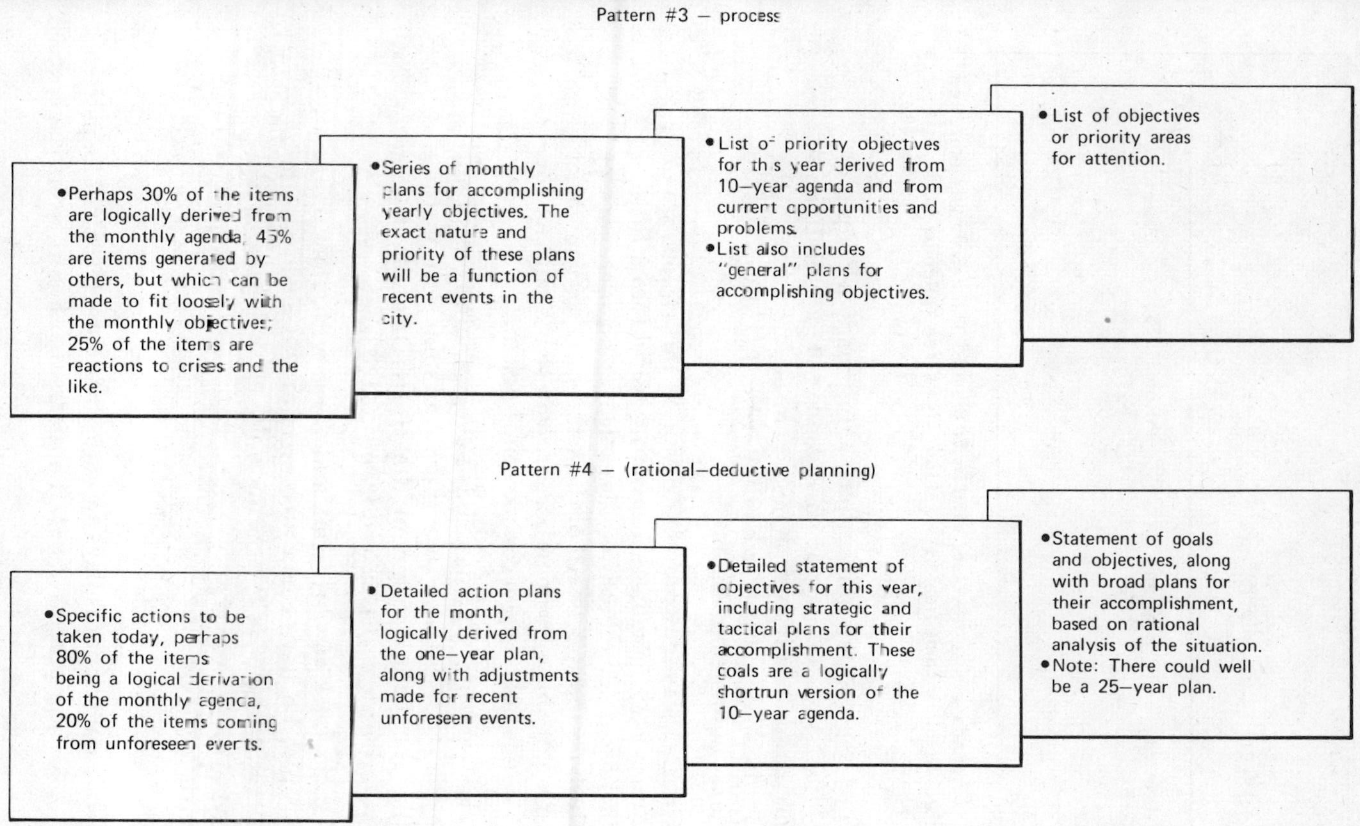

Pattern #3 – process

- Perhaps 30% of the items are logically derived from the monthly agenda, 45% are items generated by others, but which can be made to fit loosely with the monthly objectives; 25% of the items are reactions to crises and the like.

- Series of monthly plans for accomplishing yearly objectives. The exact nature and priority of these plans will be a function of recent events in the city.

- List of priority objectives for this year derived from 10–year agenda and from current opportunities and problems.
- List also includes "general" plans for accomplishing objectives.

- List of objectives or priority areas for attention.

Pattern #4 – (rational–deductive planning)

- Specific actions to be taken today, perhaps 80% of the items being a logical derivation of the monthly agenda, 20% of the items coming from unforeseen events.

- Detailed action plans for the month, logically derived from the one–year plan, along with adjustments made for recent unforeseen events.

- Detailed statement of objectives for this year, including strategic and tactical plans for their accomplishment. These goals are a logically shortrun version of the 10–year agenda.

- Statement of goals and objectives, along with broad plans for their accomplishment, based on rational analysis of the situation.
- Note: There could well be a 25–year plan.

Figure 4-2 Agendas (Continued)

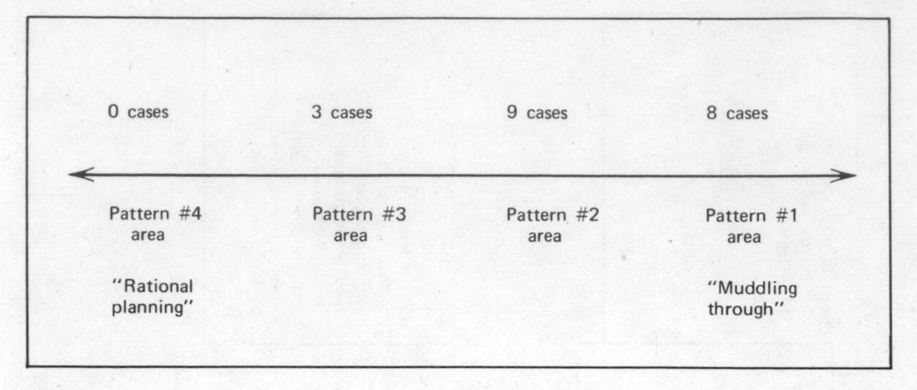

Figure 4-3 Agenda setting processes used by 20 mayors. The data in this figure and in similar figures to follow come from personal interviews (see Appendix A).

> So I'd go to my office after having made a couple of stops, and I'd have an agenda of appointments prepared in advance. I never closed my door to the public, regardless of who they were. I always kept my name in the telephone book.
>
> On the way downtown I'd notice the streets. Some streets may have been beginning to fold up a little or there may have been too many leaves on some lots, or trash on the streets. All of these things. . . . You've got to keep your eyes open because you're the only mayor. There is nobody you can pass the buck to.
>
> Then during the day I'd have appointments and usually every lunch time there was some sort of thing like the United Fund or the Heart Drive. Someone would write a speech, and I would give it.
>
> I'd go back to City Hall and meet with some more people. I'd have committee meetings to deal with the street problem or the crime problem, or whatever had come up.[3]

This brief statement displays a number of characteristics of a pattern #1 agenda setting process. First, it appears that Schiro's daily agenda

[3]Tape-recorded interview.

was set by people coming to him with requests, followed by his choosing whom to see. This reactive mode is inherent in his "ribbon cutting," appointments with citizens, luncheon talks, and committee meetings (to deal with what had "come up"). The elements of his day are short-run oriented, and they involve small discrete issues; the mayor thought it was important for him to keep an eye on streets and to deal with individual citizens. Those we interviewed who knew Schiro well say that he never really had a long-run agenda. Even his monthly and yearly agendas contained only general statements about "helping the average guy." Although the strictly logical connection between his daily agenda and his yearly agenda was not very tight, his yearly agenda of "helping people" was serious and sincere, and the entire process apparently made sense to Schiro.

THE #2 AGENDA SETTING PROCESS

The mayors who used a #2 agenda setting process tended to focus less on daily activities and more on monthly and yearly activities. As a rule, they were pursuing projects of a type that could be completed in a month, a year, or a few years at most.

William O. Cowger, mayor of Louisville between 1961 and 1965, used a pattern #2 agenda setting process. After 28 years of Democratic control of the city of Louisville, the Republican party won the 1960 elections for mayor and county judge (mayor of the county). William Cowger and Marlow Cook ran a very aggressive campaign, attacking the opposition for lack of movement and progress. In the process of talking to thousands of people and interacting with the various groups and institutions in the city, Cowger fitted a number of items into his "medium-run" agenda.

- To create a Human Relations Commission
- To create a separate (outside the mayor's office) Urban Renewal Commission
- To bring youth and drive into the city government staff
- To build Louisville a zoo
- To spur the economy and bring in new business.

The criteria Cowger used to select these items for his agenda were probably the following:

- Is this project of concern to a large number of people?

- Does it make sense for Louisville? Is it a good use of resources?
- Is it feasible? Can I do it?
- Can the project be completed or near completion in 2 or 3 years? (The mayor cannot succeed himself in Louisville.)

Cowger articulated these agenda items as campaign promises and used them in winning the election. This process of using agenda items in the campaign is very typical of mayors whose agenda was set with a #2 process.

Once in office, Cowger filled in the rest of his short-run agenda and continued to add midrange items as some of the original ones were accomplished. He established as a major one-year agenda item the passing of a bond issue, the money being earmarked for the university, for parks, for the hospital, for a museum, and so on. As in the campaign, in placing items on his agenda, Cowger listened carefully and made his own judgments.

THE #3 AGENDA SETTING PROCESS

The mayors who used a #3 agenda setting process went even further in the direction of a proactive, long-run, holistic, logically interconnected process. As opposed to their colleagues who used the #1 or #2 processes, these mayors created 5-, 10-, or 15-year agendas, as well as midrange and short-run agendas, in different periodic cycles. Contrast the following description by Milwaukee mayor Henry Maier with the typical day of Victor Schiro:

MORNING

- Soon after he arrives, his personal secretary enters his office. . . . She presents him with the early morning papers that he must sign and a picture he has been asked to autograph.
- He looks at his list of incoming calls left over from late the previous afternoon, and asks about the call from the building inspector. The inspector wants to see him as soon as possible. The Mayor says that he'll see him immediately.
- After the inspector has left, the Mayor spends the next hour reviewing some reports on his desk. These concern his operational plans, the priorities for action that he has established,

and involve a number of decisions. He tells his secretary that he wants to see the planning coordinator and the economic development director in the late afternoon.

- Coming through the door is a secretary who will be in and out of the Mayor's office several times during the day. He is the combination press secretary, troubleshooter, appointments secretary, political secretary, and operational subchief of staff. The secretary mentions a number of people whom the Mayor ought to see. The secretary informs him that the evening paper is doing a story on organized labor's influence in local government and wants to interview him on his labor appointees. He informs the Mayor that a reporter wants to know if he will answer the governor's apparent criticism of the city. He says that up until now the communications media have not shown much interest in the Mayor's charter message, but it is still early. He recommends acceptance of several civic invitations. The Mayor discusses all items with him, accepts or rejects his suggestions, then with a grin tells him to get busy and turn out some work.
- Later, taking a breather, the Mayor walks around the outer offices. He exchanges pleasantries. . . . He winds up discussing some of the latest endeavors of the division of economic development and then returns to his office.
- At noon he enjoys a luncheon with some members of the Common Council. He seeks out their reactions to various proposals and, where differences exist, tries to find a common ground.

AFTERNOON

- Back in his office after lunch, the Mayor answers some of the telephone calls that have piled up since late morning. He meets briefly with the civil defense director. While a television camera looks on, he takes part in the ceremonial signing of a proclamation in his office.
- After a while he leans back in his chair to relax for a moment, but his secretary flashes him on the intercom. "There is a gentleman here who insists on seeing you," she says, and gives him a name. "Send him in," he answers. The door opens and a citizen walks in. He wishes to talk about a problem of much concern to him

and his neighbors. "A number of people in our neighborhood want to meet with you to discuss trucking on our street," the citizen says. "All right, we'll hold the meeting, the Mayor says, "but all of the reports from our departments indicate that nothing can be done until the expressways are completed." He schedules the meeting, even though the local alderman has already informed the Mayor of the problem, regretfully remarking that there is no way to satisfy the citizenry immediately.

- To his office now come his chief aide, the director of economic development, and the planning coordinator. Their discussion concerns all of the Mayor's immediate dreams for the city, here in the form of 26 top-priority projects listed on the cards that lie before him on a table. The list includes matters as forward-looking as a long-range fiscal plan for the city, as prosaic as a proposed new system for combining the collection of garbage and refuse, as colorful as a potential world festival.
- When the meeting is over, the Mayor turns to the material he is preparing for a major policy speech. He calls two staff members for projections of estimated revenue needs for the next ten years.
- Exit staff men. Enter the reporters assigned to the city hall beat.
- When the reporters leave his office, he continues to think about a variety of things touched on during their visit. Where can he gather support to put across his state tax distribution program? How can urban renewal be speeded up? Delays resulting from the paperwork necessary between the local and federal governments seem to be causing much concern in areas slated for demolition. He wonders at what points he can compromise on his reorganization plan without giving too much away.
- The typewriters are covered in the outer office and most people have gone home for the day. The Mayor is once again discussing a number of problems with his chief aide. He promptly decides some questions which require an immediate answer. They agree that several areas need further exploration before a decision can be made, and assignments are made for those who are to gather the facts.
- Later, an old personal friend and wise political advisor drifts in, and the remaining time turns into a congenial discussion of politics.

EVENING

- Finally, his security officer reminds him that he has a dinner engagement soon.
- At the convivial evening banquet, the Mayor is applauded by the audience. Afterwards, of course, there are those who stop him to lecture or advise. "Why don't you . . . ?" "Why haven't you . . . ?"
- At home, his wife asks, "How did it go today?" "Oh, so-so," he answers. He makes a few telephone checks on various items, and then he finally relaxes. His day is over.[4]

In this example, Maier has described an 11-hour day in which perhaps 5 hours of the mayoral agenda were set in the proactive mode. Reviewing reports, talking to the council, and meeting with the planning and economic coordinators were activities that had been proactively put in the agenda because they logically had to be done to move the mayor toward accomplishing items on his longer-run agenda. On the other hand, such activities as his initial time with his secretary, his time at and after the banquet, his meeting with the citizens, and his ceremonial signing, appear to have been agenda items set in a reactive mode. That is, these activities, which took up perhaps 4 hours of his day, were initiated by others, dealt with short-run and discrete issues, and did not necessarily help him advance his future agenda. Finally, some activities—seeing the building inspector, talking to reporters, talking to an old friend and to his political secretary—were agenda items set by a method between the extremes. The items were initiated by someone else, but Maier used them to further his own future agenda. This combination of agenda setting types is fairly typical of the way a pattern #3 process looks on a daily basis.

THE #4 AGENDA SETTING PROCESS

Although no mayor in this study used a pattern #4 agenda setting process, the Goals for Dallas program initiated by former mayor Erik Jonsson is a good example of what such a process might look like. This

[4]Condensed from Henry Maier, *Challenge to the Cities* (New York: Random House, 1960), pp. 3–15, with deletions. Copyright © 1966 by Henry Maier. Reprinted by permission of Random House, Inc.

program began in December 1965 with the creation of a steering committee of prominent citizens. With the aid of technical specialists, urban experts, and local writers, 13 essays were produced on current conditions in Dallas. In June 1966 a conference of about 90 community representatives and technical experts met to talk about the essays and create a first list of "goals." In November–December of 1966 more than 6000 Dallas residents attended neighborhood meetings to examine and revise these goals. Between May 1967 and May 1968, a technical consulting group and a 300-man task force under the direction of the steering committee drafted a plan of "proposals for achieving the goals," which was reviewed by large numbers of citizens. Meanwhile, subtask forces began producing more detailed documents for specific areas. For example, the Economic Potentials Committee worked with the National Planning Association and the SMU Institute for Urban Studies to create better urban statistical information for Dallas.

The output of this process was a series of agendas with more than 100 goals of various durations—20, 10, 5, and 1 years—broken down into the areas of government, design, health, welfare, transportation-communication, public safety, education, cultural activities, recreation and entertainment, and the economy. The agendas also included plans in varying amounts of detail for achieving these goals. Such plans involved the action needed, costs, timing, and so on.

Had Erik Jonsson adopted the entire package of goals and plans as his mayoral agenda, and then created his daily and monthly agenda using a similar process, he would have been using a pattern #4 agenda setting process. In reality, he adopted only portions of that program and behaved in the manner we have described as a pattern #3 agenda setting process.

PREREQUISITES OF THE PROCESSES

The four agenda setting processes appear to require different inputs or resources if they are to "work." Thus they place very different demands on a mayor. As the foregoing description indicates, the #4 process calls for considerable technical expertise, time, and energy. It seems to demand a very dynamic and future-oriented person like Erik Jonsson to keep it in motion. Furthermore, the short-run tasks on the agenda must be actually accomplished and not bottlenecked. It appears that Jonsson's primary reason for not adopting the #4 process, opting instead for #3, was inability to complete the enormous number of tasks listed on the #4 process agenda.

At the other extreme, the #1 agenda setting process seems to require little technical expertise, time, or capacity to finish all the tasks. It does, however, require a mayor who is comfortable with the short-run orientation (like Schiro) and an information system that is *very* sensitive to today's problems (recall Schiro driving around looking at the streets). The ability to move very quickly on small, short-run tasks is also needed.

The two processes in between require varying degrees of the same elements that appear to be relevant in the #1 and #4 processes.

THE MAYOR'S DOMAIN

A mayor's domain is the sum of those areas in which the mayor behaves *as if* he has some responsibility. The larger the domain, the larger the mayor's job. For example, a small domain might include responsibility for attending ceremonial affairs and council meetings. A larger domain might include responsibilities in the following areas: five or six public service organizations (e.g., the fire and police departments); the health, housing, transportation, education, and employment of the city's population; local short-run crises; and the entire city's future—10 to 100 years from now.

It will be of no surprise to most people that the domains of the 20 mayors in the study varied considerably: some mayors consciously tried to narrow their impact; others operated in very large domains.

One would expect the size of a mayor's impact area to be a function of the city charter, since this document spells out a mayor's responsibilities. Indeed, in examining our data we find that mayors with city manager charters tended to have smaller domains than mayors in cities with weak and strong mayor charters. However, charter alone does *not* explain some significant variations in the size of the domain of our 20 mayors. Erik Jonsson (Dallas), for example, operated in a domain considerably larger than that of Victor Schiro (New Orleans), even though Dallas has a city manager charter and New Orleans does not. However, if we take into account a second factor—the mayor's agenda setting process—we have a fair explanation for the variations noted in mayors' domains (see Figure 4-4).

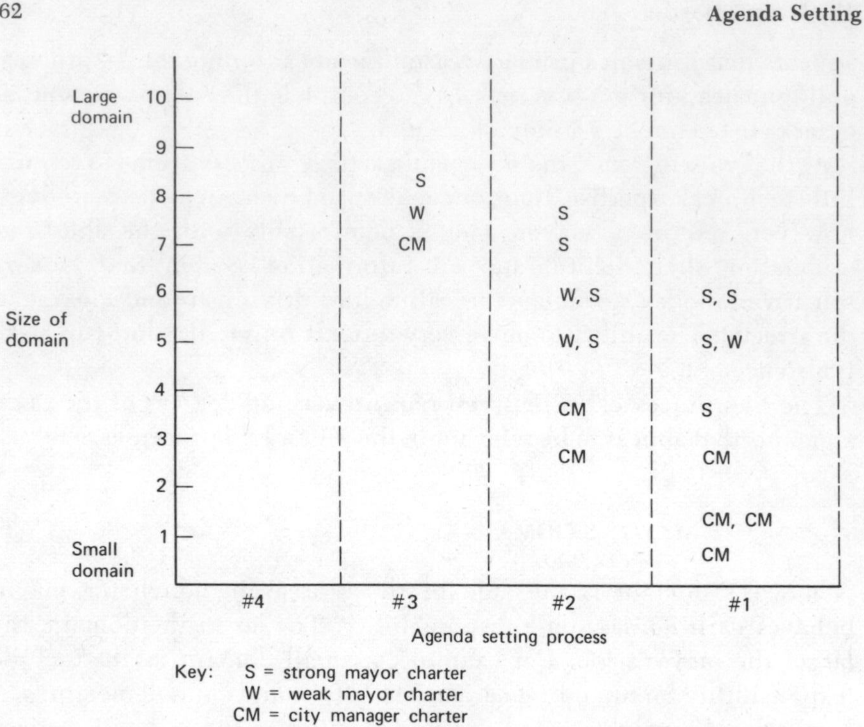

Figure 4-4 Relationship of the mayor's domain and his agenda setting process.

Mayors using a #1 agenda setting process tended to have smaller domains than mayors using #2 process, who in turn tended to have smaller domains than mayors using a #3 agenda setting process. This finding seems quite reasonable. The language with which city charters enumerate a mayor's responsibilities is seldom very precise. Thus a mayor has considerable latitude in defining his own domain. Newspapers are full of examples of mayors trying to change their domain or to clarify its boundaries. The mayor with a small domain often reacts with statements like, "No, that's not the duty of the mayor. That's the duty of the State Board of Education," or "I'm afraid, gentlemen, that that is outside my jurisdiction. There is nothing I can do about it."

In the original distinction between "muddling through" and "rational planning" we noted that the former was more concerned with parts, the latter with the whole. Precisely because the rational planning process deals with the whole, it is very difficult (if not impossible) to apply it in a limited domain. A city is a complex set of interdependencies. To use a #4 process on only part of it is to deny those interdependencies and to engage in an irrational act, unless the part on which the mayor is focusing is somehow completely under his control. However, since no mayor in this study had a restricted domain over which he had complete control, the results of Figure 4-4 are not surprising.

For example, suppose a mayor would prefer to have a very narrow domain in which he sets his agenda with a #3 process. He has only one concern. He would like to build an international trade building at the city's port facilities and significantly increase the port's multinational trade. He sees this as an 8-year project or program. As he begins to set his agenda and plan in a rational-deductive way, he soon discovers the following facts:

- The city council is less than enthusiastic about this program, and since they control money for special expenditures, he cannot ignore the political arena in his domain.
- Although a site that is ideal for the building is already owned by the city, the public transportation facilities to that site are negligible. A staff assistant tells the mayor that the trade building, as they envision it, would require a significant change in the current transportation system (streets, buses, tunnels). The mayor decides that the city's transportation system will have to be included in his domain.
- A consultant's study shows that because of the unique nature of the proposed trade building, construction during years 5 to 7 will cause major complications in the daily activities of the port. Grudgingly, the mayor accepts the port as in his domain.
- A study of the most successful international trade building in the world points out that such a building produces a great demand for multilingual employees. Given the size of the building being planned, 5000 multilingual office personnel would be required. The mayor learns that the city's school system is cutting back on an already inadequate language program. Add the schools.

Because of such interdependencies, the more a mayor uses a rational deductive agenda setting process, the larger the domain he creates for himself.

OTHER ASPECTS OF THE IMPACT OF DIFFERENT AGENDA SETTING PROCESSES

In the original distinction between a rational-deductive process (#4) and a disjointed-incremental process (#1), we noted that the former tends to produce larger changes than the latter. And this trend was confirmed by the results of our study. Mayors using a #1 agenda setting process tended to have a smaller direct impact on their cities than mayors using a #3 process; moreover, #1 administrations seemed to be more concerned with maintenance. Atlanta, for example, changed significantly during Ivan Allen's tenure, and those changes seem to be associated with Allen's agenda and his #3 agenda setting process. Fort Worth, on the other hand, appears not to have changed at all as a result of Tom McCann's actions and his #1 agenda setting process.

Furthermore, in cities whose mayor was using a #3 process, there tended to be more short-run tensions and problems traceable to the mayor's actions than in cities whose mayors used a #1 process. For example, recall that during a typical day of a mayor using a #3 process, a citizen complained to Milwaukee Mayor Henry Maier about trucking on a neighborhood street. The trucking, a result of Maier's expressway building program, was making life in the short run uncomfortable for the residents of that street. All the mayors in this study who used a #3 process tended to complicate the lives of some group or groups of people in the short run. Those groups include merchants being somewhat ruthlessly displaced by urban renewal; lower-middle-class whites being attacked socially, economically, and psychologically by a changing civil rights climate; and blacks being consigned to poverty while airports and freeways are given priority.

It also follows that the mayor who uses a #1 agenda setting process will often help create some long-run problems by not looking toward the future. This is exactly what we found in our study. Economic decline, riots, and transportation and water crises, all have some roots in the behavior of mayors who simply ignored the signs of trouble in the future.

Although it might seem possible for a mayor to set his agenda in a way that would not create any negative consequences, none of the mayors in the study did so.

CHAPTER 5

NETWORK BUILDING AND MAINTENANCE

In the second key process in our framework, we deal with the mayor's access to critical resources: votes, money, laws, human skills, and task accomplishment capacity. To be reelected, to accomplish specific objectives, and merely to prevent chaos, all mayors try to build and maintain a network of positive relationships with certain groups, organizations, and institutions. The "network members" usually include various segments of the population (e.g. the rich, the white working class, the Irish), formal governmental bodies (the state government, the city council, the city bureaucracy, etc.), some major interest groups (business, labor), and perhaps a few key institutions (the press).

A typical network appears in Figure 5-1, a graphic display of H. Roe Bartle's (Kansas City) network in and around 1957. The relationships shown change over time (and Bartle's did), but they are relatively stable in the short run. That is, major fluctuations occur, at most, yearly.

As in the case of the agenda setting process, the means of network building used by our 20 mayors varied considerably. Unlike the agenda setting process, however, we cannot talk of these variations along a single continuum. We must use three.

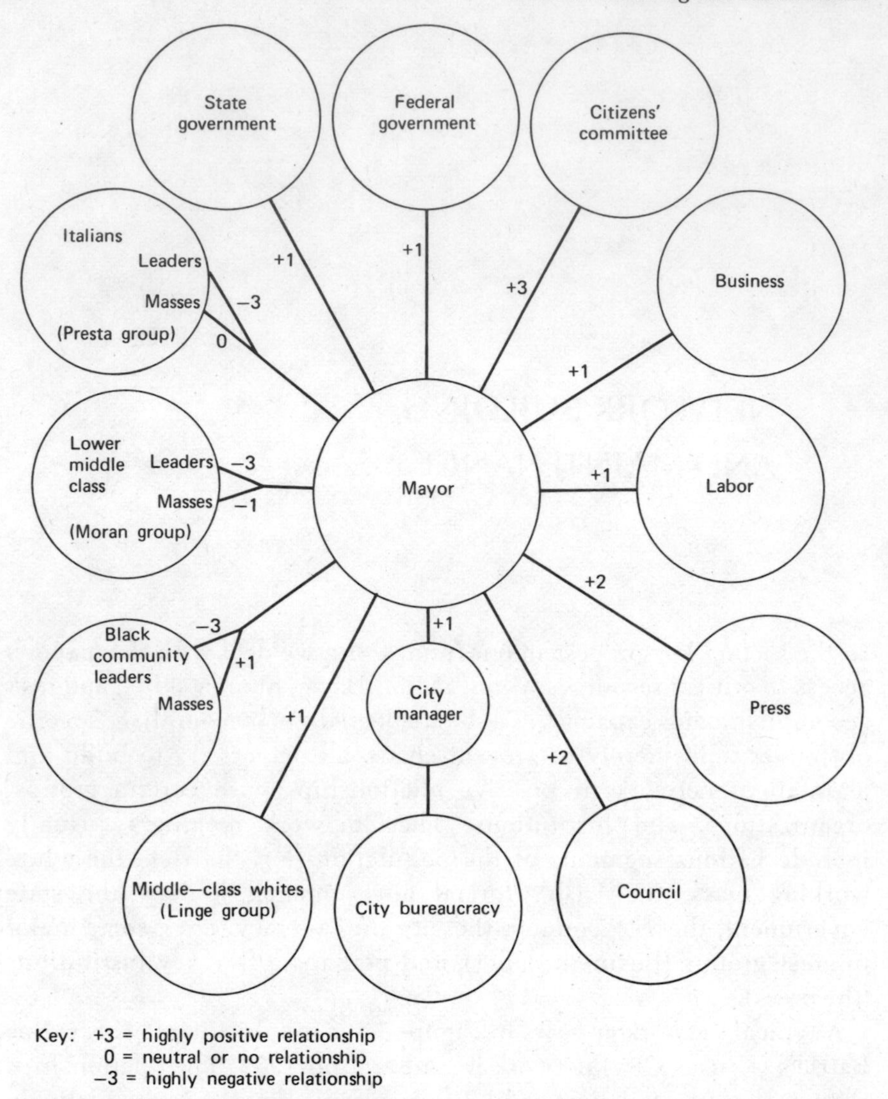

Figure 5-1 Bartle's network in 1957.

The network building processes used by the 20 mayors differed with respect to the types of cooperative relationships the mayors tried to create, how actively the mayors tried to reshape their network, and the kind of staff (the mayor's office) the mayors hired.

ESTABLISHING COOPERATIVE RELATIONSHIPS

In this study we have identified nine distinctly different cooperative relationships that mayors established with members of their networks (Table 5-1). All these relationships are based on different criteria, are established through different processes, and have slightly different effects.

Table 5-1 Types of Relationships Mayors Established with Their Network Members

Type of Relationship	Basis	Number of Mayors Who Used It Very Frequently
Utilitarian	Discrete exchange which is negotiated ("I give you something, you give me something.")	11
Coercive	Fear ("You give me this or else I'll. . . .")	4
Purposive I—for	Coalition for a common cause or goal (can be explicit or implicit)	9
Purposive II—against	Coalition against something (the competition)	2
Cooptative	Absorbing someone from a network member group into the mayor's policy-setting group	4
Personal I—reference group appeal	Appealing to reference group loyalties ("I am Irish, you are Irish, cooperate with me.")	7
Personal II—friendship appeal	Appealing to old and new friends	11
Personal III—charismatic	Appealing to superegos ("He's my ideal picture of a mayor.")	5
Formal/legal	The city charter and other legislation which says that in certain matters A has formal authority over B	4

Utilitarian Relationships

The most common type of cooperative relationship we found was based on a negotiated discrete exchange.[1] Indeed, this is what many people associate with "politics." Mayors often use this type of process to establish and maintain cooperative relationships with their councils, their bureaucracy, and their political party.

For example, Allan Talbot has reported that after Richard Lee's (New Haven) election in 1954 he negotiated with the local Democratic party a relationship of cooperation (an "arrangement") that included the following points:

> 1. Lee would clear all his appointments with John Golden, the local party chief.
> 2. Golden would handle political arrangements with the state machine.
> 3. Steps would be taken to assure that Golden's insurance business would be given favorable consideration whenever the city needed such services.
> 4. Golden's candidates would be given serious consideration for available city jobs and patronage.
> 5. Lee would have full control over redevelopment decisions and jobs, although he would clear major decisions affecting the party with Golden and Arthur Barbieri.
> 6. Arthur Barbieri, the Town Democratic Chairman, would be made Public Works director.
> 7. The party, of course, would help Lee as he needed them, in traditional ways.[2]

We did not encounter the ultimate example of this type of process because powerful political party machines no longer existed in the

[1]All the nine processes described here can be thought of as exchange processes in the broad sense. See Blau (1964). We feel that the concept is more useful if limited to the tangible and the zero-sum.

[2]Talbot (1967).

cities studied. Some of the old bosses were reported to be masters at giving discrete services in exchange for votes, legwork, or even money. They often distributed Christmas baskets, helped their people get on relief or the WPA, stood between them and the police in minor cases of law violation, provided social centers in the wards, bought coal for the faithful during the winter, and performed thousands of other services. A typical contract might have been a job with the city in exchange for 3% of one's pay and so many hours per week working for the party.

Three conditions are required for the successful utilization of this type of process. First, a mayor needs some resources or capital which he can exchange—favors, jobs, money. The mayor who has little of this political capital, as is often the case in a city manager government, seldom relies heavily on the utilitarian relationship for cooperation.

Second, the mayor needs network members who are willing to engage in the process. Some define it as legitimate, others do not. For example, European immigrant groups have generally been willing to engage in this process, whereas Anglo Saxon Protestants have not. Politicians usually accept it, but business leaders tend to denounce it publicly. The local labor council may well be willing to engage in it, but the local newspaper often will not.[3]

The final key to the successful use of a discrete exchange process involves a skill that some mayors develop much more effectively than others. It is not enough to have resources and a willing partner, since these political resources can be lost just as an entrepreneur can lose money. The mayor who is successful at this process is a good "power broker."[4] He has a sensitivity in negotiating relationships that can increase his power.

This type of cooperative relationship, like the others, has both advantages and disadvantages. Its greatest advantage is concreteness; it includes a fairly clear picture of the obligations of each party and, unlike some of the other processes, it involves relatively little risk. "I give you, you give me" is clear, simple, straightforward. The biggest drawback is that the process can be very expensive. To use this process to create and maintain positive relationships with everyone in a network takes a lot of resources. Most mayors today have a very limited

[3]There are sensible historical reasons behind the development of these patterns. See Banfield and Wilson (1963).
[4]See Banfield (1961).

supply of such resources, and they are often pressed to use those resources in the task accomplishment process.

Coercive Relationships

A second type of relationship identified in this study is a coercive one. Compliance is based on the fear of negative sanctions, such as withdrawing something valued (a job) or giving something unwanted (pain). That is, cooperation is exchanged for not acting.

We found little use of the coercive process alone, although people enjoy telling anecdotes that supply many examples of it. Undoubtedly we rarely encountered raw coercion simply because it is based on a form of blackmail that, today at least, is not sanctioned by most of our society. In relying on the coercive process, therefore, a mayor risks public disclosure and furnishing the competition with a weapon that can be used against him.

It is not uncommon for coercion and the simple exchange process to be used together very effectively. The key is the simultaneous punishing and rewarding of a group, which then becomes cooperative for two good reasons: cooperation is based on the implicit promise of future rewards and the threat of future punishment. For example:

> Lee's first departmental encounter was with the Police Board, a seven-member group of which he automatically became a member under the city charter. The Police Commissioners convened on January 4, 1954, to meet their new member and to ratify a private and not entirely apolitical decision, the appointment of a new Assistant Police Chief. During the closed-door caucus before the official meeting, Lee promptly challenged their choice, announced his own candidate, and gave two warnings: if the Commissioners did not go along with his candidate, he would throw the public meeting into an uproar, and he would keep their votes in mind when it came time for reappointments. This surprise maneuver, although infuriating to the Commissioners, had the desired impact. This is how one observer described the public meeting which followed:
>
> "They were very subdued, even solemn. Dick's

> candidate was nominated, seconded, and approved. Then Dick suddenly started paying a glowing tribute to the guy the Commissioners wanted for Assistant Police Chief. Then he proposed two motions—one establishing a new position of Assistant Chief for Plainclothesmen, the other nominating the Commissioners' man to fill it. Well, the heads had been bowed, you know, but suddenly they looked up in surprise, I guess, and quickly seconded and approved Dick's motions."[5]

It appears that by combining the coercive process with the discrete exchange process, a mayor can win some of the benefits of the coercive process with less risk.

Purposive Relationships—For

The third type of relationship we observed was purposive, and it was based on a coalition.[6] The mayor gains cooperation from a network member group based on the belief that they are working for a common cause or objective having payoffs for many individuals. Sometimes a coalition is formed by a mayor's explicit appeal to a group to join him in a venture, as when George Christopher (San Francisco), William Cowger (Louisville), and Roy Martin (Norfolk) each formed a coalition with parts of his network around the issue of downtown renewal. Sometimes it takes the form of a more implicit pact, based perhaps on a network member's observing the results of the mayor's past actions in certain areas and cooperating because he liked those results. Such was the case of Louis Welch's (Houston) cooperative relations with some of his constituency.

The main bases for coalitions during the 1960s included such problems as downtown redevelopment, transportation, civil rights, honesty in government, and economic development.

There seem to be two key elements in the successful creation of this type of relationship. The most obvious is an appropriate agenda setting process in the #2, #3, #4 areas—that is, a process generating

[5]Talbot (1967), pp. 30–31. Copyright © 1967 by Allan R. Talbot. By permission of Harper & Row, Publishers, Inc.
[6]See Dahl (1961).

appropriate middle- or long-term objectives. Stable coalitions, by definition, are based on interests that demand action beyond today's agenda. Since a mayor using a #1 agenda setting process has no clear middle- or long-term goals, it is *almost* impossible for him to establish such a relationship. The second key is a viable communication system among the network members with whom the mayor wants to create a coalition. Without both these elements, the coalition process is probably doomed.

The use of this purposive process has one major advantage for the mayor. Unlike a relationship based on discrete exchange, which has a certain zero-sum nature, this process can create power continuously without new fuel.[7] Whereas one's ability to maintain cooperative relations with the discrete exchange process requires *giving* more of a valuable, limited resource to a network member, a mayor can appeal to the same coalition-based objective over and over again to maintain cooperation with no tangible cost. This type of power is expandable and extensible (in time).

The process entails some very clear risks, however. A mayor cannot appeal to the same goal again and again without producing evidence that he is progressing toward the goal. Because of the complexity of the arena in which the mayor must live and because of the decentralization of power, there is always the chance that he will not be able to accomplish anything in a given area. The mayor risks not only losing a cooperative relationship, he may also become saddled with an extremely uncooperative one from a group of irate citizens. A number of the mayors in this study fell victims to this risk. Arthur Naftalin's (Minneapolis) relationship with the local press and Louis Welch's (Houston) relationship with the local black community eventually turned hostile basically for this reason.

Unfortunately, too, the purposive process affords the mayor less flexibility in agenda setting than any of the other seven network building processes.[8] By creating a relationship based on certain purposes, he commits those purposes to his agenda. If he ever decides to shift his agenda by dropping those items, however, he must also sacrifice the original cooperative relationship.

[7]The concept of zero-sum was first expressed by von Neumann and Morgenstern (1944).
[8]For a good discussion of the constraints placed on goal setting by interorganizational relationships, see Thompson and McEwen (1958).

Purposive Relationships—Against

The fourth type of relationship is a variation of the third. It is a purposive relationship based on a coalition *against* something. Such coalitions are usually in opposition to the competition either because of their purposes or because of personal qualities of their mayoral candidate or leader.

As a mayoral candidate, for example, Lester Maddox clearly established this type of relationship with some groups in Atlanta based on a coalition against changes in the status and rights of the black population. In New Orleans, some of the political opponents of Victor Schiro formed such a relationship with parts of the wealthier groups in the city who found Schiro "embarrassing." Hugh Addonizio increased his positive relationship with the Italian community in Newark during his 1962 election campaign by exploiting a statement by his opponent which could have been interpreted as anti-Italian.

This type of network building process relies on sensitivity to what really scares, outrages, and offends people; more than many people realize, a very subtle skill is involved.

Since the mayors we studied used this process only as a last resort, it seems to have some very real drawbacks, compared with the others. The main risk is that a bad judgment can be very costly. Such negative tactics have never been consciously sanctioned by our culture. Therefore, if a mayor misjudges a group and makes an appeal that doesn't "grab them," they may react against the mayor for trying something that is "wrong."

Because of its tenuous social legitimacy, it is difficult to maintain a negative purposive relationship over time. To do so requires more than just one brilliant extemporaneous emotional appeal at a crowded gathering. It requires planned, continuous effort, which is almost impossible to sustain; thus the cooperation based on this type of relationship tends to die out. None of the mayors in the study were able to maintain a negative purposive relationship over time.[9]

[9]It has been reported that former Mayor Hague of Jersey City managed to maintain such a relationship with four or more massive parades or gatherings each year. The enemy was "communism." After the marching and band playing and flag waving, Hague would announce: "The people of Jersey City are sustaining their mayor in opposing any invasion by those Reds."

Cooptative Relationships

The fifth type of relationship, which we call cooptative,[10] involves cooperation with some group based on their belief that the mayor has absorbed some of their own elements into his policy-making process.

From our observations, the process that establishes this type of relationship can occur in one of at least three different ways. In the first, the mayor selects someone from the group in question and makes him a part of his staff. Only a few mayors in our study were found doing this, possibly because they sensed that the price to pay for a group's cooperation in this case was too high. Alternatively, the mayor maintains a cooperative relationship with a certain group by allowing key people in that group to be his "informal advisors." Belief that they have a "direct line" to the mayor helps create cooperation. In the most common cooptative process, however, the mayor enlists various types of citizens' groups to "advise him." For example:

> One of Cermak's chief techniques as officeholder was his continual use of citizens' advisory committees, invariably packed with distinguished names. Through these committees Cermak went through the motions of public consultation and power sharing. However, the committees were usually so well organized, through the appointment of a few key Cermak men plus the control of the agenda and of full-time committee experts, that recommendations to which Cermak himself was opposed seldom eventuated. The use of these committees may be reckoned as a chief weapon in Cermak's successful drive to enlist the support of "the forces for good."[11]

The risk involved in using this process is obvious. The coopted party or parties may influence the mayor's agenda in a way that he perceives as incorrect or in a way that produces conflicts for him. That is, this

[10]For the original study of this relationship see Selznick (1949).

[11]Alex Gottfried, *Boss Cermak in Chicago* (Seattle: University of Washington Press, 1962), p. 349.

type of relationship will allow a mayor less agenda setting autonomy, therefore possibly creating a difficult, incongruent, unstable situation. More than one mayor in this study spent sleepless nights trying to devise a method of diverting a committee he had established or burying its report.

Personal I—Reference Group Appeal

We found that mayors use three kinds of *personal* relationships to create cooperative bonds between them and their network members. One is based on appealing to some reference group, another to friendship, and the last to a group's "ideal" concept of a mayor.

Reference group appeal can be successful if the people being appealed to feel strongly about that group and if the mayor is indeed a part of it. The reference group might be the Republicans or the Irish or the liberals. Arthur Naftalin was very successful at gaining cooperative relationships with the liberals and intellectuals in Minneapolis through reference group appeal. Richard Lee used his Irish–Democrat heritage to his advantage in New Haven. In San Diego, Frank Curran even experienced moderate success in appealing to the "common man" in this manner.

Personal II—Friendship Appeal

The second type of personal relationship mayors created was based on friendship (both casual and intense). Walton H. Bachrach, the former mayor of Cincinnati, used to walk down a crowded city street and greet nearly everyone by name. The mayors who succeeded in creating cooperative relations based on friendship tended to have many friends before they were elected, as well as a personality and style that made acquiring new friends easy. In some cases, an important aspect of this process was having friends in the right places—that is, in positions of leadership and power. Lee's close personal friendship with Yale President Whitney Griswold was clearly a significant part of the relationship that existed at one time between the mayor of New Haven and the administration of Yale University.

Creating and maintaining a large number of acquaintances and friendships is a time-consuming task. Many of the mayors in this study reported that they spent nearly every evening at a political or social function. Mayors often use ceremonial activities to meet and befriend people. Others use dinners and banquets. A few attended thousands of wakes.

Personal III—Charismatic Appeal

The third type of personal relationship is based on an appeal to the voters' image of an ideal mayor or person.[12] Such appeals are usually termed charismatic. None of the mayors in this study had the charisma often attributed to, say, a Kennedy, but a number did achieve some cooperation with specific groups in their networks based on charisma.

All these personal relationships depend on man's willingness to cooperate with someone he trusts—whether he thinks the trusted person is a friend, similar to himself, or God-like. An excellent example of the power inherent in this source was given by a Minneapolis politician in describing former mayor Hubert Humphrey:

> He would get up to speak to some gathering of people and he'd tell them, in a way that they felt was legitimate, exactly how they felt about two or three key issues. By the time he was through they would all be nodding their heads and smiling and saying "He understands!"
>
> He would turn around and go to give another speech with people who were the archenemies of the first group and he'd do the same thing. Without ever promising to do a damn thing, he got more people to line up in back of him. . . .

Personal relationships have a number of clear advantages. They do not require tangible resources to create and maintain them. They can generate reasonably powerful bonds of cooperation. Perhaps more than any other type of relationship, they usually permit mayors considerable flexibility in agenda setting. Indeed, this is why many politicians like such relationships the most.

[12]This is what psychoanalysts might call an appeal to the superego, or to the ego ideal. According to psychoanalytic theory, it can elicit a very strong response.

At the same time, personal relationships have two drawbacks. For some mayors, they are nearly impossible to create because the mayor does not have the necessary prerequisites—perhaps he does not have a personality that is charismatic to his network members; he may not have a lot of friends (or lack a tendency to make friends quickly), or he may be without a clear reference group linkage. Yet even if he does have these attributes, establishing personal relationships can be very time-consuming.

Formal/Legal Relationships

The final type of cooperative relationship established by mayors with network members was based on people's belief that in certain matters the mayor had the legitimate authority to direct their actions, usually because of explicit legislation to that effect. Members of a city bureaucracy who automatically take orders from a mayor, and city councilors who always cooperate and obey the mayor on certain matters, often do so because this type of relationship exists.

Formal/legal relationships are *the* basis for cooperation within classical bureaucratic organizations. The Public Executive model we examined in Chapters 2 and 3 did not address the issue of obtaining resources mainly because it assumed that a mayor would automatically have a formal/legal relationship with necessary resources, as does a private executive (in theory at least).

In one respect, the process of establishing this type of cooperative relationship is very different from the eight preceding cooperation building processes. One must convince others that there indeed exists a "legitimate" basis for such cooperation, but the largest task in building the relationship lies in creating the "legitimate" basis if it does not exist. In the case of a mayor, this usually means seeing that major legislation is passed or changing the city charter. By changing from a city manager to a strong mayor charter, for example, a mayor could establish this type of cooperative relationship with the city bureaucracy.

There appear to be two reasons why mayors relied relatively little on this type of cooperative relationship. First, the basis for it was rarely found. Even the strongest city charter, from the point of view of the mayor, gives a mayor only limited formal authority over the city bureaucracy and perhaps a little over the council. It gives him virtually no formal control of the other members of his network. Also, creating the basis for this type of relationship is very difficult. No mayor in this study was successful at changing his city charter in a major way.

Our discussion of relationship building processes is summarized in Table 5-2. Besides the two processes that were the focus of the Power Broker and Coalition models in Chapter 2, we have identified six others: coercion, cooption, reference group appeal, friendship appeal, charismatic appeal, and formal/legal appeal. Each process apparently has different prerequisites for its use, as well as different advantages and disadvantages.

Table 5-2 Processes Mayors Use to Establish Cooperative Relationships with Their Network Members (Summary of Discussion in Text)

Network Building Process	Prerequisites	Advantages and Disadvantages
Discrete exchange	Resources to exchange	Low risk, but "expensive."
Coercion	Few	Can get dramatic, quick action for little cost, but has risks.
Purposive appeal—for	A #2, #3, or #4 agenda setting process	Provides mayors some power but has risks (must eventually perform) and entails some loss of autonomy.
Purposive appeal—against	Few	Like coercion, can provide inexpensive, dramatic short-run results, but is risky.
Cooption	Usually need a #2 or #3 agenda setting process	Is cheap, but requires some loss of autonomy and control, which can create problems.
Reference group appeal	Network members must *feel* a part of some reference group which mayor is in, too	With the prerequisites, is fairly inexpensive and safe.
Friendship appeal	Friends or capacity to make friends quickly	Very low risk, but involves costs in *time.*
Charismatic appeal	Charisma	With the prerequisites, is very low risk.
Formal/legal appeal	City charter or other legislation	Takes almost no maintenance, but is difficult to obtain prerequisites.

SHAPING NETWORK MEMBERS

The mayors in this study did not build their networks only by trying to establish cooperative relationships with groups and organizations as they existed. Some mayors also tried to change the very nature of their networks by creating, eliminating, restructuring, or reconstituting (changing the membership) certain groups or organizations. These actions always seemed to have one of two purposes; either to make it easier to establish cooperative relationships with a given resource or to create a resource that did not exist but was needed by the mayor.

In this study, five mayors did virtually no network shaping, twelve engaged in little network shaping, three engaged in some, and none made a major effort to extensively mold his network (Table 5-3).

All the mayors in this study appeared to recognize that their success at building cooperative relationships was to some degree affected by their competitors. Regardless of the number and size of the political organizations in a city, each mayor faced some very real competition for any and all the resources he wanted—money, support, votes, and talent. As we have seen, some of the cooperation building processes carry the risk of perhaps providing fuel for competitors, thus making cooperation building more difficult. As a result, all the mayors in this study took some steps to eliminate the competition by simply not aiding it. All consciously considered the impact of their actions with respect to the competition. The thinking that produces this behavior is aptly summarized in a quotation attributed to former mayor William

Table 5-3 Shaping Network Members

Amount of Network Shaping Done by Mayor	Number of Mayors in Category	Shaping Method Used	Network Member(s) Process Aimed at
Almost none	5	Some eliminating	Competition
Little	12	Mostly reconstituting (changing the membership of a group)	City bureaucracy, city council, political parties
Some	3	Some use of creating, eliminating, restructuring, and reconstituting	Almost all network members
Extensive	0	Considerable use of creating, eliminating, restructuring, and reconstituting	All network members

Hartsfield of Atlanta: "Boy, don't ever make a mistake they can take a picture of."

The dozen mayors who engaged in "little" network shaping usually attempted to change the membership of the city bureaucracy, the city council, and their political party, to their own advantage. To do so they utilized their appointive powers, their skills in the campaign process, and other resources. They tried to get their friends elected to the city council. They appointed as many allies as possible to positions in the city bureaucracy. They did what they could to make sure that key positions in their own party were held by friends. These mechanisms have been used traditionally by many mayors.

The behavior of the three mayors we have listed as having engaged in "some" shaping was less routine. For example, Erik Jonsson's Goals for Dallas program clearly had a shaping effect on almost all the members of his network. Although the program certainly did not have as much effect as Jonsson would have liked, it exerted clear impact on the council, the city bureaucracy, and the mayor's constituency. It changed the time orientation of these groups toward the longer range, and it produced more value and goal consensus among them and with them.

When first elected, Richard Lee (New Haven) faced an unorganized and fairly apathetic business community that was structured such that developing a strong cooperative relationship with its members was difficult. Lee's solution was to organize the business leaders from whom he knew he could elicit cooperation. By carefully selecting a chairman and working hard to secure the participation of all the "big names," he created the Citizens' Action Commission (CAC). The very process of this group meeting together and with Lee helped create some of the organization and linkage he wanted. The rest he created by myth. He went out of his way to tell people how strong the CAC was, how it represented business, and how it was definitely on his side.

Lee also did more to restructure the city bureaucracy than any of the other mayors in this study.[13] His restructuring had two major elements. First, he divided the bureaucracy into two parts and put a "deputy mayor" in charge of each. One part contained the more traditional city services; the other contained the old and new departments that related directly to redevelopment. His second major change was to centralize

[13]For a good description of Lee's restructuring of the city bureaucracy, see Talbot (1962), Chapter 3.

as much as possible the overall bureaucracy, especially the half that contained the traditional services. It is interesting to note that this structure appears to have been very useful to Lee in the following years.[14]

None of the mayors in this study made extensive changes in the shape of their network members, although we heard many stories of how mayors in the past had done so. Indeed, the powerful machine mayor actively shaped his network to assure himself of continued tight control. Mayor Hague (Jersey City) is alleged to have been very skilled in keeping certain groups from forming, in disorganizing others (like unions), in electing his own men officers in still others, and in doing favors for or buying off the rest. In his book on Hague, McKean tells the following story about a threat by the business community to organize itself against Hague:

> They recounted all their grievances against his administration: high taxes, high assessments, inefficient government, poor schools, and all the rest. They made their complaints, and then they asked him what he was going to do about them. He arose and told each man what favors he had received from the organization, what laws he was violating or had violated, or what money he owed to banks of which the Mayor was a stockholder or director. He reminded others of the relatives they had on the public payroll, and he told some of them of business practices in which they had engaged that would not make good publicity. Then he put on his hat and walked out.[15]

It was said that Democrat Hague even controlled part of the Republican party.

Extensive network shaping can *give* the mayor considerable power, but it also *takes* a great deal of power to do the shaping. No mayor in this study appears to have been that powerful.

[14]The structure is one that the organization theory of Lawrence and Lorsch (1967) would predict to be "effective."

[15]Dayton D. McKean, *The Boss: The Hague Machine in Action* (Boston: Houghton Mifflin, 1940), p. 186.

THE MAYOR'S OFFICE

One final aspect of the network building process as we have observed it is the creation of the mayor's office. In some cases, usually in the city manager cities, the mayor had no staff or office. When there was a mayor's office, however, its makeup varied considerably.

The mayor's staff can give essential help in agenda setting, network building, and task accomplishment. That is, the staff can be important in extending what the mayor can do and in *adding* to what he can do. For example, consultant Edward Logue and his staff were tremendously useful to Lee in helping him at agenda setting. Lee developed a #3 process, which demands a certain amount of "technical expertise"; Logue and his staff helped provide it. Lee's staff also supplied essential help in other areas. First Herman Averill, and later others, managed the traditional city services for Lee on a daily basis (task accomplishment process). This was an important job for which Lee did not have the time. Taylor, Appleby, Adams, and others managed his link to federal funds in Washington, obtaining more renewal funds per capita than any other city in the United States.

Each of the mayors in this study seems to have felt the need for an office that could help him perform the three key mayoral processes by extending himself and making up for his weaknesses. What is striking in the data is not the few examples of a mayor successfully creating a useful office, but the overwhelming number of cases in which this *did not* happen. As Table 5-4 reveals, in only 2 of our 20 cases did a mayor create an office whose resources were significantly useful to him.

Table 5-4 Mayor's Offices

Mayor's Office	Number of Cases in Study
No office	8
Loyal staff of very limited resources	6
Staff contains some resources of worth	4
Staff contains key resources for helping mayor with three processes	2

There seem to be at least three reasons for the failure of most mayors to create the type of office found in Lee's administration. One we have already noted—a number of the mayors are given no staff under their city charters. A second reason is that quite a few mayors displayed little managerial talent in selecting the type of staff they wanted.

Nevertheless, the most important reason seems to be a desire above all else for a loyal staff which is controllable. Reminded daily of the frustrations caused by not having complete control over situations that affect his agenda items, a mayor seems to be driven to eliminate uncertainty from as many areas as possible. In regard to a staff, this means hiring a group whose main qualification is their *loyalty* and their reliability in executing orders. If this was the main criterion in their selection, other criteria would have to be compromised. The result is usually a mediocre but loyal staff. Gottfried's description of former Chicago mayor Cermak is typical:

> He rarely made errors in his selection of personnel, either as public official or party functionary. As public official it was his habit to make some very good appointments. There is no case on record of any important Cermak-appointed subordinate who had to be removed for dereliction of duty. It is true that Cermak never allowed good appointments to occur in such numbers as to hamper his freedom of action in matters of patronage and spoils; nevertheless, such appointees made possible a minimum of effective government by the various Cermak administrations, lending the color of respectability to Cermak as public official. As party functionary Cermak selected workers largely on the basis of effectiveness, but it is noteworthy that most of the men closest to him could be described as being of mediocre talent. Cermak took no chances on building up a rival or possible successor. In a very few cases when some lieutenant showed either unusual qualifications or ambition, he was eliminated, either by a promotion to a nonlocal office or by less subtle means. As a result of his policy of personnel selection, Cermak at no time in his career had to face rebellion in his own ranks; and upon his

death no Cermak lieutenant was qualified to step into his shoes.[16]

IMPACT ON THE NETWORK

The direct impact of the network building processes we have been describing is, of course, on the network they build or maintain. The networks created by these processes appear to have served many functions for different mayors. For example, they often:

1. Provided access to financial resources.
2. Provided access to and control over an implementation capacity that could handle the projects his agenda generated.
3. Provided enough support for reelection.
4. Provided access to important power centers that might stand in the way of his agenda items.
5. Provided agenda setting "advice."[17]

Not unexpectedly, the mayoral networks identified in this study varied considerably in their structure and makeup. Some networks allowed the mayor access to very few resources, whereas others gave him access to many resources. At one extreme the networks of some of the mayors were characterized by weak positive relationships, some neutral relationships, and a few negative relationships. At the other

[16]Alex Gottfried, *Boss Cermak in Chicago* (Seattle: University of Washington Press, 1962), p. 348.

[17]The reader who is familiar with Parsons's work (1957) will notice that the network, as we have now defined it, sounds very Parsonian. One could hypothesize that an effective network is one that provides the vehicle for allowing a mayor to help the city solve Parsons's four social system problems: adaptation, goal attainment, pattern maintenance, and integration. That is, the network gives the mayor access to resources (adaptation) and implementation capacity (goal attainment). The network itself provides for integration, and the maintenance of the network provides for community pattern maintenance. From a Parsonian point of view, the mayor's role as we have defined it seems to aid cities when their organizations and institutions are having difficulty with the four problems that a social system must solve to survive.

extreme, the networks exhibited many strong positive relationships, no neutral relations and often one or two strong negative ones.

The network building processes that were used to create these two extreme kinds of networks were also very different. Specifically, the network building pattern associated with the "strong" networks had the following characteristics:

1. More of the nine relationship building processes were used (than in the case of the weak network), and more relationships were based on multiple processes. For example, a "strong network" might have a strong positive relationship between the mayor and his council based on discrete exchange, coercive exchange, cooptation, and personal friendships. A "weak network" might have a weak positive relationship between the mayor and his council based on discrete exchange alone.
2. The nine relationship building processes were used more efficiently and effectively in the "strong networks." That is, the mayors with strong networks were simply more successful at correctly utilizing each of the processes they employed. They had the skills necessary and the material and nontangible resources available; and they were good at predicting what would appeal to different network members.
3. The mayors with "strong networks" tended to engage in more network shaping and/or office building activities than did the mayors with "weak networks."

None of these observations is very startling, although all are important. In Figure 5-2 we have charted the relationship between network building processes and their impact. In general, the more relationship building, member shaping, and office building are successfully accomplished, the more resources are accessible to the mayor in a network of strong positive relationships.

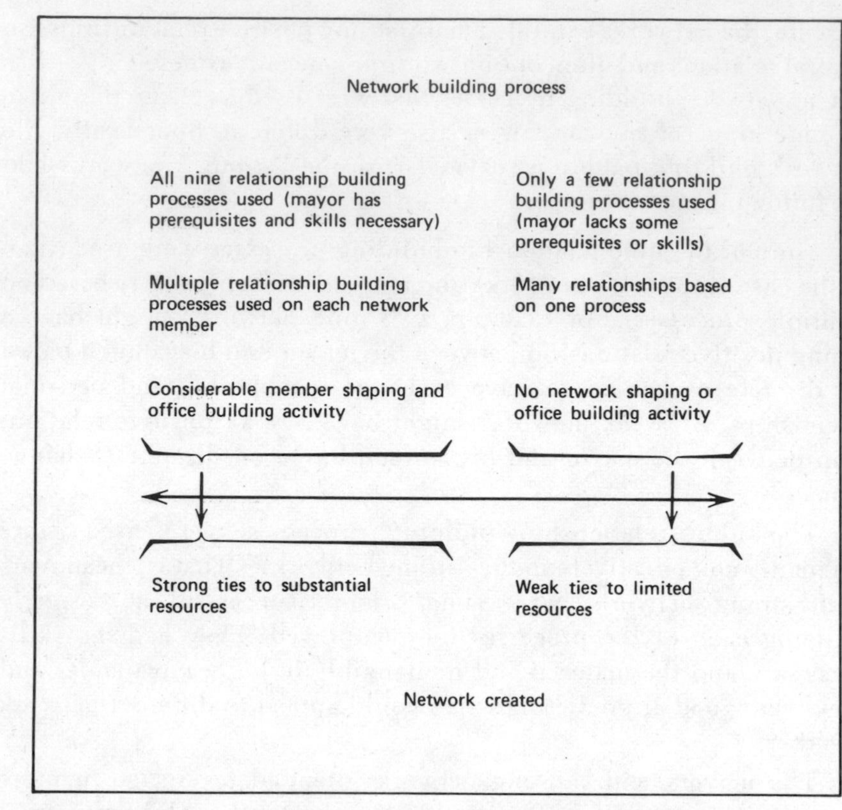

Figure 5-2 Relationship of the building process and the network it creates.

CHAPTER 6

ACCOMPLISHING TASKS

The third and final key mayoral process comprises the behavior in which a mayor undertakes the tasks on his agenda. In the 20 situations studied, three distinct task accomplishment processes have been identified: bureaucratic, entrepreneurial, and individualistic. A mayor involved in a bureaucratic process behaves like a leader in a bureaucracy—he directs, delegates, evaluates, controls (as in the Public Executive model in Chapter 2). A mayor engaged in an entrepreneurial process behaves like an entrepreneur—he hustles, promotes creates, and attempts to enlist the aid of certain others (as in the Public Entrepreneur model). A mayor involved in an individualistic process simply undertakes the task by himself—he doesn't try to delegate it or enlist someone else to do it.

These three approaches are very different. The individualistic process, unlike the other two, relies solely on the mayor's personal time, energy, and resources for task accomplishment Using a bureaucratic process, a mayor behaves as if he had formal authority or strong control over the nonpersonal resources he needs. In an entrepreneurial process, on the other hand, the mayor acts as if he lacked formal authority or strong control over the resources required for task accomplishment.

All three accomplishment processes can be described as taking a task, breaking it into subparts, bringing specialized resources to bear on the subparts, and coordinating the activities of specialized resources. In an individualistic approach, any subdivision of the task and subsequent coordination of activities go on only in the mayor's mind, since he alone accomplishes the task. Using a bureaucratic style, the mayor orders others to do most of the work and relies on formal organizational mechanisms to perform most of the division and coordinations. The entrepreneurial mayor induces others to do most of the work, and he himself somehow makes provisions for task division and coordination.

Table 6-1 shows to what extent each of our 20 mayors utilized these task accomplishment processes. Overall, the individualistic process was used most, the bureaucratic next, and the entrepreneurial the least.

THE BUREAUCRATIC PROCESS

The mayor who is engaged in the bureaucratic process behaves in a manner most people associate with a chief executive. This behavior has been studied over the years under a number of names, the most general being "management."

The mayor who engages in a bureaucratic process normally does so as he uses the city bureaucracy to work on his agenda. Occasionally, however, the mayor will use this process to direct his council, his party organization, and other network members.

George Christopher (San Francisco) is a good example of a mayor who relied heavily on an aggressive form of the bureaucratic process to work on the tasks in his agenda. The following instances described by George Dorsey's book are fairly typical:

> The voters had approved a bond issue for Brooks Hall, a huge underground exhibit area connected with Civic

Table 6-1 Extent to Which 20 Mayors Utilized Three Task Accomplishment Processes

	Extent of Use (number of mayors)		
Process	Very little	Some	Considerable
Bureaucratic	5	7	8
Entrepreneurial	9	7	4
Individualistic	0	7	13

Auditorium. The hall was considered crucial in competing with other cities for conventions, one of San Francisco's biggest industries.

By the time bids were called on the $4,500,000 project, the low figure was $700,000 over the the city's cost estimate. The mayor brought in the heads of the departments concerned, and was advised that the only thing to do was to submit another bond issue to the voters.

"Hell, by that time, the costs will go up another $700,000," Christopher growled.

The other officials shrugged. They insisted there was no other legal way to obtain the additional funds.

Christopher turned to cigar-chewing Harry D. Ross, the city's shrewd old controller.

"Listen, Harry, I don't care how you do it. But find the funds—legally."

Ross looked impassively at the mayor, then grunted, "I'll see what can be done."

Ross discovered that sewer-line changes that had boosted the cost of the project could legally be paid for out of surplus sewer funds in the city's treasury. He found that street funds could be applied to certain of the buildings adjuncts, such as sidewalks. By the time he was through, the finances were set. The contract was let, and construction began to roll. The completed building was dedicated on April 11, 1958.

A smaller project provided the ultimate example of official procrastination. For fourteen years the city had been planning to build a North Beach branch of the public library. Previous mayors had appointed site committees, which usually fell to wrangling. If they finally agreed upon a site, other North Beach residents protested that it was all wrong.

So, rather than offend anyone, each of Christopher's predecessors had shelved the project. Nearly a generation of North Beach children were deprived of a library of their own; they traveled to other neighborhoods or to the main branch—or they did without library books.

"I am going to appoint one last committee, and give it three weeks," Christopher announced soon after taking office. Sure enough, the members were soon fighting among themselves. When the committee asked that action be deferred another year, Christopher vigorously shook his head. "No, you just tell me the sites various ones of you favor, and I'll choose one of them."

Of the three sites submitted, Chrostopher, after his own survey, chose a corner of the North Beach Playground on Columbus Avenue. Real-estate prices had skyrocketed over the years, and the mayor saw here a chance to obtain a site "free," since the city already owned the land. But immediately he ran into a howl from the Recreation and Park Commission.

"Now, listen," Christopher told the commission, "I want that corner turned over to the library. That's an order."

Reluctantly the commission followed the mayor's "order."

CHRISTOPHER. "When are we going to start the Palace of Fine Arts?"

CITY ATTORNEY HOLM. "The state is hesitant about approving the contract. It is still being studied in Sacramento."

CHRISTOPHER. "Can't we go ahead with the plans meanwhile? The public is rightly critical when a bond issue is approved and then years go by before anything gets done." (He turned to his executive secretary.) "Write this down: If the city attorney's office doesn't hear from the state in a week, we'll raise Cain with someone in Sacramento."

With his background in accounting, Christopher was at his most incisive in budget sessions. He had little patience with city officials who were poorly prepared to answer questions on dollars-and-cents items. When Health Department officials couldn't supply the information he wanted on a proposed project in their budget

> that spring, he snapped, "Come back next year when you have learned more about it and we'll discuss it."
>
> A grand-jury committee, after a superficial study, reported that San Francisco Hospital was overstaffed "in a shocking degree."
>
> Christopher quickly challenged the statement.
>
> "Both the University of California and Stanford University medical schools," he said, "have warned the city that the hospital is not adequately staffed and have threatened to withdraw their accreditation.
>
> "The San Francisco Medical Society believes it is understaffed, and the last three chief administrative officers [of the city] have said it was understaffed. Outside experts I have called in have agreed.
>
> "I can't afford to take any chances with the health of the people."
>
> There was no retreat on the hospital budget.[1]

Four types of skills or abilities or knowledge appear to be particularly important to the mayor who uses the bureaucratic process. The first is an understanding of the issues and tasks with which he must deal. It is clear that Mayor Christopher was not ignorant of economics, construction, and budgeting. The mayor who does not comprehend at some minimum level the tasks with which he must deal is forced to blindly accept the advice of others. When he receives conflicting advice, he has little basis for choice. Those who have argued for years for the city manager form of local government see such skill or knowledge as central to good local government.

A second element that appears important is a thorough understanding of the organization or group that the mayor is trying to manage. He needs to understand exactly what resources and capabilities the organization commands, where they are, and how he can mobilize them. Stated a different way, he needs to understand how people and functions are apportioned in the organization, how they are coordinat-

[1]George Dorsey, *Christopher of San Francisco* (New York: Macmillan, 1962), pp. 152–153, 199–200. Copyright © George Dorsey, 1962, reprinted with permission.

ed, and who has authority and responsibility for what. Without this knowledge he can easily find himself "shooting in the dark," giving the wrong instructions to the wrong people. He will base his plans on incorrect assumptions about what he can or cannot do. He will continually violate the expectations of others, frustrating everyone. In this study we heard many stories of mayors who thought they were making effective use of a bureaucratic process and the city bureaucracy when, in actuality, nothing was happening.

It is not very difficuult to understand why many mayors have this problem. City bureaucracies are often gigantic, not particularly "logical" organizations. Mastering one is a big chore, and one the mayor is usually expected to complete in a short period of time. The corporate executive who "knows" his organization usually has been in it for 15 to 40 years. Very often the mayor has *never* really been a part of the city bureaucracy.

The third skill that appears important to the bureaucratic process is the ability to delegate—knowing what to delegate, how much, and to whom. The data from our study suggest that lack of this skill is fairly common. Garrett's description in the following passage on La Guardia is typical:

> La Guardia, himself, was not the world's greatest administrator. This was true not only because he often created tension and resentment around him; he also fell down because he could not apportion his energy and time wisely and often got bogged down in trivia. Part of the trouble lay in his impulsiveness; like a child he tended to follow what interested him at the time. But much of his difficulty came from the fact that he found it hard to delegate power and responsibility; most likely he was motivated by a feeling that only he could do a task the way it should be done; perhaps, too, Fiorello was not uninfluenced at times by an unconscious desire to hog the spotlight on his administration.
>
> He began his first term by insisting that nothing should be done in his administration without him. This, of course, was impossible; work had to go on, commissioners had to act. What happened was that the administrative heads acted anyway, but God help them

> if they made the wrong decision. Gradually the Mayor gave in to necessity, but he never learned the art of efficient administration. He, himself, had to make out the dinner menu for the celebration of the *Normandie's* arrival on her maiden voyage. He personally had to lead a raid on an alleged house of prostitution in Brooklyn. The new City Charter which went into effect in 1938 contained a provision for the appointment of a Deputy Mayor by the Mayor for the purpose of giving the latter some relief from his chores. In La Guardia's hands this provision became a dead letter. Henry Curran, whom La Guardia first appointed Deputy Mayor, has written that in the beginning the Mayor turned over to him a few miscellaneous matters, but he got through with them in a month, and in the end, "the job came swiftly down to handling some of the mail and sitting for the Mayor in the Board of Estimate. That was all."[2]

Closely related to the ability to delegate, the final important skill in using the bureaucratic process is knowing when to use it and when not to try. Under certain circumstancces it is ineffective or inefficient to use this process instead of one of the others. Specifically, using it on a task that the mayor could easily handle by himself can be very inefficient. Using it when the mayor does not have formal authority or strong control over the resources he needs can be very ineffective.

One of the difficulties experienced by George Christopher, among others, seemed to be related to the mayor's almost constant use of the bureaucratic process to the exclusion of the entrepreneurial one. Some times when he did not control the resources he needed, people did not follow his "orders" and the tasks simply did not get done.

THE ENTREPRENEURIAL PROCESS

When the mayor uses the entrepreneurial task accomplishment process he behaves like an entrepreneur. This process has received less

[2]Charles Garrett, *The La Guardia Years: Machine and Reform Politics in New York City* (New Brunswick, N.J.: Rutgers University Press, 1961), pp. 131–132, reprinted with permission.

attention from academics than the previous one. Nevertheless it has been studied under the names of entrepreneurship and project management.

The reality of a mayor's role is that under all present charter forms he has limited formal authority. At best he is given some control over the city bureaucracy (some appointive powers, control of the budget, etc.), some control over the council (prepares agenda, veto, etc.), and a few limited legal powers over the rest of the members of his network. In the network building process, the mayor uses a variety of methods to increase his formal powers by creating cooperative relations with people. Nevertheless, the most powerful mayor in the study had relatively *minor* control over most of the parts of his network compared with, say, the amount of control a business manager exercises over his subordinates. Here the entrepreneurial process becomes important. We noted earlier that the bureaucratic process is often ineffective when the mayor lacks strong control or formal authority over a resource he needs. The entrepreneurial process has emerged over the years to deal with just such a situation. Louis Welch, former mayor of Houston, Texas, has been described by many people as fairly adept at using this process to get things done. For example:

> The first thing he does is to figure out who would benefit from whatever he was trying to do. Then he'd go to them and talk them into helping him. You see, this way he builds his own highly committed temporary organization around each task.
>
> When carrying out the specific steps necessary, if anyone gets in his way, he'd try selling them first, and if that didn't work, he'd try arm twisting.
>
> He understands, for example, that certain types of people are actually rather flattered when they are asked to do something for the city. He's particularly good at using the resources that can be available because of that. For example, when the City was in the process of trying to put in a computer, Welch went to a number of corporations and received the assistance of a team of computer experts at no cost to the city.[3]

[3]Research interview notes.

Another mayor in our study who was particularly successful in using the entrepreneurial process was Richard Lee of New Haven. In the following example, reported by Talbot, Lee was trying to secure a major department store for his main downtown renewal site.

> Lee began dashing off personal notes to New York store executives to see if they might be interested in the project. Rather predictably they were not. He then focused his attention on finding an individual who might be helpful, and, quite accidentally in early 1962 he found a pressure point.
>
> Among the Yale Fellows who had played roles in the Yale loan commitment was J. Richardson Dilworth, a nephew of the former Mayor of Philadelphia, an executive in the Rockefeller Fund, and a man whose investment skills had placed him in the upper echelons of what Lee, with gleaming eyes, would call "the big New York money." Dilworth and Lee were having lunch at Mory's to discuss Lee's future plans when Dilworth revealed that he was on the board of R.H. Macy & Co., Inc. Lee immediately invited Dilworth to tour the project area where he had "just the right site picked out for a Macy department store." After showing Dilworth the site, which was next to Malley's, Lee drove him around the highway network and showed him the city's new parking garage. Dilworth was sufficiently interested to set up an appointment for Lee with Donald B. Smiley, the Treasurer of Macy's. Lee's meeting with Smiley went smoothly, and the official agreed to dispatch several of his staff to take a closer look at New Haven.
>
> The young Agency staff prepared a full-blown presentation based on the way Macy officials like their information organized, for coincidentally it happened that the economic consultant to the Redevelopment Agency, Larry Smith, was also an economic consultant to Macy's. The New Haven meeting and subsequent sessions in New York went extremely well. The store officials were particularly impressed by the highway network and the city parking garage, which offered

direct access to the site Lee was offering to Macy's. An event that occurred at this time indicates how much the Macy transaction meant to Lee. One day some Macy staff members, city officials, and an overall project design consultant, one of several consultants who had a part in the project during its stormy history, were gathered in Lee's office discussing the proposed store. Suddenly the consultant suggested that Lee's site was not the one Macy's should choose, that they should locate at a different end of the project. He was just as suddenly interrupted by Lee, who politely asked him to step into a nearby office, where Lee backed him against the wall, grabbed him by the lapels, and through clenched teeth muttered:

"Look, you Viennese S.O.B., one more word from you on a different Macy site and I will hammer you into that site, where you will be a human pile for the store."

By summer's end the Macy staff was sold on New Haven and on Lee's site. In September, 1962, Lee announced that Macy's would build a $5,000,000, four-level department store.[4]

Some of the attributes of a successful enterpreneurial style can be seen in the previous examples. Most of all, it requires imagination, drive, and a wide range of influencing skills. These skills are much the same as those we discussed in the last chapter (cooperation building) with some important differences. The skills we are describing here are really sales skills, as opposed to public relations and marketing skills. The mayor needs to be able to convert whatever resources he has into fairly specific actions by other people. He needs more than the ability to build general bonds of cooperation. Indeed, just as a salesman can use good public relations as a resource in making a sale, a mayor can use a cooperative relationship to help achieve what he wants. And just as a salesman can sometimes sell an item to a person he has a neutral or even negative relationship with, so can a mayor. For example:

[4]Allan R. Talbot, *The Mayor's Game* (New York: Harper & Row, 1967). Copyright © by Allan R. Talbot, 1967. By permission of Harper & Row, Publishers, Inc.

> [La Guardia's] combativeness and quick sense of timing were the chief components of his political skill. As soon as he took the oath of office in 1934 he plunged into a fight with Governor Lehman and the State Legislature. He requested authority to upset the budget planned for 1934 by the previous Tammany administration in order to cut payrolls and reduce his deficit. As a dramatic ploy he raised the spectre of an increase in the five-cent subway fare if his request was not granted. He also dashed off to Washington and got a promise of millions in PWA funds contingent on a balanced budget in New York City. He hurled all of this at Albany daring them to block him and face the consequences. He then went on the radio and attacked Tammany Hall as having padded city payrolls with political hacks whom he wanted to bounce. Better to "save a home than save a politician," he cried. He finally got modified approval from the State to write his own budget. He had succeeded only because of his use of all of the resources of influence at his command.[5]

Mayors use literally dozens of techniques to influence people to do specific things: logical persuasion, charm, coercion, bribery, pleading, and so on. In the previous examples, Welch was reported to be good at appealing to self-interests, strong arming, and flattering, and Lee was shown to be skilled at sales and coercion.

A second significant element in any entrepreneurial process is an understanding of the task itself. Without such understanding, it is almost impossible for a mayor to figure out what discrete subtasks must be initiated, and in what order. Some of the problems mayors in this study had when using an entrepreneurial process can be traced to a lack of understanding of the task. This was especially true of tasks in areas that were new and different. In the early 1960s many a mayor was unsuccessful in accomplishing tasks associated with race relations for these reasons.

A final ability relates to understanding the network member with

[5]Irwin C. Hargrove, "Dramatizing Reform," in *Political Leadership in American Government*, James D. Barber, Ed. (Boston: Little, Brown, 1964), p. 106.

which the mayor is interacting. The same kind of skill was discussed earlier in relation to the bureaucratic process. In this case, however, the skill is more closely associated with understanding informal arrangements. More precisely, the mayor needs a keen understanding of the social structure and key individuals in the parts of his network with which he wants to use an entrepreneurial process. A number of instances in our data suggest that the lack of this ability severely restricted a mayor's capacity to accomplish specific tasks, but perhaps even more importantly, this lack of understanding inhibits mayors from even trying.

It is important to recognize that sometimes the mayor can behave in a bureaucratic process, yet get things done in an entrepreneurial style. For example, if Lee had assigned a task to his staff using a very bureaucratic process, they might have worked on it using an entrepreneurial process—New Haven's early successes in obtaining federal funds were based on diligent research and negotiation carried out by Lee's staff (an entrepreneurial process). The staff also attacked specific renewal projects with a variety of entrepreneurial processes:

> The team operated from a neighborhood office, and, using the Housing Code as a weapon and persuasion as a device, they visited each house, convincing owners not just to improve their buildings to code standards but to enhance them by aesthetic standards.
>
> What operators they were! "My, Mrs.———, won't your home look lovely if we point the bricks and paint the trim white?" The architect would show the woman a painting of her home as it would look if she followed his suggestions. "Would you like the painting, Mrs. ———?" Indeed she would, and she would fix up her house, too. Such unusual attention was in itself a flattering persuader. With others the architect would sometimes play neighbor against neighbor. "Now, Mr.———, Mr. Jones down the street is putting up shutters." "What! That cheap Jones is putting up shutters? Well, I'm not only going to put up shutters. Draw me a picture of what a new roof would look like, too." There were some who wanted nothing to do with

> rehabilitation at first. But once a few of the homes were done, the fear of being the last to improve took over. Neighborhood pride began to replace individual isolation.[6]

It is also important to recognize that Lee, for one, used an entrepreneurial process to deal with *all* the members of his network at one time or another. He hustled business, Yale, the Irish, the Italians, the state government, and everyone else.

THE INDIVIDUALISTIC PROCESS

The "individualistic" process refers to the way in which the mayor works on specific tasks by himself. He does not try to enlist the aid or consent of others. He does not manage or hustle. He acts as "himself" or as a person with some special expertise or skill.

Mayors typically approach a variety of tasks from the individualistic standpoint. The ceremonial tasks in an agenda are perhaps the most obvious, but they are by no means the only ones. Some mayors, like Arthur Naftalin (Minneapolis), spent time doing "staff"-type work on policy issues. Some, like Frank Lamb (Rochester) and Walton Bachrach (Cincinnati), acted as regular members of the city council. Some, like Ralph Locher (Cleveland), personally arbitrated conflicts between interest groups. Others, like Victor Schiro (New Orleans), spent time just listening to people, in an almost clinical-therapeutic role. Finally, many of these mayors, like Ivan Allen (Atlanta), used the individualistic process to deal with crisis situations or sudden tragedies, such as a riot or the death of an important person.

In all these cases the issue of interest is focused less on skills or abilities than before. Certainly if a mayor uses this process in an area that requires skills he does not have, he will run into trouble. However, we found few instances of this happening. In fact, these men seemed to use an individualistic process in activities for which they had special skills, avoiding its use where they did not.

[6]Talbot (1967), p. 139. Copyright © by Allan R. Talbot, 1967. By permission of Harper & Row, Publishers, Inc.

Of more importance, perhaps, is the "opportunity cost" associated with this process. A mayor, generally speaking, can accomplish fewer and smaller tasks using this process than he can with the other two. Therefore, when he chooses the individualistic approach, in a sense, he is reducing his overall task accomplishment capacity. Consequently the use of this process entails an important cost.

MOBILIZATION OF RESOURCES

The different task accomplishing patterns found in this study appear to have had very different impacts on their networks. At one extreme, some patterns tended to mobilize a minimum of resources to accomplish relatively small tasks. At the other extreme, some patterns tended to mobilize very large quantities of resources to accomplish very ambitious tasks having a substantial impact on the city (see Figure 6-1).

Figure 6-1 confirms our expectation that in general the more a mayor uses any of the processes, the more resources he mobilizes, and the greater his impact on the situation. Also, the more he uses the bureaucratic or entrepreneurial process instead of the individualistic one, the more resources he mobilizes, and the greater is his impact. These statements are true almost by definition.

In Figures 6-2 and 6-3 we display two simplified networks to further clarify the differences in impact of the extreme task accomplishment

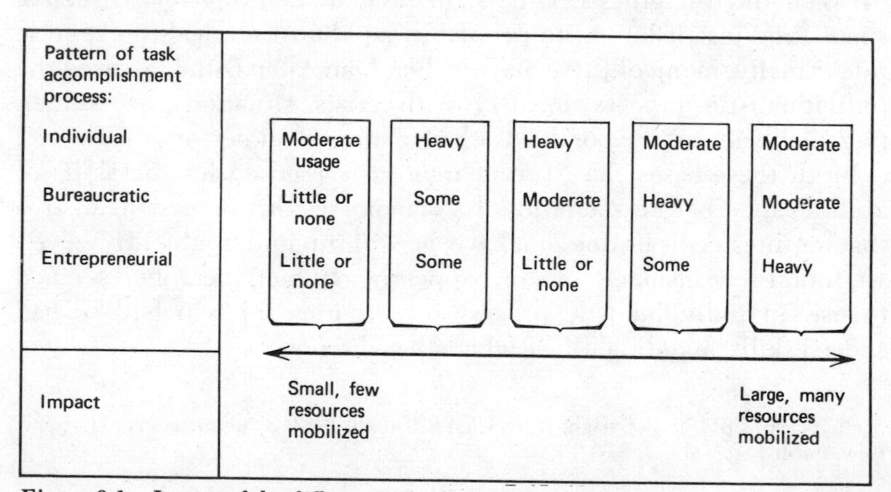

Figure 6-1 Impact of the different task accomplishment patterns.

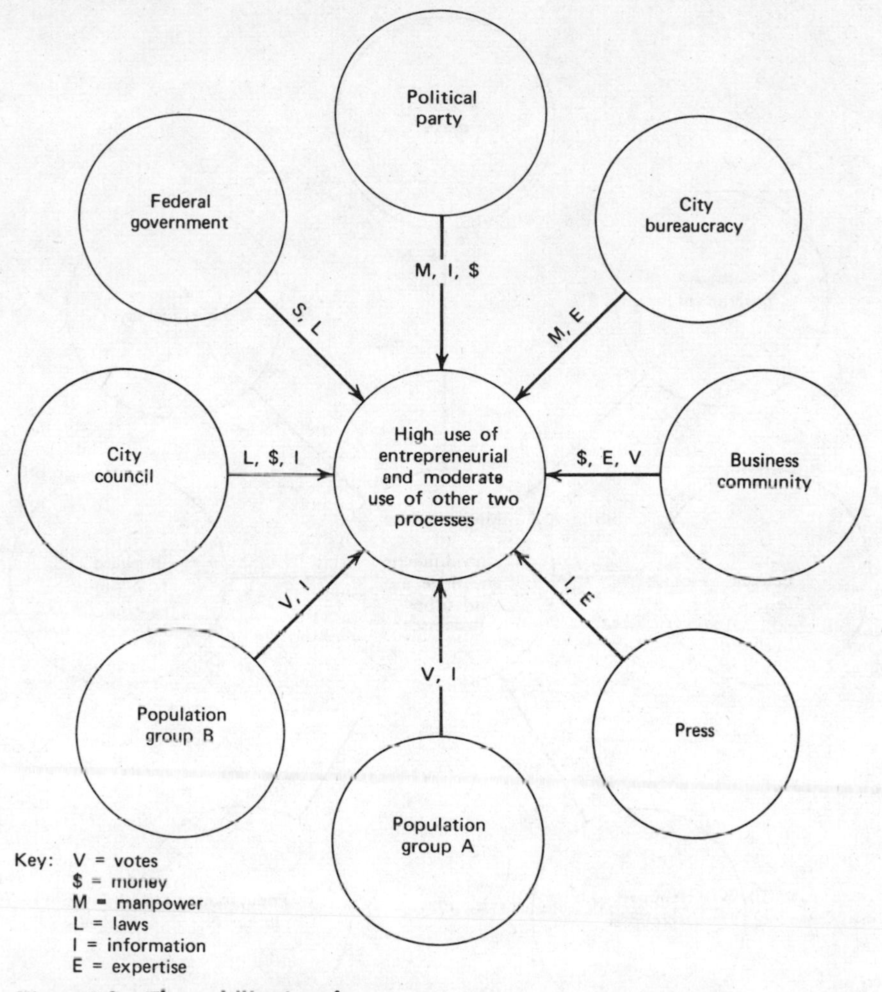

Figure 6-2 The mobilization of many resources.

patterns. In Figure 6-2, the mayor's pattern is characterized by heavy use of the entrepreneurial pattern and moderate use of the bureaucratic and individualistic patterns—he has mobilized a large number of resources with this pattern. In Figure 6-3, the mayor's pattern reveals moderate use of the individualistic process alone. As a result, he mobilizes few resources from few network members.

The mayors who used more processes more often acted in three different ways. First, they simply spent more time on task accomplishment processes. Second, they used their staffs as multipliers of their own actions. Earlier, we noted how Lee used his staff to carry on an

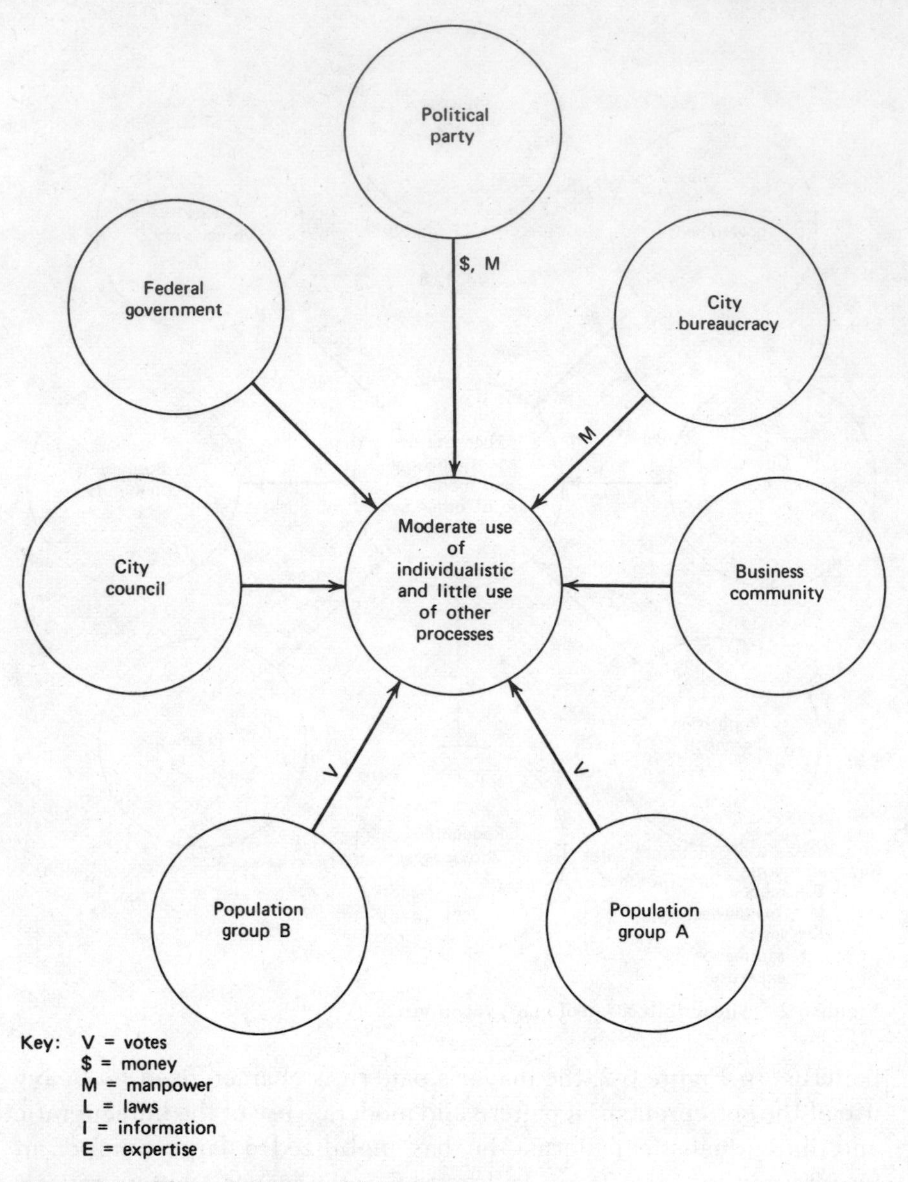

Figure 6-3 The mobilization of few resources.

entrepreneurial process in some areas. Finally, the mayors engaged more intensely in these processes. The mayors who used all three processes tended to work simultaneously on multiple agenda items. That is, while involved in one activity (e.g., attending an awards

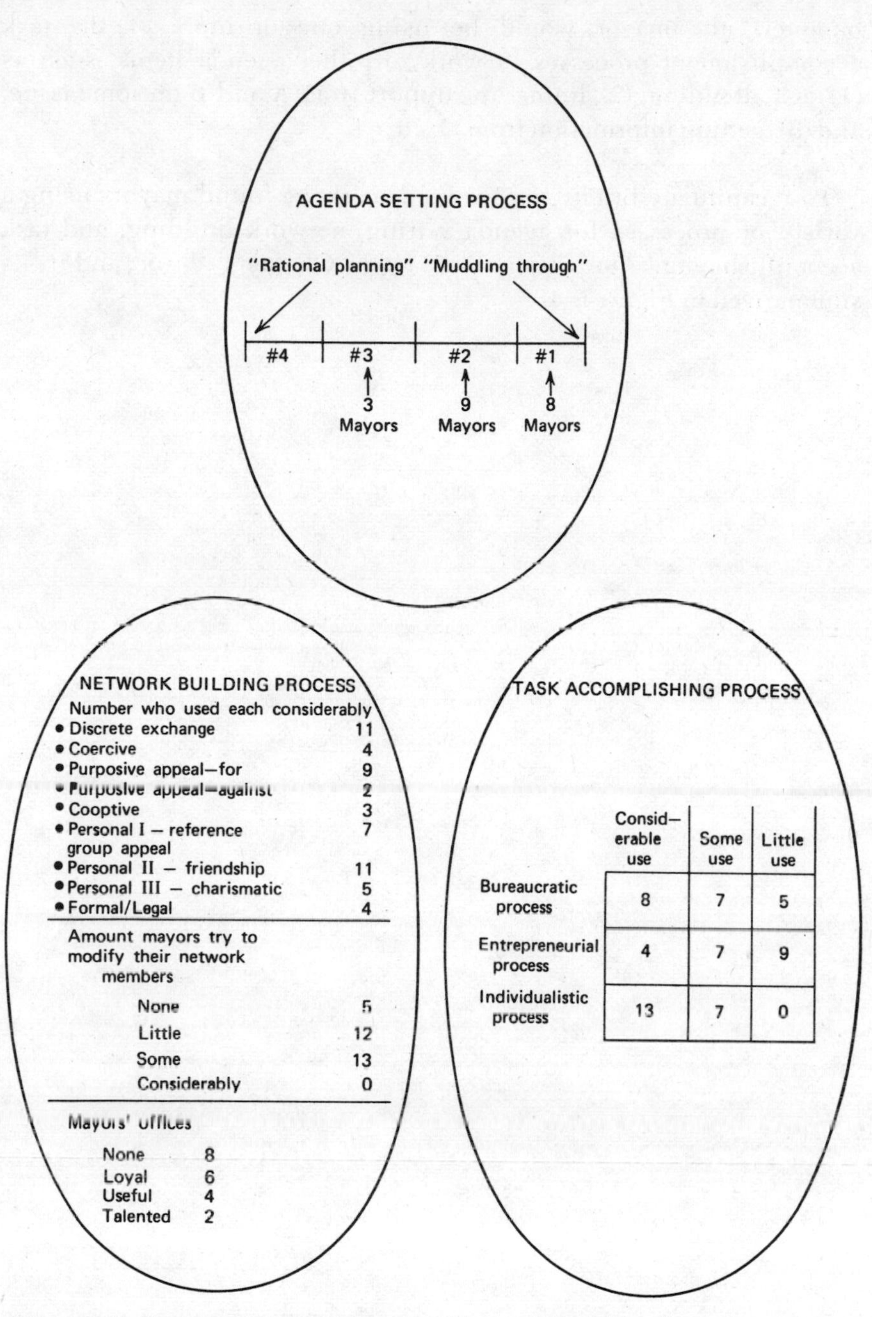

Figure 6-4 Summary of main findings in Chapters 4, 5, and 6.

banquet), the mayor would be using one or more of the task accomplishment processes to work on other agenda items, such as (1) just attending, (2) lining up support from A and B on some issue, and (3) getting information from C, etc.

To recapitulate briefly, in our field work we found mayors using a variety of processes for agenda setting, network building, and task accomplishment. Our discussion from Chapters 4, 5, and 6 is summarized in Figure 6-4.

CHAPTER 7

PATTERNS OF BEHAVIOR: THE IDENTIFICATION OF FIVE TYPES OF MAYORS

Since the processes adopted by mayors for their agenda setting, network building, and task accomplishing tended to be stable (i.e., they changed little or infrequently), we can usefully talk about a particular mayor's pattern. For example, a hypothetical mayor could be described as follows: #2 agenda setting process, high use of discrete exchange plus personal appeal network building processes, little effort to modify network members, no staff, heavy use of bureaucratic and individualistic task accomplishing processes, but no entrepreneurial behavior.

Each of the three key mayoral processes can assume a number of forms; thus the total number of overall patterns that could develop, in theory at least, is very large. Nevertheless, in this study the combined processes adopted by our 20 mayors clustered around only five patterns. That is, from the point of view of the behavior defined by our framework as key, five types of mayors were found in our study. For convenience, these can be called: Ceremonial, Caretaker, Personality/Individualist, Executive, and Program Entrepreneur.

THE CEREMONIAL PATTERN

The first pattern appears to describe what is commonly called the Ceremonial mayor. This type of mayor adopts a #1 agenda setting process (muddling through) and relies heavily on personal appeal processes in his network building. He has no staff or office of any consequence and does not try at all to mold or modify his network members. He tends to have a number of neutral relationships in his network—perhaps with the state, county, and federal governments. He tends to ignore the bureaucratic and entrepreneurial processes, relying on the individualistic process for the moderate number of tasks he undertakes (Figure 7-1).

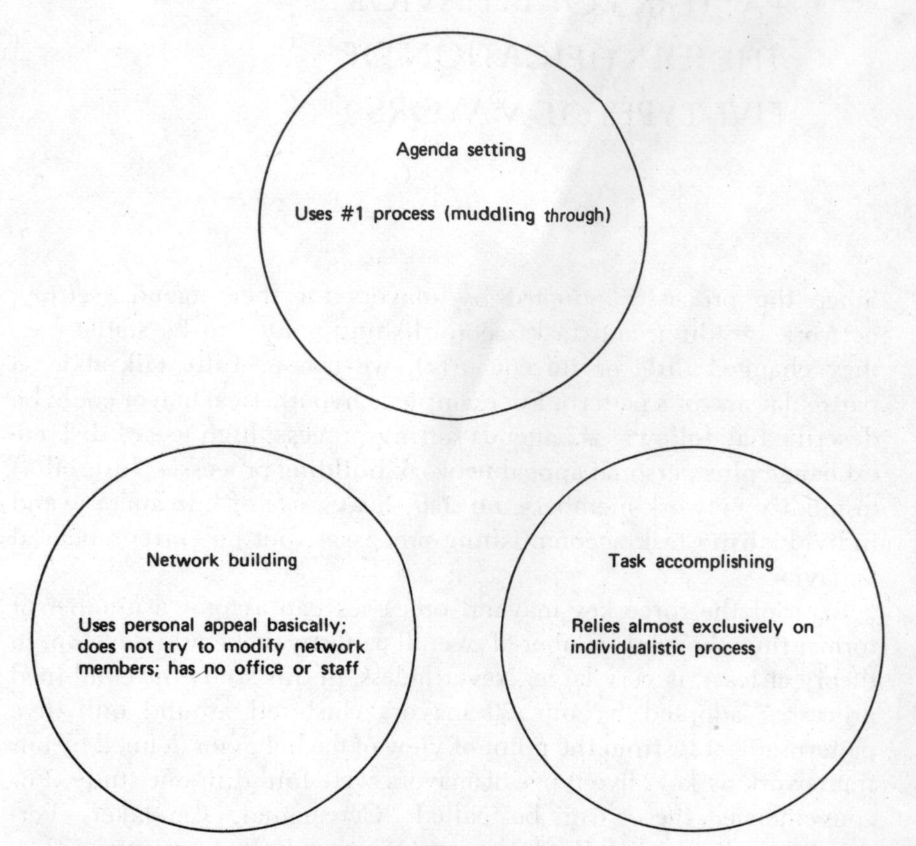

Figure 7-1 **The Ceremonial mayor. Examples from this study: Walton Bachrach (Cincinnati), Tom McCann (Fort Worth), Frank Lamb (Rochester), Frank Curran (San Diego). Patterns for McCann, Lamb, and Curran were slightly different from that described.**

Walton H. Bachrach of Cincinnati is the prototype mayor in this category. Bachrach was described to the researchers in this way:

> Walt was a very personable guy and just about everybody loved him. He'd walk down a crowded street and say hello to nearly everyone—by their first name.
>
> He was very conscientious as councilor and mayor. He had limited abilities, but he was honest and took his job seriously.
>
> As mayor he spent nearly all of his time in ceremonial activities. He gave speeches at banquets, he welcomed conventions, he cut ribbons at all types of openings, he gave out keys to the city, and so on. He really looked the part and he played it with grace and dignity.
>
> Walt never hid the fact that he enjoyed those ceremonial activities. He really did. He had said a number of times, in public even, that if Cincinnati decided to change its charter from a city manager form to a strong or weak mayor form, he'd retire immediately.[1]

Compared with the other four mayoral types we have identified, the Ceremonial mayor's behavior is the least complex. Agenda setting is very straighforward. Only short-run agendas are generated. Council meetings are automatically scheduled in, as well as most requests for the mayor's time (to perform ceremonial affairs). If there are too many requests for the time available, the mayor must make some fairly simple decisions.

The Ceremonial mayor relies on personal appeal processes to create a "low-key" network. Bachrach's appears in Figure 7-2. Given the nature of his agenda, he does not need a large number of strong positive links to potential resources. To continue his pattern (i.e., to survive), all he needs is weak positive links to a majority of the city's electorate. Although the city charter usually gives him no staff (an

[1]Source: interview notes.

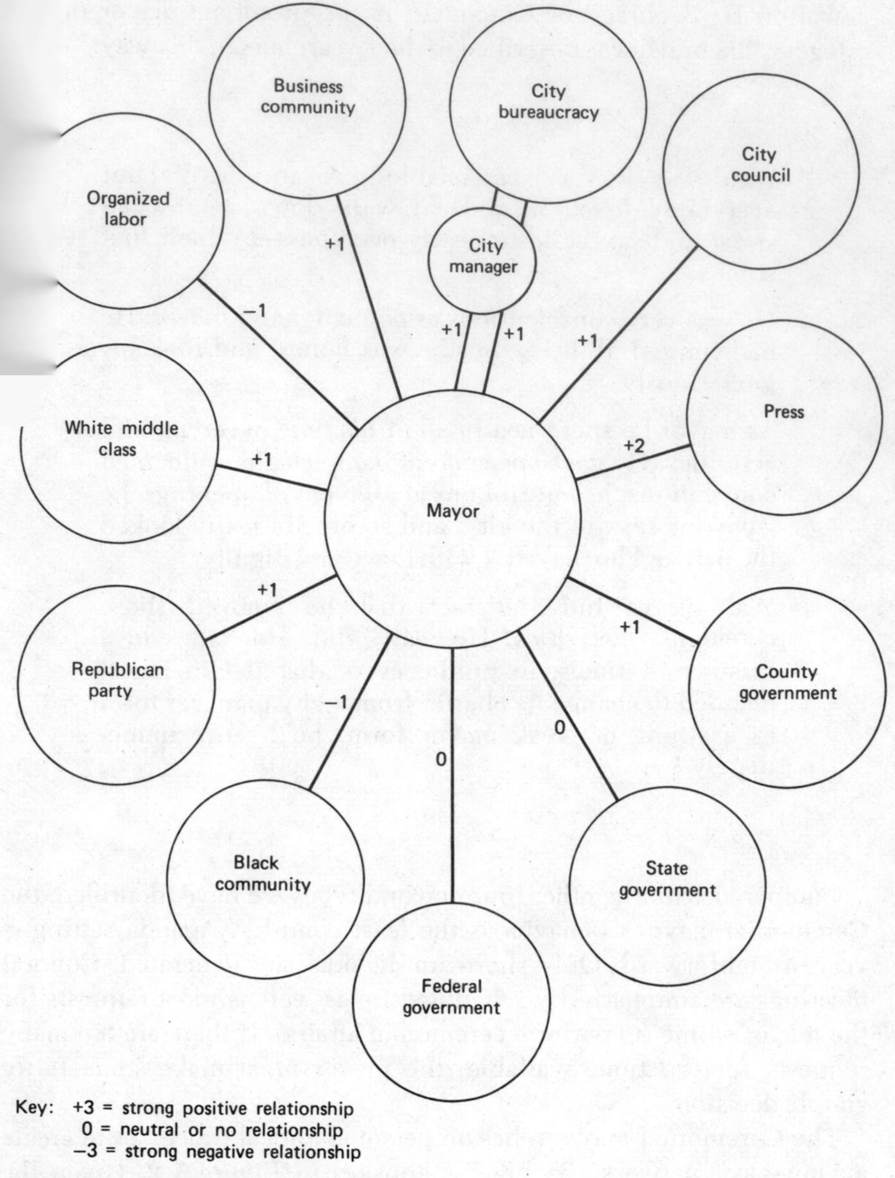

Figure 7-2 Bachrach's network in 1965.

office), this is no drawback because he has no need of those resources, either. Furthermore, the Ceremonial mayor could not mold or shape his network members much even if he wanted to, since to do so requires a fairly strong power position.

It is not surprising to find that this type of mayor relies basically on personal appeal processes for building his somewhat weak network. Of all the cooperation building processes, it is the most attractive. To use the discrete exchange process, a mayor needs resources (jobs, money, important favors) to exchange. To use a coercive process, he needs enough strength to survive the risks involved. To use the purposive appeal process, or even the cooption process, a mayor needs an agenda setting process of the #2, #3, or #4 type. With none of these prerequisites, the Ceremonial mayor is left with personal appeals.

It is quite clear why the Ceremonial mayor uses only an individualistic task accomplishment process. The city charter seldom gives him authority to manage a city bureaucracy, and his agenda does not include the types of tasks that demand the resources an entrepreneurial pattern can mobilize.

The Ceremonial mayor is in a sense a minimum mayor. He operates in a restricted domain, creates a weak network of relationships, and has a small direct impact on his city. Of the five types of mayors identified in this study, this type has the least observable impact, good or bad, on his city.

THE CARETAKER MAYOR

The second pattern discernible in our data describes what might be called the Caretaker mayor. This type of mayor has a #1 agenda setting process. He relies on a discrete exchange process for network building and, as much as possible, on a personal appeal process. His attempts to modify his network members tend to be limited (always the city bureaucracy). He builds a loyal staff with relatively few resources. He employs the bureaucratic and individualistic task accomplishment processes to moderate degrees (Figure 7-3).

The prototype of this kind of mayor, Ralph Locher of Cleveland, is described by almost everyone who knows him as "an honest, dedicated public servant who is an awfully nice guy." Locher recalls a "typical day" as follows:

> I would get up and then dress and go walk our dog. When I came back I'd have a cup of coffee with my wife and at 7:30 sharp a *Cleveland Press* reporter

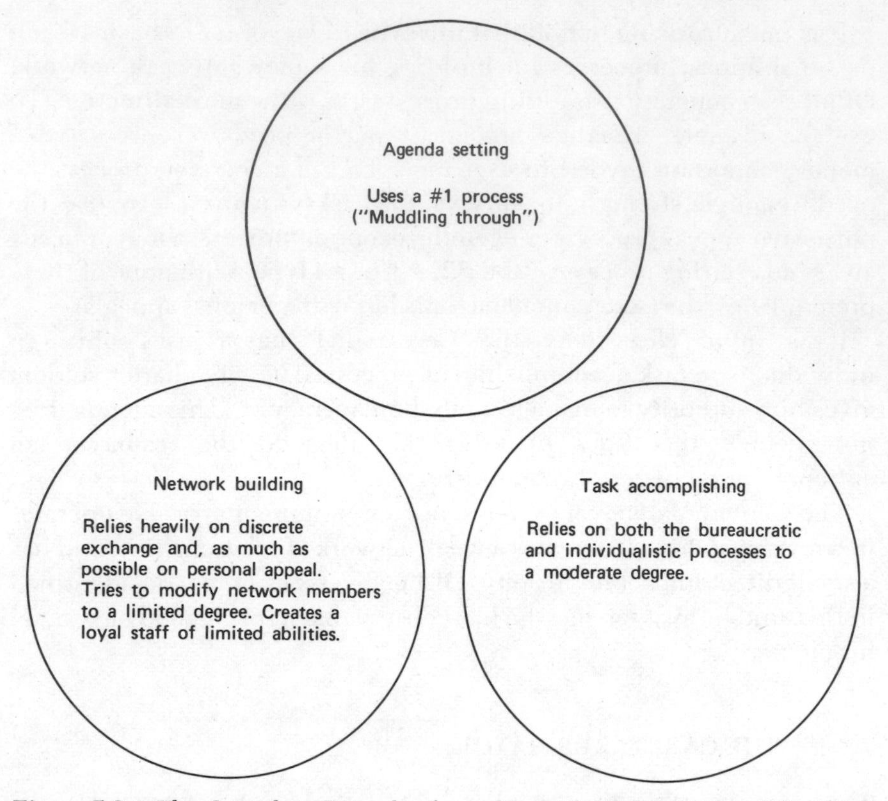

Figure 7-3 The Caretaker. Examples from this study: Ralph Locher (Cleveland), Victor Schiro (New Orleans), Chester Kowal (Buffalo), W. Ralston Westlake (Columbus), Hugh Addonizio (Newark). Patterns for Kowal and Westlake were slightly different from that described. Addonizio's pattern changed while in office.

would phone me to ask a few questions. After my car would arrive, the driver would take me downtown. I would make it a point to go a different route almost every day to see if the services were getting done. You really can't delegate, as I found out in the last three years. I'd always go down by the port usually to see what ships were in. It's really a delight to go through the port and see the many products that are shipped in and out. When I got to the office I would go through the mail. I insisted on seeing everything, even the advertisements, and certainly all the invitations. I would pass them on myself by writing approval or OK. On the ones that required a response, I would dictate

> one. Frequently the letter required a meeting with a cabinet member and a commitment to make, if it had to do with streets, resurfacing and such matters as that. Then after that on Friday we'd have a cabinet meeting which would last until about 11:30.
>
> Then we'd let the reporters in to ask us questions. Every other day I would have a meeting with the radio and TV people at about 10:00 in the morning. After that the luncheon engagement was usually with some of my aides or with some convention group that was meeting. Upon returning to the office in the afternoon, there would be perhaps a meeting with the director of some delegation who wants something corrected or changed or improved or who is complaining about something that is going wrong. I tried to get home in time to get a little bit of rest, because virtually every night there was some meeting of some special interest group, so to speak.[2]

Locher's agenda setting process, as the passage suggests, was a #1 type. He tended to create only short-run agendas by choosing among the initiatives made by others. He dealt with what "came up." He did not initiate changes or projects but tried to effectively maintain, or take care of, that which existed. As Locher told the researcher,

> "You know, I suppose it could be said that Burke [another mayor] and I were custodial mayors. We tried to keep the city clean and swept and policed. Some say that wasn't enough. Let me just say this about that complaint. You can't nurture flowers and good thoughts and ideals when you're living in a rat-infested squalor and your city services aren't being done."[3]

[2]Source: interview notes.
[3]Ibid.

Locher and the other Caretaker mayors tended to rely heavily on the discrete exchange process for network building. As opposed to the Ceremonial mayors, these men had some resources for exchange, and they used them. They played power broker with favors and jobs. The Caretaker mayors resembled the Ceremonial mayors in their willingness to use personal appeal to reference groups and friends. This combination of network building processes is characteristic of what has often been described as the ethnic politician.

As Locher's typical day suggests, he relied moderately on both individualistic and bureaucratic task accomplishment processes. By himself, he attended functions, talked to people, and arbitrated disputes. As a bureaucrat, he directed his cabinet to perform the basic city services and to react to specific problems.

Like the typical Caretaker mayor, Locher made some adjustments in his network members, basically around the city bureaucracy. That is, he used the power given to him in the city charter in staffing the bureaucracy and his mayor's office. The Caretaker mayor operates in a moderate-sized domain, with a network of moderate strength (see Figure 7-4). His impact on the city, which is considerably larger than that of the Ceremonial mayor, tends to come in many small ways along traditional lines. As the name implies, the Caretaker's focus is on maintaining what exists, not on change.

THE PERSONALITY/INDIVIDUALIST

The third pattern observed in this study represents what might be called the Personality/Individualist mayor. This type of mayor uses a #2 agenda setting process. He relies mostly on personal appeal and to some extent on purposive appeal in network building. He has no staff and does not try to shape his network members. He tends to count heavily on an individualistic task accomplishment process and only occasionally on bureaucratic and entrepreneurial processes (Figure 7-5).

Somewhat typical of this pattern is former Mayor Roy Martin, Jr., of Norfolk. Martin was described as a strong-willed, honest and straightforward, abrupt, hard-working mayor. Although the mayoralty in Norfolk is supposed to be a part-time job, he spent at least 30 hours a week in that role. People saw him not as an "idea man" but as one who picked up and aggressively pursued good projects initiated elsewhere.

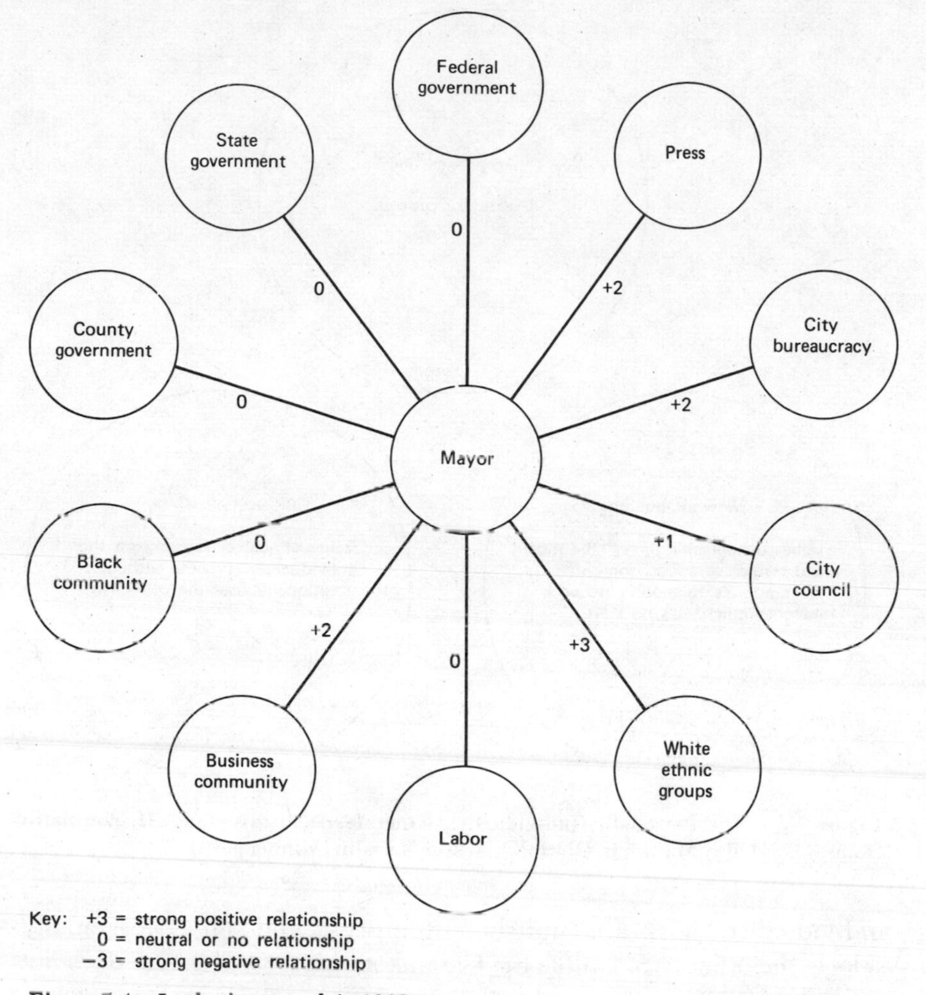

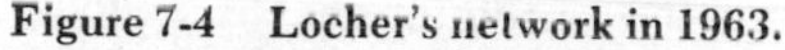

Figure 7-4 Locher's network in 1963.

As one would expect of a project-oriented mayor, Martin used a #2 agenda setting process. Unlike the Ceremonial and Caretaker mayors, he had a middle-run agenda containing projects that he established and modified. Martin's agendas, for example, included items associated with urban renewal, the Chrysler art collection, the sports arena and theater, and the sales tax.

The Personality/Individualist mayor tends to pursue his projects and attack his daily agenda items as a solo actor. He aggressively uses the

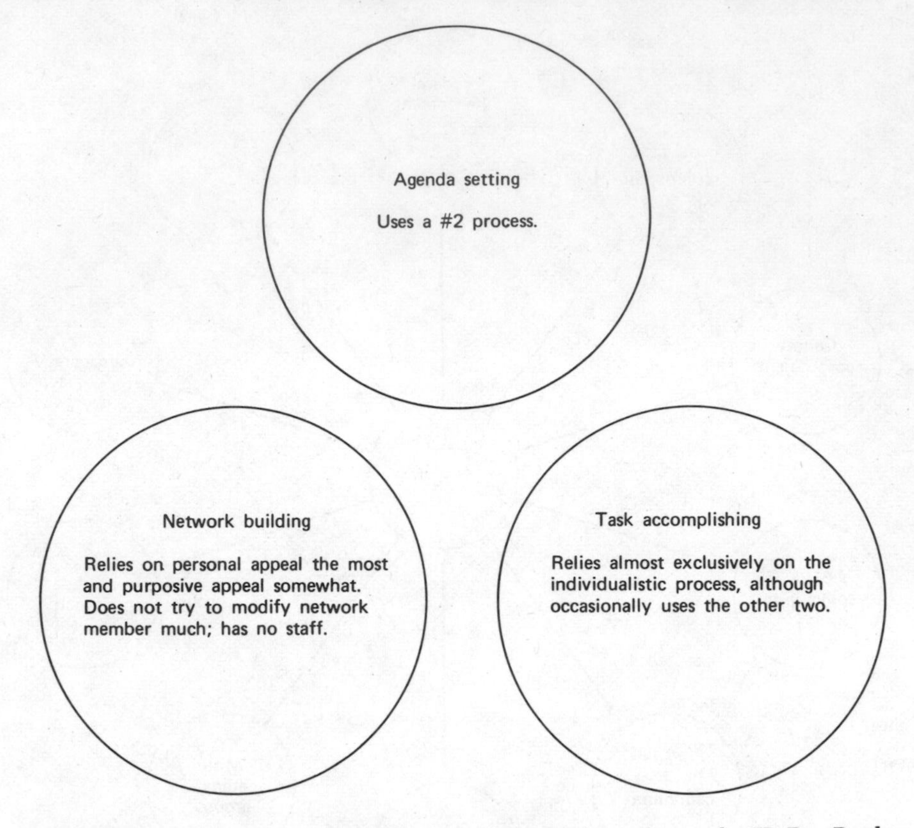

Figure 7-5 The Personality/Individualist. Examples from this study: H. Roe Bartle (Kansas City), Roy Martin, Jr. (Norfolk), Arthur Naftalin (Minneapolis).

individualistic task accomplishment process and only occasionally selects the other two. Unlike the Caretaker, this type of mayor does not as a rule receive much formal authority over a bureaucracy.

Although the city charter gives him little formal power, Roy Martin was not a weak mayor. His close association with the business community on a friendly and purposive coalition basis was a source of considerable strength (see Figure 7-6). In general, the Personality/Individualist's use of the personal appeal processes and the purposive appeal process provides a network that is considerably stronger than the Ceremonial mayor's.

In many ways, this type of mayor is simply a Ceremonial mayor who has become more aggressive and has enlarged his job by (1) changing to a #2 agenda setting process, (2) using the resulting projects in a

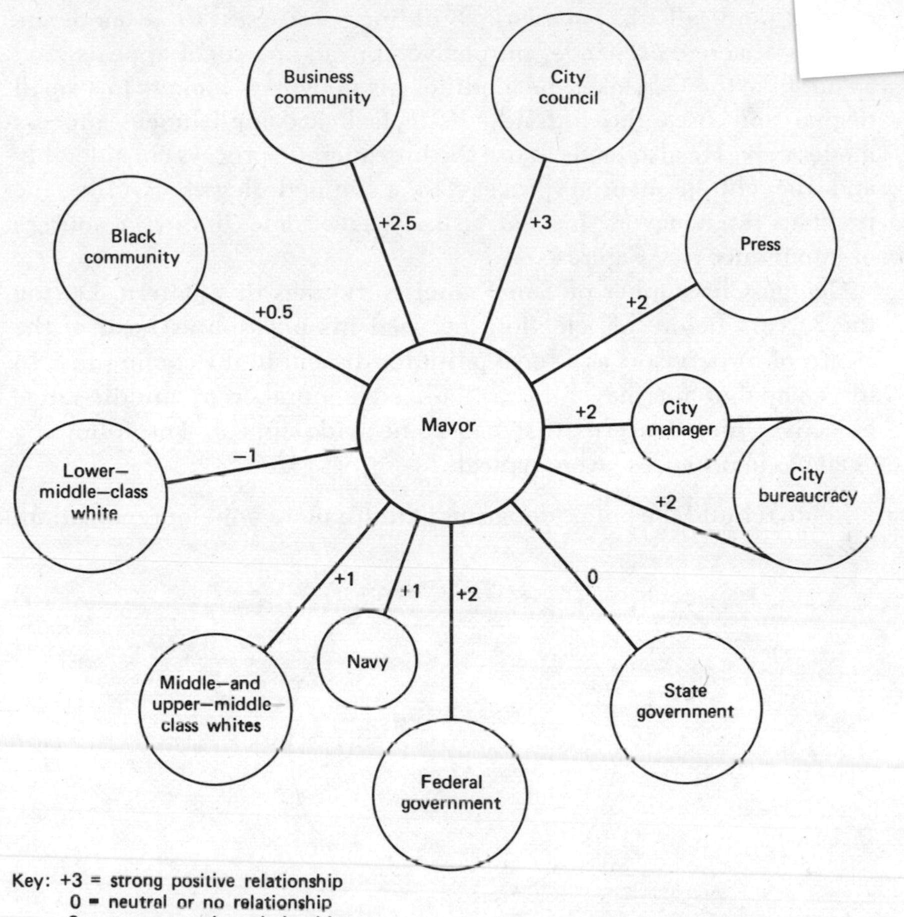

Figure 7-6 Martin's network around 1968.

purposive appeal process, and (3) increasing his involvement in individualistic task accomplishment. Thus he achieves a larger impact on his city than does the Caretaker mayor, and the impact tends to change things instead of maintain them.

THE EXECUTIVE

The fourth type of pattern describes what we call the project-oriented executive, or simply the Executive. He uses a #2 agenda setting process and all the network building processes to a moderate degree—discrete exchange, purposive appeals, personal appeals, and so on. Like the Caretaker, he modifies his network members to a small degree and uses the individualistic task accomplishment process moderately. He also tends to use the bureaucratic process considerably and the entrepreneurial process to a limited degree. Unlike the previous three mayors, his staff usually have some (limited) resources of importance (see Figure 7-7).

George Christopher of San Francisco typifies this pattern. During the 2 years before his election, he used his position as head of the Board of Supervisors as a focal point for dissent in the community. In his campaign for mayor he articulated a number of middle-range objectives and concerns that had some wide appeal. The following "campaign promises" were typical:

> to rebuild the police department into a more honest organization.

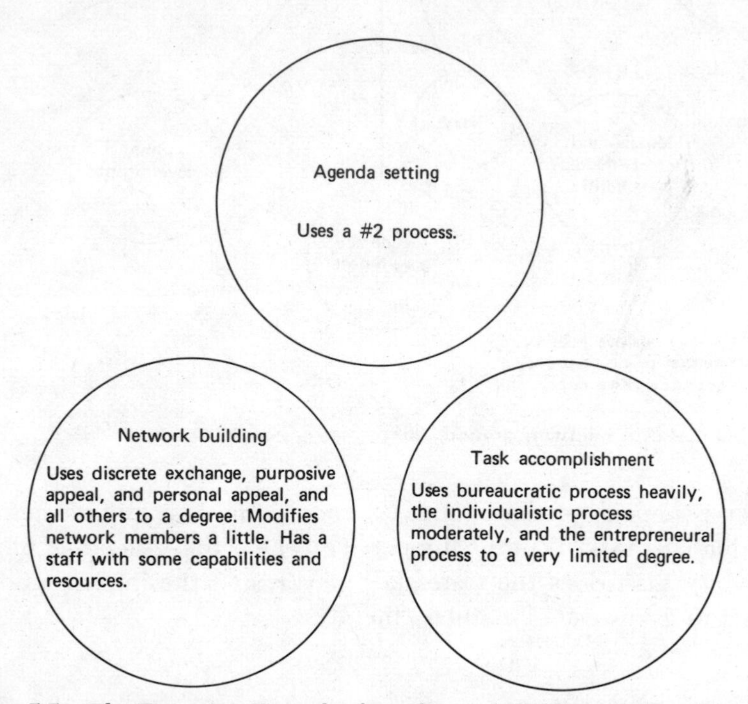

Figure 7-7 The Executive. Examples from this study: William Cowger (Lousiville), George Christopher (San Francisco), Charles Boswell (Indianapolis), Thomas Whelan (Jersey City), Louis Welch (Houston). Patterns for Boswell, Whelan, and Welch were slightly different from that described.

- to stimulate physical building and redevelopment (especially with regard to a few specific projects).
- to get the city bureaucracy to run on more of a basis of fiscal economy.

When elected, Christopher proceeded to set his agenda in the fashion we have labeled a #2 process. The mayor's daily agenda was established with an eye on his middle-range projects, and new ones were added as the original objectives were accomplished.

The Executive tends to use most or all of the network building processes to some degree. Christopher utilized his middle-range projects for purposive appeals, placing lesser reliance on discrete exchange, coercion, and cooperation. That is, he occasionally "made deals," "twisted arms," and "enlisted the aid of various groups" (see Figure 7-8 for Christopher's network).

In Chapter 6 we quoted a long description of Christopher's approach to tasks on his agenda. That approach was the prototypical bureaucratic task accomplishment process. The Executive tends to rely heavily on this process, moderately on the individualistic process, and somewhat on the entrepreneurial one.

In many ways, the Executive mayor looks like a Caretaker who became more aggressive and enlarged his domain. The difference between these two mayoral types is much like the difference between the Ceremonial and the Personality/Individualist mayors. That is, the Executive uses a #2 agenda setting process, as well as more network building and task accomplishment processes. As a result, the Executive operates in a larger domain than any of the three previous mayors, has a stronger network than any of the other three, and has a larger impact than the others. Like the Personality/Individualist and unlike the other two, this impact tends to be toward some change instead of maintenance.

THE PROGRAM ENTREPRENEUR

The fifth and final pattern we identified describes a mayor we call the Program Entrepreneur. This type of mayor uses a #3 agenda setting process. He utilizes nearly all the network building processes very skillfully, especially the purposive appeal process. He tends to actively try to modify some of his network members, and he surrounds himself

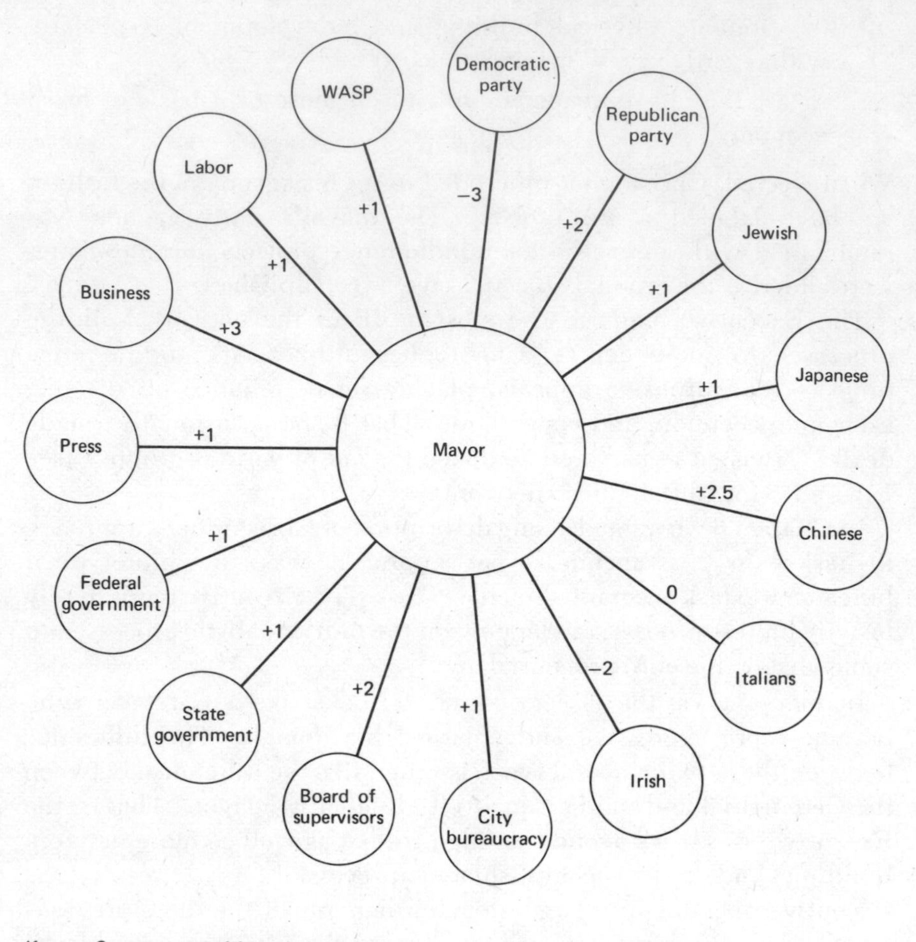

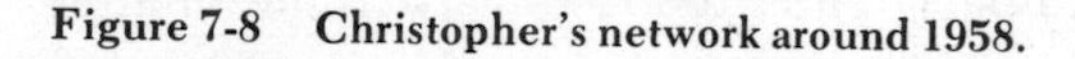

Figure 7-8 Christopher's network around 1958.

with a staff of important and useful resources. He uses all the task accomplishment processes, expecially the entrepreneurial one (see Figure 7-9).

Richard Lee (New Haven), whom we have mentioned often in the previous three chapters, is characteristic of this type of mayor. In Chapter 10 we look in detail at Ivan Allen of Atlanta, another mayor who was found to use this pattern.

Lee lost two extraordinarily close elections for the mayor's office in

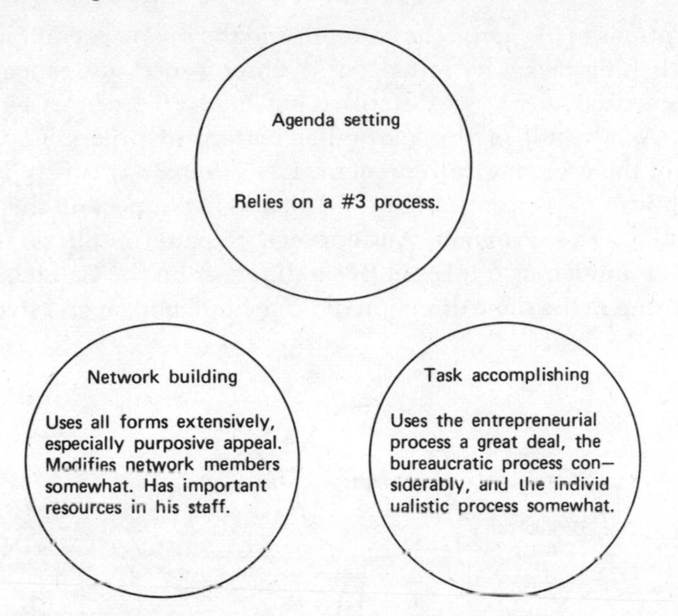

Figure 7-9 The Program Entrepreneur. Examples from this study: Ivan Allen (Atlanta), Richard Lee (New Haven), Erik Jonsson (Dallas), Louis Welch (Houston). Welch fits somewhere between this pattern and the Executive pattern.

1949 and 1951. In a city with a heavy Italian and Irish population, he used the agenda setting process that was common among ethnic politicians—a pattern #1 process. His opponent used the same process, and both races were rather run-of-the-mill contests.

Sometime in 1952 or 1953, however, Lee began developing the idea of "rebuilding the city." It is not clear how this actually happened. In an iterative process of talking to friends and getting favorable reactions, Lee began to develop his program and to use it to build positive relationships with the various groups and organizations of importance in New Haven. He ran for mayor again in 1953 and won easily.

Once in office, Lee called in Edward Logue, assembled a topnotch staff, and used an old city master plan developed by Maurice Rotival to help him set an agenda in a pattern #3 process. As we noted in Chapter 5, he used all the network building processes rather extensively. He bargained, he coopted, he coerced, he charmed, he appealed to superordinate interests. He put together a talented office staff, he extensively reshaped the city bureaucracy, and he made minor modifications to his party, the council, and the business community. In accomplishing tasks, he relied on all three processes, especially the entrepreneurial one. As we described in Chapter 6, Lee was a masterful hustler. As a result of this particular pattern of processes, which is typical of the program Entrepreneur, Lee's domain was very large, his network was very strong (Figure 7-10), and his impact on the city was substantial. The Program Entrepreneur's pattern differs from the Executive's much as the Executive's differs from the Caretaker's. It is another step in the same direction of larger and more aggressive action.

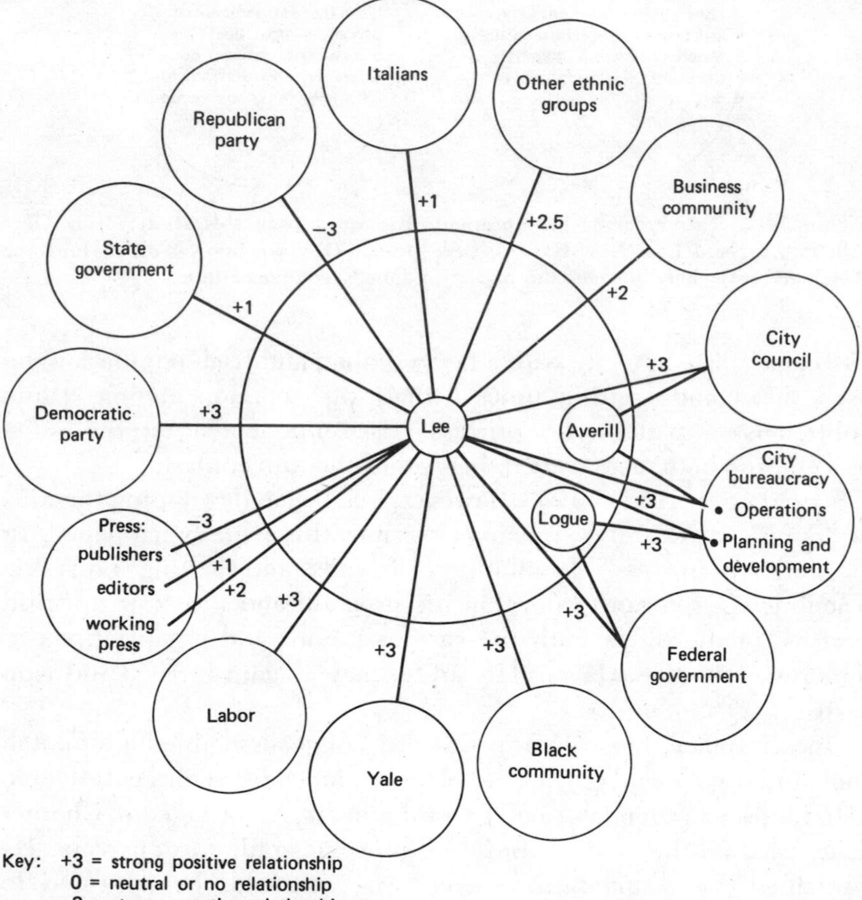

Figure 7-10 Lee's network in 1958.

SUMMARY

We have identified five mayoral types. Each has a different behavioral pattern as defined by his agenda setting, network building, and task accomplishing processes. In this study of 20 mayors we found approximately four representatives of each type.

Even though we have not directly addressed the overall question of pattern impact, it should be clear that different types of mayors appear to have very different impacts on their cities. The question of pattern emergence, however, requires clarification. Why does one type of pattern develop or emerge in a particular situation? We will explicitly address this question in Chapter 11. To prepare for that discussion, we next explore the overall dynamics of the phenomena we are studying.

CHAPTER 8

PATTERN DYNAMICS: CONSTRUCTING A MODEL OF MAYORAL BEHAVIOR

A SUMMARY AND SYNTHESIS

In our analysis and discussions in the previous chapters we have been evolving a detailed model of mayoral behavior (see Figure 8-1), which can be summarized in the following nine points:

1. The mayor's behavior can be thought of in terms of three key processes: an agenda setting process, a network building process, and a task accomplishment process.
2. The agenda setting process can take on many configurations, and in a sense, all are variations along a continuum. At one extreme (#1 or muddling) it is reactive, part oriented, continuous, disjointed, and short-run oriented. At the other extreme (#4 or rational deductive planning) it is proactive, holistic, periodic, logically interconnected, and long-run oriented.
3. In any situation, certain constraints will lower the feasibility of some of the agenda setting forms. (And conversely, the availability of certain resources will make some forms possible.) Specifically, as we proceed from a #1 to a #4 process, more and more information and expertise resources are needed either from the mayor, his office, or his

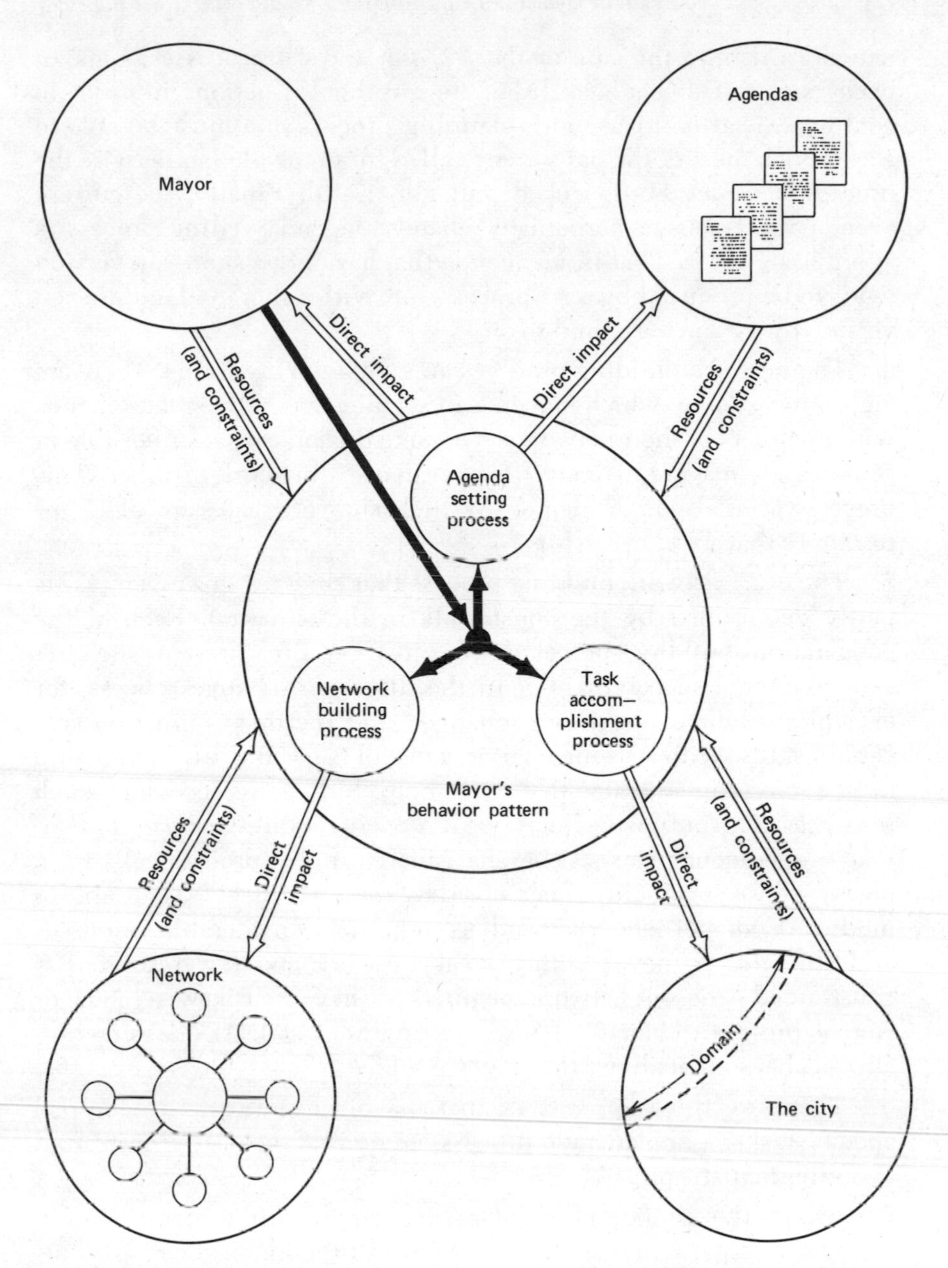

Figure 8-1 First approximation of a general purpose model of mayoral behavior.

network. Also, in the case of the #2, #3, and #4 processes, a mayor needs successful feedback from the city on his actions in order to continue. That is, to use any planning process one must be able to accomplish most of the daily steps called for in the plan; otherwise the process becomes bottlenecked and not useful. Finally, the current agenda itself acts to perpetuate whatever agenda setting process is appropriate for it. That is, an agenda that has only a short-run version tends to be produced by a #1 process, one with a short and middle-run version by a #2 process, and so on.

4. The network building process can take on many forms. There are eight processes by which mayors can secure cooperative relationships with members of their networks. To make the job easier, or feasible in some cases, mayors actively try to reshape a network member. This process varies also in the degree to which a mayor creates an "office" of resources that are of use to him.

5. The exact network building process that emerges in a given case is partly determined by the constraints in the situation. Each of the cooperation building processes requires certain "prerequisite" resources for its successful use. In the discrete exchange process, for example, resources must be exchanged and the mayor must possess certain skills. With a strong charter, a mayor can achieve a relationship to the city bureaucracy that will help him gain access to such resources. The purposive (for) appeal process requires some middle- or long-range agenda items. The charismatic appeal process calls for a mayor whose personality is perceived by some as "ideal." To be able to modify or shape network members requires considerable resources and strength. A mayor with a weak network and few resources is constrained to accept network members as they are. Likewise, a mayor cannot build an "office" of resources without at least one prerequisite—a charter that allows the mayor an office.

6. There are three approaches that mayors can use to accomplish specific tasks: a bureaucratic process, an entrepreneurial process, and an individualistic process.

7. Again, the configuration of task accomplishing processes that emerges in a particular situation is partly a function of the constraints in that situation. The agenda will dictate which tasks are to be tackled. Limitations of the mayor's own skills and inclinations may make it impossible for him to effectively use one of the processes. The shape of his network and the nature of the task will dictate which process is

most appropriate. For example, if resources that are linked to the mayor in his network with a weak positive relationship (+1) are needed to accomplish a task, an entrepreneurial process is needed, because the other two will not work.

8. Overall, the agenda setting process has a direct impact on the mayor's agenda, the network building process on his network, and the task accomplishing process on the city (or, rather, that subpart which is within his domain). The agenda, network, and city in return provide the processes with resources (and constraints).

9. Finally, all three processes have a direct impact on the mayor. That is, his behavior and its impact can be satisfying or not to his own needs, desires, and aspirations—whatever they are. In return, he provides the processes with resources (and constraints), and consciously or unconsciously directs his behavior.

The model we have developed up to this point has four contextual variables that differ slightly from the ones that were part of the framework in Chapter 3. We have combined two of the original contextual variables (formal governmental structure and distribution of power in the community) into a new concept, which we have called the network. We have retained and refined two of the original contextual variables, the mayor and the city. Finally, we have included a new concept—the mayor's agenda (or agendas).

Our model is still incomplete. As it stands, it describes how mayors behave and how short-run dynamics and constraints both affect and are affected by such behavior. We now need a better understanding of system dynamics in the long-run. What important long-run relationships influence pattern emergence? Until now we have been concentrating on relationships between the processes and the contextual variables. Let us now examine the relationships among the contextual variables themselves. In doing so, we specifically focus on relationships that are important in the long run and are of course relevant to the phenomena we are studying. There are six such relationships: agenda–network, agenda–city, city–mayor, network–city, network–mayor, and mayor–agenda.

AGENDA–NETWORK RELATIONSHIP

For our purposes, the most important relationship between the mayor's network and his agenda can be stated as follows:

> 1. If the resources accessible to the mayor in his network are not of the right kind or are not of sufficient number for undertaking the tasks on his agenda, the situation is unstable in the long run and must change.

We have a number of examples of mayors who found themselves with this type of imbalance between their networks and their agenda. Chester Kowal of Buffalo appears to be one of them.

Kowal was elected mayor of Buffalo in 1961. As a candidate, he articulated a number of promises that helped him win a three-way race with 38% of the vote. As mayor, he made these promises mid-range agenda items and adopted a #2 agenda setting process to pursue them. Kowal began his term as mayor with a city council dominated by the opposition, a city bureaucracy that had been controlled by the opposition for years, and a solid majority of the population not supporting him. He discovered very quickly that it was difficult to follow up on his original agenda items concerning police reform and redevelopment because his efforts were often slowed down and blocked. Recognizing that he needed access to more power and resources in his network, Kowal tried to increase his cooperative relations with some key people and groups in the city. Unfortunately, he was not very successful. As a result, Kowal changed over to a #1 agenda setting process. He added no new middle-range objectives and slowly abandoned his original ones. That is, an imbalance between an agenda and a network led to Kowal's changing his agenda to erase that imbalance.

It is evident that to create and follow mid-range and long-range agendas (to plan), a mayor *must* have some control over his network. The more items and details he has in his future agendas, the more control he needs to pursue them. The entrepreneur who is struggling to keep his small business financially above water does not create long-run agendas for good reasons. On the other hand, the corporate executive who has control of various resources and who has some control over his customers and suppliers may well have an unbelievably detailed agenda for the month, year, and decade.

The issue, more precisely, is simply that when a mayor does not have control over resources and key decisions, he is forced to operate on a local, short-run basis where he can take advantage of whichever opportunities may arise. To use a military analogy, the commander-in-chief may use a #3 or #4 agenda setting process, the general directing an invading army may use a #2 or #3 process, the lieutenant directing some men will probably use a #2 or a #1 process, and the lone soldier will certainly use a #1 process.

A more subtle aspect of this same relationship is implied in the word "accessible" in the original relationship statement. Different types of "positive" or "cooperative" relationships allow the mayor slightly different types of access to the resources held by a network member. Just because a mayor has a strong cooperative relationship with a network member does not mean that he can always "use" it. A few examples will clarify this issue.

Ralph Locher (Cleveland) tended to build most of his positive relationships using discrete exchange and personal appeal. In the 1965–1967 period he faced a very tense and difficult situation which included a fairly large racial riot. Many of the people who have criticized Locher argue that he should have behaved more like New York's Mayor John Lindsay or Atlanta's Mayor Ivan Allen, Jr. That is, they felt he should have mobilized massive human and financial resources to meet the "problems." Such critics fail to realize that purposive appeals are non-zero-sum; thus only a network based on such appeals among other things, is capable of supplying human and financial resources on a large scale and in a fairly short time. With Locher's network, had he tried to follow his critics' suggestions (perhaps he did), he probably would have failed. Having established a relationship with a group of people based on quid pro quo, only an unrealistically large number of favors can induce behavior from the group thus solicited comparable to the behavior of people rallied by a purposive appeal. Old line party workers could not come close to mobilizing the support that McCarthy and McGovern forces obtained from the young, basically because the former had a discrete exchange network whereas the latter created a purposive appeal network.

H. Roe Bartle (Kansas City) also faced a very difficult (but different) problem in his second term. After 19 years of Citizens' Association dominance, in 1959 the factional remnants of the old Pendergast machine won a majority of the city council seats. Since these factions were not a cohesive group, and since Bartle's Citizens' Association was historically responsible for Pendergast's downfall, something not far from chaos ensued.

Bartle's critics argue that he should have taken a strong stand and brought order out of what developed into a virtually uncontrollable situation. However, even though Bartle's network was fairly strong, it was not of the type that could achieve "order" goals in a relatively short period. Bartle's cooperative relationships were based primarily on personal appeal with some purposive appeal. The ideal network to achieve moderate-sized "order" goals is based on coercive appeal and discrete exchange, among other things. With muscle and money it would have been relatively easy to create order in the council room.

Thus a mayor needs not only a positive link to the resources called for in his agenda, he also needs the kind of link that will allow those resources to be mobilized in the situation of the moment.

AGENDA–CITY RELATIONSHIP

The key relationship between the mayor's agenda and his city can be stated as follows:

> 2. If the future planning in the mayor's agenda is too far out of line with the feasibility and payoff of planning in his domain, the situation is unstable in the long run and must change.

To understand this statement we need to introduce a conceptual tool adapted from the work of Charles Perrow.[1] If we think of a mayor's domain as a source of information, we can characterize a particular domain in terms of two dimensions which describe that information—variety and analyzability (see Figure 8-2). The larger the domain and the more heterogeneous it is, the greater the variety of information it will produce. The more we know about cause and effect relationships

[1]Perrow (1970).

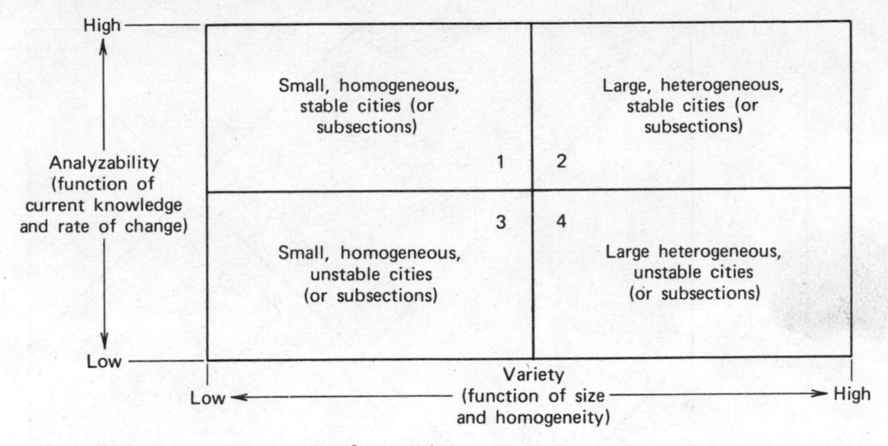

Figure 8-2 Information coming from a city.

in the domain's subsystems and the more stable they are, the more analyzable is their information.

The analyzability dimension helps us determine the feasibility of planning ahead. If the information a mayor receives about his domain is completely unanalyzable, planning ahead is all but impossible. To plan ahead one must make assumptions about cause and effect relationships and about the possibility of certain uncontrollable events occurring. If the information one has to plan with is not readily analyzable, making good assumptions and guesses is very difficult.

The variety dimension relates to the payoff received from planning ahead. The greater the variety (complexity) of information coming from a subsystem, the greater the possibility that the mayor and others will not be able to perceive the full implications of their current acts on the future of that subsystem and on others. Indeed, planning ahead pays off the most when conditions are so complex that people cannot easily see the future consequences of their current acts. Without planning, they will take actions that later evaluate as mistaken and inefficient.

Combining these feasibility–payoff thoughts, we can draw the conclusion concerning the relationship between the agenda and the city which was stated earlier and is shown graphically in Figure 8-3. At one extreme, if the information about a mayor's domain has low variety and low analyzability (point A), the most rational agenda is one that involves little planning (a #1 type). In this case, planning ahead is risky and does not yield much payoff. At the other extreme, if the

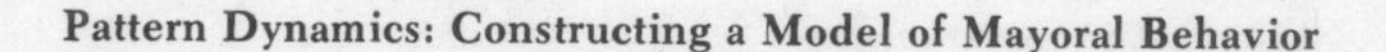

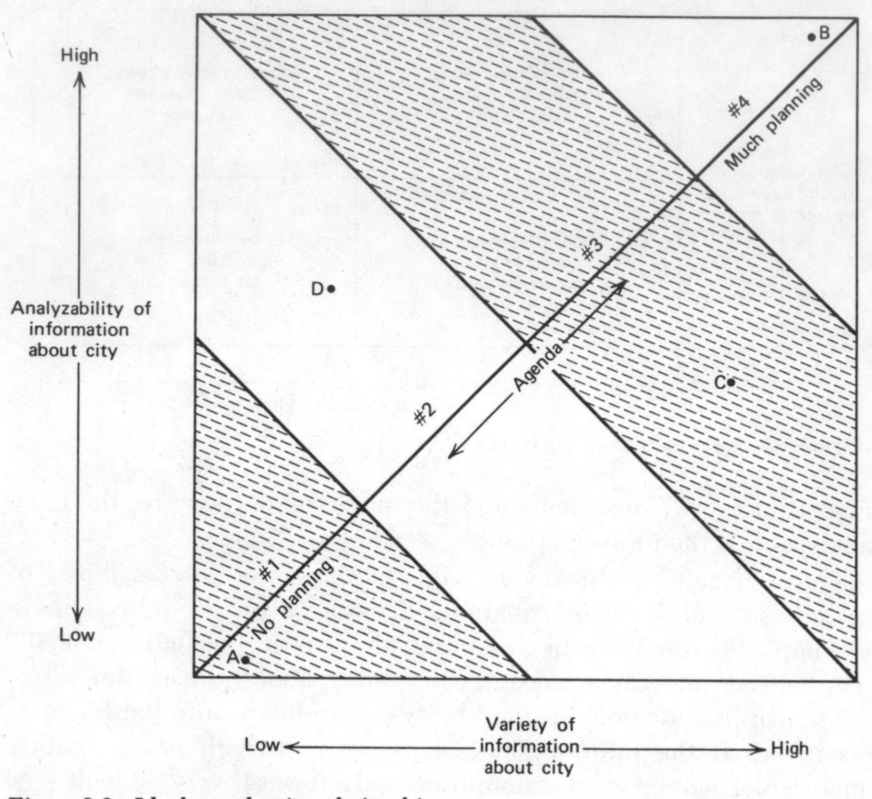

Figure 8-3 Ideal agenda–city relationship.

information has much variety and is highly analyzable (point B), the most rational agenda is one that entails a great deal of planning (a #4 type). In that case, planning ahead is very feasible and very profitable. In between, if the variety is relatively high (three-quarters down on the continuum) and the analyzability is moderate (the halfway point on the continuum), we have point C on the figure, which falls in the #3 agenda setting area. With the same amount of analyzability but fairly low variety, we find point D, which falls in the #2 agenda setting area.

The mayor whose agenda and city are thus misaligned may face numerous problems. If his agenda has less planning in it than his domain ideally calls for, he will eventually be severely criticized for "missing opportunities, not thinking ahead, and wasting resources by attacking problems piecemeal." This is what happened to Victor

Schiro and W. Ralston Westlake, among others. If, on the other hand, a mayor has more planning on his agenda than the information from his domain suggests, he will sooner or later become bogged down in delays caused by his own mistaken assumptions and will often have to deal with a disappointed public. No mayor in the study seriously suffered from this problem, although Lee had some difficulty with it near the end of his tenure.

CITY–MAYOR RELATIONSHIP

> 3. If the mayor's cognitive orientation is such that he is unable to understand at least the major events occurring in his city, the situation is unstable and will change.

There are many ways of bringing information into the mind and then using it. According to one conception of this process, developed by James McKenney, Peter Kenn, and others, man's "cognitive orientation" is perceived along two dimensions: intuitive–systematic and preceptive–receptive.[2] The latter refers to how a person brings information into the mind, the former to how he then uses it. The systematic–receptive person focuses on details, takes in small amounts of information, and deals with it in very systematically. Such an orientation is common to what we often call "technicians." The systematic–perceptive person screens a large amount of information for patterns, then selectively brings in information which he deals with in a very systematic manner. Such an orientation is common to "engineers." The intuitive–receptive subject, who focuses on detail and deals with it intuitively, is often an "artist or craftsman" type. Finally, an intuitive–preceptive person screens large amounts of information looking for patterns and deals with that information in an intuitive way. This orientation is often that of the "professional" (Figure 8-4).

[2]Keen and McKenney (1973).

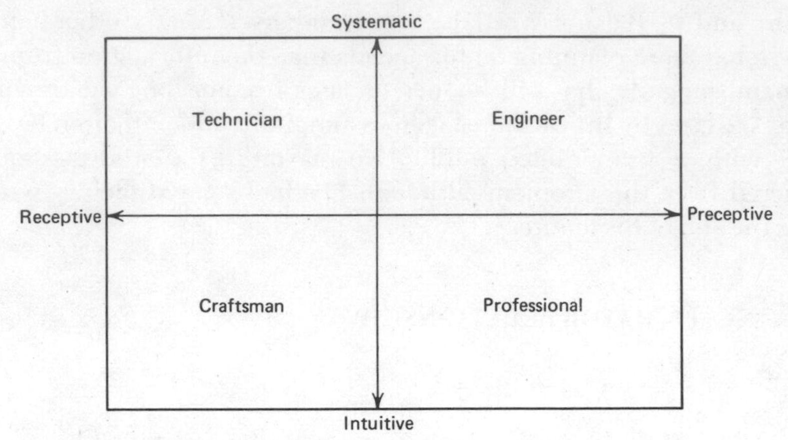

Figure 8-4 Different cognitive orientations.

Each cognitive style or orientation seems to deal best with one type of phenomenon or problem. Each is best equipped to gather and process information with certain characteristics. For example, the systematic–receptive person (technician) is oriented to deal best with a small amount of analyzable data. His receptive information-gathering mode can accept only a limited amount of information because of its focus on detail. His systematic information-processing mode is frustrated if the information cannot be processed logically and systematically (i.e., if it is not analyzable).

In the city–mayor "ideal" relationship (Figure 8-5), we see that different city types can be understood best by different types of mayors. If the city and mayor are significantly out of line with each other, the mayor will not be capable of understanding or sensing accurately what is happening. He will therefore sometimes act inappropriately. In a crisis especially, the negative consequences of such actions can be severe.

For example, Ralph Locher (Cleveland) faced a number of crises during his last few years in office. Most of these were directly associated with an increasingly militant black community. Indirectly they were the result of large demographic and economic changes that had been occuring in Cleveland for at least 10 years. In reacting to these crises, Locher made a number of disastrous decisions. At one point in 1965, his police chief publicly supported retaining the death penalty in Ohio, stating that society needed to protect innocent whites against blacks who wanted to kill them. Predictably enough, some civil

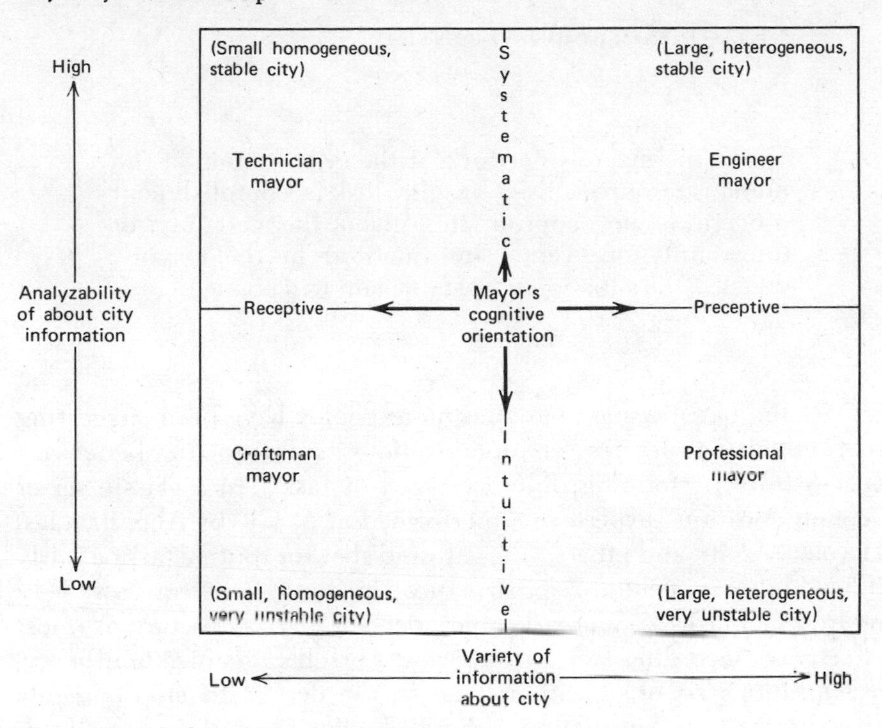

Figure 8-5 Ideal city–mayor relationship.

rights groups hurried to city hall to confront the mayor. Locher refused to see them, and they picketed his home one Saturday in June. Locher reacted by doing "exactly what I did every Saturday—I cut my grass." During the 1966 riot in the Hough section of Cleveland, Locher ordered the police to shoot down a helicopter which he assumed was part of the rebellion. Luckily, the police did not shoot, for the aircraft turned out to be a TV helicopter.[3]

In these and other instances, Locher's critics usually tried to explain his behavior by using terms like "bigot." Such an explanation in this case is not only naive, it is unfair. We found no evidence to suggest that Locher fully understood what was happening during these crises. Locher received his municipal and political "education" as the protégé of one of Ohio's best known politicians, Frank Lausche. Lausche's style was very successful in his day. In 1965, however, Cleveland was a very different city and required the services of a very different kind of mayor.

[3]Source: interview with Ralph Locher.

NETWORK–CITY RELATIONSHIP

> 4. In the mayor's network, if the organization of the human resources used in the task accomplishment process is not appropriate, given the certainty or uncertainty of events (information) in the mayor's domain, the situation is unstable and will change.

Over the past decade more and more people have been suggesting that certain structures or organizations seem to be better for successfully performing different types of tasks. In a classic set of "communication" experiments performed at M.I.T. by Alex Bavelas, Harold Leavitt, and others, it was found that for routine tasks a fairly inflexible and centralized structure is best, whereas for very nonroutine tasks a more flexible, decentralized structure is most effective.[4] According to Lawrence and Lorsch's organization theory, organizations or organizational parts that deal with environments characterized by "uncertainty" should be flexible and decentralized, and organizational parts dealing with "certain" environments should be fairly inflexible and centralized.[5] If one organization must deal with environments that are very different (certain–uncertain), its internal structure must reflect these differences; that is, there must be differently structured subunits to deal with the various environmental parts.

Going back to our conceptualization of the mayor's domain, we find that if it is highly analyzable with very low variety, it is quite "certain" in the Lawrence and Lorsch sense. If it has low analyzability with great variety, it is quite "uncertain" (see Figure 8-6). With this background, we can now state the ideal network–city relationship:

> 1. If the mayor's domain is a fairly certain environment, the implementation capacity in his network should be fairly centralized and structured.

[4] Leavitt (1962).
[5] Lawrence and Lorsch (1967).

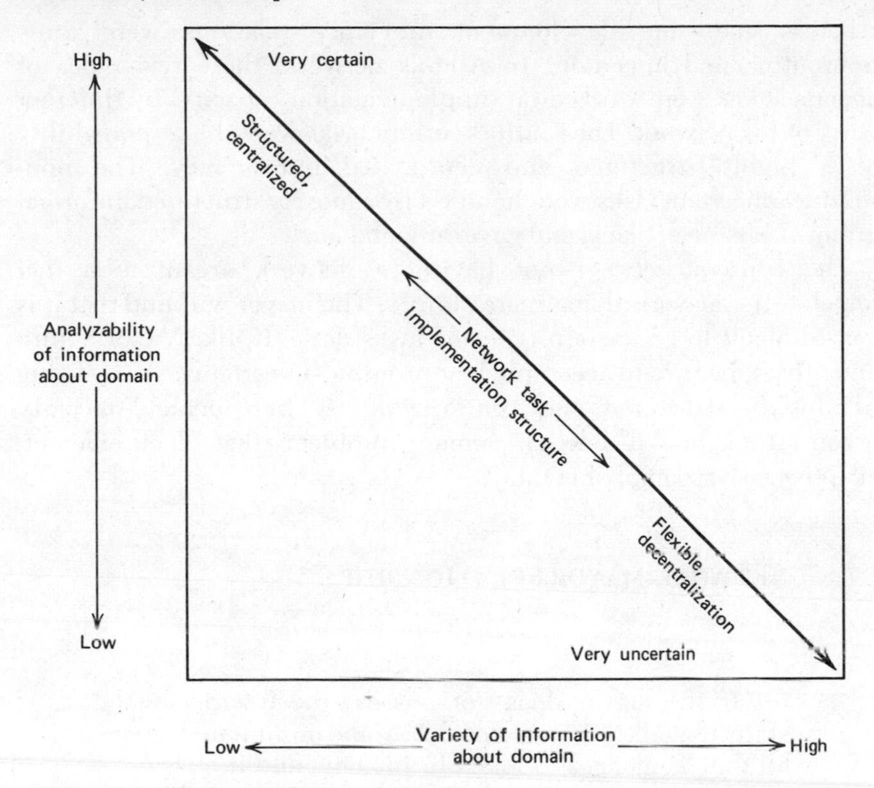

Figure 8-6 Ideal network–city relationship.

> 2. If the mayor's domain is an uncertain environment, his implementation capacity in his network should be fairly decentralized and flexible.
> 3. If the mayor's domain has large elements in it which are very different on the certain–uncertain dimension, his implementation capacity should be split (differentiated) into at least two parts, which are structured quite differently.

An example should help clarify this relationship. Ivan Allen's domain (Atlanta) was very large relative to that of most of the other mayors in this study. Thus it is not surprising that it contained a wide variety of elements, both very certain and very uncertain. For example, the delivery of basic city services was quite routine and certain, whereas economic development and race relations were quite nonroutine and uncertain. In Allen's network, these two types of agenda items were worked on (implementation capacity) by different parts of his network. The routine–certain tasks were the responsibility of a highly structured and centralized bureaucracy. The nonroutine–uncertain tasks were handled by a loosely structured, informal group of business, black, and governmental leaders.

The consequences of not having a network organization that matches the mayor's domain are simple. The mayor will find that it is very difficult to get certain types of tasks done. If, like Victor Schiro and others, he tries to accomplish nonroutine–uncertain tasks by using his highly structured and centralized city bureaucracy or party organization, he will encounter many problems that block efficient, effective task accomplishment.

NETWORK–MAYOR RELATIONSHIP

> 5. If the mayor does not possess the interpersonal skills that allow him to speak to some minimum degree all the "languages" spoken in his city, and if he is not highly competent in the language of his most powerful network member (if there is a "most powerful" one), the situation is unstable in the long run and will change.

This was particularly striking in the data collected in our initial field study. The six cities chosen varied considerably in the heterogeneity of their populations. In one city there were only three main differentiated population groups—blacks, middle- and upper-middle-class whites, and lower-middle-class whites. In another city there were a dozen groups of importance—Irish, Italian, old Yankee Protestant, business, university, labor union, and so on. The mayors also varied a great deal with respect to the breadth of their interpersonal "language" skills. Some could talk or behave in one language, others could behave in many. For example, one mayor always behaved like a corporate executive regardless of the setting, whereas another had a very flexible style and personality. The latter (Lee) was described by one of his aides in the following way:

> When he is with the Irish, his ethnic background comes out and he looks like he grew up in Dublin. When he is at the university, he is a wise old man. Over at the Chamber he is a shrewd capitalist. With the unions he is a cigar-chomping tough guy. He's not just "acting" either. He really knows how to talk the language of each of those groups.

The three mayors in the initial study whose interpersonal language skills did not "match" the languages spoken in their networks appear to have had serious difficulties not encountered by their colleagues. The consequences of a poor match were twofold. First, the mayors had difficulty in building and maintaining their networks. Being able to speak a group's language seems to be almost a prerequisite to establishing and maintaining a strong, positive relationship with its members. Second, the mayors had difficulty "hearing" some network members and interpreting their expectations, ideas, and demands. To some degree, at least, a "good" city is not defined in the abstract. It is good to the people who live in it. If the mayor cannot hear or understand their concerns, not only will he take actions that make people angry but this behavior may have a negative impact on his city.

Lee is a good example of a mayor whose interpersonal language skills served him well in a very heterogeneous city. George Christopher, on the other hand, lived in an even more heterogeneous city (San Francisco) but had a narrower repertoire of interpersonal skills. Indeed, his chief interpersonal asset was that his predominant language (business) was the same as that of the most powerful subgroup in the city. However, Christopher suffered as a result of this mismatch. By the time he retired after 8 years as mayor, a number of subgroups in the city were quite upset with him. That is, he had not been able to maintain a cooperative relationship with them over time. The city also suffered. As a result of not "hearing" some parts of the city, Christopher built the Embarcadero Freeway, which is considered by many to be one of the city's greatest liabilities.

It is interesting to note that the backgrounds of the mayors who had a rather broad language capacity were quite different from the personal histories of mayors whose language skills were limited. The mayor with the broadest personality (Lee) spent his developmental years working and living in one group after another. He was born in an ethnic subculture, took his first job at a newspsper, his second at the Chamber of Commerce while he also worked as an alderman, and his third at Yale University. Before he became mayor, he knew all the languages of the city, had had experience with all the major differentiated groups, and could demonstrate success at working with each of them. Two of the mayors with fairly narrow personalities had spent the 20 years prior to their first election in the same subculture—one in a boardroom (Jonsson) and one in an insurance office (Schiro).

MAYOR–AGENDA RELATIONSHIP

> 6. If the mayor's agenda calls for him to have many interpersonal or cognitive skills which he clearly lacks, the situation is unstable in the long run and must change.

If the mayor is not the right man for the job (agenda), there is a problem.

In the case of Erik Jonsson (Dallas), there was very good alignment between the mayor and his agenda. Jonsson had spent the decade prior to his election as mayor of Dallas as the head of a growing, multi-million dollar instrumentation company. He had demonstrated very unusual talent at creating and implementing large and aggressive programs that produced enormous change in the direction he desired (growth for his company). His orientation was holistic, logical, and middle- to long-run oriented. Jonsson's mayoral agenda was characterized by large, future-oriented programs and projects like the Goals for Dallas program described in Chapter 4. His agenda also included the slow and difficult process of building a more adaptive and technically sophisticated city bureaucracy. Under his leadership, Dallas and Fort

Worth built the largest and most technically advanced airport in the world.

In other situations in this study, the alignment between agenda and mayor was not as good. If the misalignment is too great, the usual consequence is that the mayor is very ineffective or very inefficient in carrying out his agenda. In either case, poor performance tends to upset people and to waste resources. The mayor's typical reaction is to change his agenda to bring it more in line with his own personality and skills.

To a large degree the case of Victor Schiro fits this pattern. Prior to his work in New Orleans city government, Schiro was an insurance salesman. His basic cognitive orientation was that of a craftsman. He thought in terms of small systems and small groups of people. He tended to see problems as caused by and affecting discrete individuals. His interpersonal orientation was geared to the middle- and lower-middle-class white community. He did not speak the languages of the black community, the old-line wealthy, or the highly educated.

After his second election campaign was over, Schiro's agenda included three midrange projects: one dealing with riverfront development, one with a stadium, and one with a jazz festival. To follow through on the first two required some capacity to see the city as a whole and to understand the complex, large-scale interdependencies involved. To follow through on the first and third (and somewhat on the second) required competence to deal with the old-line money interests in New Orleans. Schiro did not have these cognitive or interpersonal skills, and after an awkward period of fighting and name calling, he abandoned all three agenda items.

ALIGNMENT, NONALIGNMENT, COALIGNMENT

We have found at least one key relationship between each of our contextual variables. Those relationships are such that if any two contextual variables are not "aligned," the consequences of that nonalignment eventually create problems for the mayor.

In a sense, nonalignments produce "amplifying problems" for a mayor. A large nonalignment between the mayor and the city, for example, means that the mayor cannot completely understand the signals sent by the city about possible problems, opportunities, and crises. As a result, he will create an agenda, react to people, and behave, on the basis of false information. At first, these actions will produce only minor problems—an annoyed citizen and a few "stupid" decisions. Yet in time these problems add up, and in a crisis situation such actions can be disastrous (as with Locher's reaction to the riot).

If all four contextual variables of a mayor's system are aligned simultaneously, we have a state of "coalignment." None of the mayors in this study could be said to have created and maintained a completely coaligned system, although some came close (Figure 8-7). None created large multiple nonalignments, either.

Nonalignments that go uncorrected over time tend to lead to a mayor's demise. If the mayor cannot somehow eliminate the

Mayor	Coalignment results	Election results
	Complete coalignment ↑	
Allen		Retired after 2 terms
Lee		Retired after 8 terms
Cowger, Bachrach, Martin		Retired after 1, 2, and 3 terms
Welch, Jonsson		Retired after 5 and 3 terms
Lamb, Boswell		Defeated after 2 terms; retired after 1 term
Christopher, Naftalin		Retired after 2 and 4 terms
Curran, Whelan, Addonizio		Defeated after 2 terms; in jail; in jail
Schiro, McCann		Retired after 2 terms; defeated after 2 terms
Bartle, Locher		Defeated after 2 and 1 terms
Kowal, Westlake		Retired after 1 term; defeated after 1 term
	↓ Large multiple nonalignments	

Figure 8-7 Coalignment and election results.

nonalignment, people generally look to the electoral process to correct the situation by replacing the mayor. As Figure 8-7 indicates, there is a fairly clear relationship between election results and coalignment results.

There are undoubtedly several reasons for the failure of the mayor's survival and his coalignment results to correlate completely. The most important relates to "slack."[6] Insofar as a mayor is able to command slack "vote resources" in his network, he may be able to survive regardless of nonalignment problems. Some of the old "machine" mayors are reputed to have maintained their position by having and using such slack resources.

This issue of coalignment is important, and we continue to explore it in some of the chapters that follow.

THE NEW MODEL SUMMARIZED

We now have the model of mayoral behavior shown in Figure 8-8; it contains only two elements that have not been discussed at some length. A mayor's values and aspirations, and his needs and drives, must be included in our model because they provide internal energy and direction to a mayor's behavior.[7] We have more to say about them later.

The model says that a mayor's behavior can take on a number of specified forms in three key processes—an agenda setting process (described in Chapter 4), a network building process (Chapter 5), and a task accomplishment process (Chapter 6). The mayor directs this behavior in a system having four key variables—the mayor, his agenda, his network, and the city (see Figure 8-8 for definitions). These variables and the mayor's behavior are connected in a complex system of interdependencies that can be broken down into two sets of dynamic relationships. One set of relationships is between the mayor's behavior and the contextual variables, as summarized earlier. The mayor's behavior in the three processes has a direct impact on the contextual variables, whereas the contextual variables act both as resources for and constraints to a mayor's behavior. The second set of

[6]For an interesting discussion of slack in an organizational setting, see Cyert and March (1967).

[7]We have chosen to talk about "internal characteristics" using the three basic categories used by many psychologists—thinking, morals, and motivation; or ego, superego, and id.

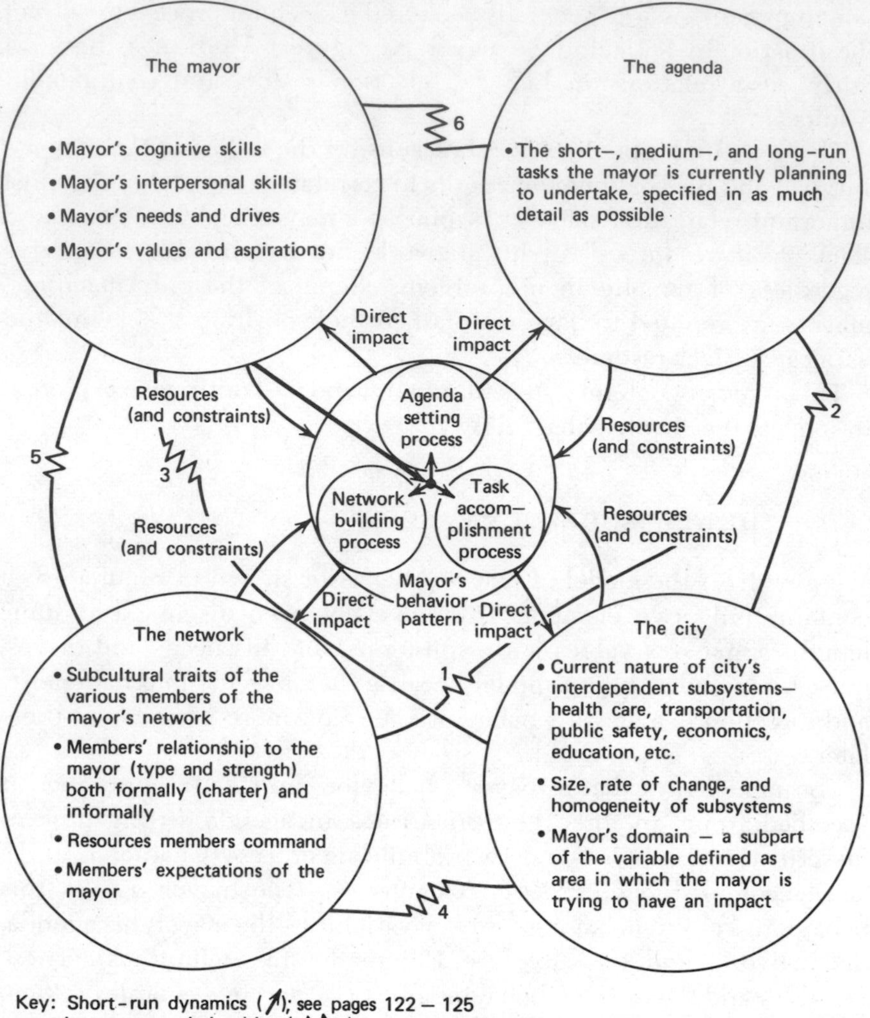

Figure 8-8 Summary of the model.

dynamics is among the contextual variables themselves. The relationships between the mayor and his network, his city and his agenda, and so on, affect the stability of the system, as well as the survival of the mayor in the long run.

Let us now move to a discussion of one mayor's behavior. We hope the following example, involving a "conspicuously successful" mayor, will help the reader gain better understanding and insight into our model.

CHAPTER 9

ATLANTA: A CASE STUDY IN MAYORAL BEHAVIOR

IVAN ALLEN, JR.

Ivan Allen, Jr., was the only son of a respected, moderately wealthy Atlanta businessman (the president of the Ivan Allen Office Equipment Company). Although the elder Allen never ran for public office, many people described him as a politically ambitious man.

As a child, Ivan was not a particularly good student, but he was highly motivated, engaging in entrepreneurial activities at an early age. After high school he enrolled in the School of Commerce at Georgia Tech, where he received fairly good grades. He was elected president of the student body, vice-president of the interfraternity council, cadet colonel of the ROTC, and president of the ODK. When he graduated from college he joined his father's business, married, and spent the war years in Atlanta working at a job on a draft board.

Allen's first experience with politics came in 1936 when Ed Rivers was elected governor. The future mayor actively campaigned for Rivers and served as treasurer of the State Hospital Authority and in other positions from 1936 to 1940. After the war he became executive secretary to Governor Ellis Arnall. Between 1948 and 1958 Allen was a member of the State Board of Education, worked in the State Department of Veteran Services, and helped lead the Georgia Chamber of Commerce in industrial development projects, all while continuing to work in the family business. In 1958 Allen investigated the possibilities of his becoming governor. When support did not arise, he backed out.

In 1960 Ivan Allen, Jr., was a typical member of the Atlanta establishment. He was 48 years old, president of the Ivan Allen Company, president of the Chamber of Commerce, and a wealthy, respected citizen. People who knew Allen at that time describe him with such words as pragmatic, honest, temperate, entrepreneurial, charming, efficient, and energetic.

When William B. Hartsfield decided to retire after 23 years as mayor of Atlanta, Allen announced he would enter the 1961 mayoralty race.

ATLANTA: 1837–1960

Atlanta, Georgia, was founded around 1837 as the end of a railroad line. It was only a small town when General Sherman's troops destroyed it in 1864. After the Civil War, Atlanta started all over again.

Growth came quickly to Atlanta after 1870. By 1900 the city held nearly 100,000 people, and by 1960 the population exceeded 400,000. Geographical factors were particularly important in creating this growth. Straight lines drawn on a map from New York City to New Orleans and from Chicago to Miami will cross just north of the city; thus Atlanta was a potential distribution center, "crossroads," and transportation hub. The city also has the second highest altitude of the major cities in the country. It has no extremes in weather, and it is accessible to the Atlantic coast and the Blue Ridge Mountains.

Atlanta's population in 1960 could be roughly divided into three groups: middle- and upper-class white; black; lower-middle and lower-class white. Atlanta has never had any significant European ethnic groups.

The central city has experienced a typical population shift in the past few decades. The percentage of the central city population that was black grew from 38% in 1950 to 48% in 1960 and 51% in 1970. This increase in black population has occurred mainly in the center of the city and to the east and west of the business district. The more affluent whites have generally moved to suburbs north of Atlanta, and the less affluent to the suburbs in the south.

William B. Hartsfield, the mayor until 1962, enjoys the reputation in

Atlanta of having been a good mayor. People speak of him as having taken good care of the city for many years. During his tenure, Atlanta prospered and grew. Retail sales, for example, increased nearly six times between 1939 and 1958. It was Hartsfield who bought a race track and built the second airport in the South.

When Hartsfield left office in 1961, Atlanta could not be described as a "sick" city by any means. There were no obvious crisis-generating problems. However, it was not a "model city," either. The economy was not booming as many felt it should. Tension between the races was growing. The downtown area looked old. Many felt that the town was not realizing its sizable potential.

Compared with most cities its size, Atlanta's community organization in 1960 was relatively simple. Outside the city government, only two stable groups of importance were organized to deal with decisions affecting the community and its governance. By far the more powerful of the two was the business community. The other was the black community.

The business community in 1960, as represented by the Commerce Club, was the most cohesive, well-organized, and powerful group in Atlanta. Historically, the leaders in the business community (the heads of banks, top Coca-Cola management, and others) had worked well together. Most Atlanta businessmen today agree that during this period six or seven men spoke for the business community. The quality of this leadership appears to have been reasonably good. These "spokesmen" were sharp, aggressive, had community spirit, and were moderate or moderate-conservative politically. This group backed Mayor Hartsfield and solidly backed Ivan Allen, too. They often operated through the Chamber of Commerce or informally at the Commerce Club.

The business community was small compared with the total population of Atlanta. Nevertheless, its strength was bolstered because the upper-middle-class and some of the middle-class white communities always followed its lead. In a sense, these three separate groups were one, with the business leaders providing the overall leadership.

The black community in 1960, although less cohesive and much less powerful than the business community, was the second major organized group in Atlanta. Under the leadership of men such as Walden (lawyer), Dobbs (Masonic leader), Borders (minister), King (minister), Wilkes (minister), Scott (newspaper owner), and Maize (Board of Education), the black community had begun to organize itself for political and community action during the 1930s. Around

1950 these black leaders achieved one of their first successes in the public arena as a result of their organized efforts. By pulling together their voting strength, they induced Mayor Hartsfield to add some blacks to the police force. It was a small victory (six policemen with little power), but a real one. Later in the 1950s a ministerial alliance began to set up, and win, segregation test cases. In the first one, six black ministers boarded a bus and defiantly sat in the front. During this time, Mayor Hartsfield, while not directly advancing their cause, was cooperative.

Examining the other ways in which Atlanta might have been organized, one finds a void. Labor has become a weak force in Atlanta in the 1970s. In 1960, because of the antilabor orientation of the South and because Atlanta was a service-industry town, labor was no force at all. Atlanta had a number of universities, but because most of them were young and small, they did not represent an organized academic establishment. Historically the church had been an organized force of importance in the white community, but this was no longer true by 1960. The church was still powerful in the black community in 1960 in that quite a few of the black leaders were ministers. But the black community at that time was organized on the basis of race, not religion. Because the city elections were nonpartisan and the city was basically Democratic, there existed no citywide political organizations.

The only other group to be reckoned with was the lower-middle-class white community, which derived some power from its large size. It was unorganized, relatively leaderless, and a much less significant community force than the business and black communities.

The only other relevant form of organization in Atlanta was the "formal" one, the city government. Atlanta's charter calls for the citywide election of a mayor and 18 aldermen every 4 years. It also creates a moderate power position for the mayor (weak mayor charter). A Board of Aldermen is in charge of each of the city's departments. The mayor appoints the chairman of each board and submits names to the board to be considered for department heads.

Historically the aldermen have not been an outstanding group, but neither have they been corrupt and self-serving. Hartsfield maintained good relations with them during his administration. In 1960 most of the board members had served for at least 10 years, and three had more than 30 years of service.

The city bureaucracy was in reasonably good condition in 1960. It was headed by a group of old-line career men who knew their jobs well and had held their positions for a number of years. The departments were rigid and not very innovative, but they performed their duties and displayed no signs of major corruption.

THE 1961 CAMPAIGN: THE EMERGENCE OF AN AGENDA, AN AGENDA SETTING PROCESS, AND A NETWORK BUILDING PROCESS

During 1959–1960, when Allen was vice-president of Atlanta's Chamber of Commerce, he developed a program that set fairly general objectives for the coming decade. As it was later summarized in literature published by the Chamber, the program was based on six points:

> 1. EXPRESSWAYS: The Atlanta Chamber of Commerce must use its every facility to press for a definite step-up in the tempo of local expressway construction. To this end it should lend its full and continuous support to local, state, and federal agencies in all possible ways. Although the Chamber takes pride in what has been completed, it must at the same time insist that progress has not been fast enough and that a substantial acceleration in the expressway program is absolutely essential to the health and well-being of the Atlanta community.
>
> 2. URBAN RENEWAL: The Atlanta Chamber of Commerce must vigorously support the city's urban renewal and housing efforts across the board. More specifically, it should: (a) urge and assist in a speedup of activity by the city and its agencies handling the current program; (b) encourage private capital to take advantage of the unprecedented development opportunities in urban renewal projects; (c) press for a further expansion of urban renewal (including an expanded program of finance) in the years immediately ahead; and (d) work with all agencies concerned in locating new housing opportunities for the Negro population.

3. AUDITORIUM–COLISEUM, STADIUM: The Atlanta Chamber of Commerce should strongly support the construction of an auditorium-coliseum and a stadium. Finance and building plans should be readied, sites selected, and operating organizations set up as rapidly as possible. The public wants these facilities, and there is no time to lose.

4. RAPID TRANSIT: The Atlanta Chamber of Commerce should take the lead in pressing for a practical, large-scale rapid-transit system for Atlanta. The scope and timing of the project calls for an immediate start at concrete planning and programming. The only alternative is even more expressways than now projected at five times the cost per mile and even further expansion of automobile traffic loads, with a breakdown in central traffic circulation by the end of the decade.

5. SCHOOLS: The Atlanta Chamber of Commerce must take a bold and firm stand on this issue. It must clearly set forth to the public at large, and the business community in particular, the full implications of the Little Rock, Norfolk, and New Orleans stories. It should officially endorse the majority report of the Sibly School Committee (favoring keeping schools open) and actively work for the passage of necessary legislation in the January session of the General Assembly. Atlanta's public schools must stay open and the Chamber should provide its share of vigorous leadership in seeing that they do.

6. "FORWARD ATLANTA": The Atlanta Chamber of Commerce should establish and vigorously carry out a three-year "Forward Atlanta" program of education, advertising, and research to carry the Atlanta story over the nation. This program should be supported by a minimum budget of $500,000 per year, raised from the Atlanta business community. Only through such a campaign can Atlanta hope to stay on top in the years ahead.

This program appears to have been the product of an interactive *process*. Allen discussed various items extensively with his friends and associates, and as ideas began to take shape in his mind, he recruited a number of "intelligent" and "creative" (Allen's words) people to help him pull his thoughts together and package them. This process lasted for nearly a year. When Allen began campaigning for mayor in 1961, he announced that if elected he would adopt the six-point program as the basis of his mayoral agenda.

The 1961 campaign began with a half-dozen announced candidates. Allen put together a campaign organization that included Hartsfield's former campaign manager, Helen Bullard, and a manpower reserve of about 400 people—the employees of the Ivan Allen Company. In trying to build the remainder of a network strong enough to secure his election, Allen relied heavily on friendship appeals and purposive appeals.

The following story, attributed to mayoral candidate Howell Smith in a conversation with Allen himself, indicates the types of cooperative links Allen developed, based on historical friendship.

> When I found out that Mills Lane [head of C & S Bank] was backing you, I figured I'd get me a bank to back me. So I called up Mr. Ed Smith over at the First National and went over there and he said, "I'd be delighted to support you because I'm sure you'd make a good mayor. But Ivan and I are very close personal friends, and our wives were born and raised together and have traveled together all their lives, so we're just committed to support Ivan." He was very gracious about it, and I wasn't too upset. I knew I had three more banks anyhow. Well, next I went to see Mr. George Craft at the Trust Company of Georgia, and he was nice to me too, said he would even support me—except, he said, you two were raised together and your daddy is a director of the Trust Company of Georgia, and Mrs. Craft and your wife had traveled together all over the world, so he was going to have to support his friend Ivan Allen, Jr.
>
> Well, that shook me up a little but I still had two more banks left, so I went to see Mr. Gordon Jones at the Fulton Bank, and he told me that you two were fraternity brothers, and his wife and Mrs. Allen had just spent the summer in Europe together. That left me

> with one more bank, the National Bank of Georgia, and I never saw anyone so gracious in my life as Mr. Joe Birnie. He said he thought I'd make a fine candidate just like everybody else had said. But then I got the same thing. "Ivan Allen and I are good friends," he said, "and on top of that, my wife and his spent the spring traveling together in Europe, so I'm going to have to support Ivan."[1]

Without dealing in specifics, Allen used his six-point program to create purposive cooperative relationships with a large number of people and groups in Atlanta. Members of the upper-middle-class and business communities liked its commitment to economic development. Members of the black community were attracted by the urban renewal, schools, and rapid transit points. Some groups in the middle and lower-middle class favored the stadium and the expressways.

With a well-financed campaign and a charming personality, Allen was able to project a mildly charismatic image. He used his program, his charm, and appeals to pragmatic self-interest to build links and friendships with quite a few black leaders. Finally, as he and Lester Maddox emerged as the top candidates, Allen urged Atlantans to unite with him *against* Maddox and "that small group who wishes to bring another Little Rock to Atlanta."

In the initial election, Allen came in first with 38% of the vote, followed by Maddox with 21%. In the runoff, Allen got 65%, Maddox 35%.

1962: THE EMERGENCE OF THE REST OF THE PATTERN, THE FAILURES, AND THE CHANGES

Allen was sworn in as the mayor of Atlanta in January 1962. He immediately began to operate in the fashion we have described as a #3 agenda setting process. He filled in the details of his six-point program and created short-run agendas that were consistent with the long-run objectives. For example, a number of his proposals required major financing, and Allen made the passage of an $80 million bond issue a

[1]Ivan Allen, Jr., *Mayor: Notes on the Sixties* (New York: Simon & Schuster, 1971), p. 51.

top-priority item on his 12-month agenda. He also created short-run strategies associated with rapid transit, expressways, and other projects.

In that first 10 to 12 months, Allen spent little time on network building and maintenance activities. In his efforts to accomplish specific tasks, he relied heavily on what we have called a bureaucratic process. This overall pattern is very similar to the one he had used as president of the Ivan Allen Company.

In retrospect, Allen has said numerous times, "My first year in office turned out to be a nightmare. We accomplished very little."

> The worst setback I suffered during that first year was the resounding defeat of my proposed $80 million bond issue. I simply failed to communicate with the voters and with the board of aldermen on the bond issue. For example, the plan for the beautification of Piedmont Park suddenly blew up in my face and became a raging racial issue. The Woodruff Foundation had offered a gift of $4 million on the project, but as always asked that it be an anonymous gift. The redneck elements started screaming that the Piedmont Park plan was really an effort to integrate the park (it had already been integrated, but they failed to mention that), and that the $4 million anonymous gift was "nigger money." We had no defense because we couldn't announce that the Woodruff Foundation had offered to put up the money. The bond issue was beaten by a two-to-one vote.
>
> I even managed to lose what had been overwhelming support in the black community through my mishandling of another disaster that first year, the Peyton Road blockbusting issue. There was a very nice white subdivision off Peyton Road, on the southwest side of Atlanta, called Peyton Forest. The developer of the subdivision became dissatisfied with the rate of development there and made some threats to people in the area (he felt that they were standing in the way of his developing the land), pointing out that Negroes were moving into adjoining neighborhoods, and he just

might start selling to them in Peyton Forest. The residents became indignant toward the developer and frightened about the encroachment of blacks in the area, and a volatile situation began to build up. It was the classic situation of a neighborhood being faced with racial transition. This took place in fifty-two separate formerly white neighborhoods in Atlanta during that one year, and often the situation was inflamed by "blockbusting" realtors and developers.

When I was advised of what was happening, I looked into the matter and saw that just north of Peyton Forest there were some eight hundred acres of unused land that had been improperly zoned commercial. Over the years it had been fairly common practice for the board of aldermen to create a buffer zone—a no-man's land—between black and white neighborhoods by simply zoning a large enough area for commercial use. The result was, Atlanta city maps were dotted with scores of these unused plots of land. And this was at a time when we needed all the good land we could find for housing. So when the developer finally sold his own home in Peyton Forest to a prominent Negro doctor, setting off a holocaust among the whites there, I promptly decided to close off the subdivision—entrenched whites on one side, encroaching blacks on the other—with a barrier on Peyton Road. I saw it as a way of accomplishing two things: calming the white people in the neighborhood and focusing attention on the unused eight hundred acres so we could get it rezoned and put to use for low or middle-priced housing. I saw it as a happy compromise between two very serious problems, and thought maybe I could be Solomon before it was over. But what I learned, once again, was that when you're dealing with the public you cannot assume they know all that you know. The people of Atlanta didn't understand all of the subtleties of the situation. They only saw a crude barricade—the "Atlanta Wall," it came to be called—stretched across a road, making a dividing line between whites and blacks. I had forgotten an axiom that William B. Hartsfield once used: "Never do anything wrong that they can take a picture of." The press had a heyday, and

> the feeling against me was understandably bitter in the Negro community. "I don't see how any decent white man can do what you have done," said the Reverend Sam Williams, who had been one of my stronger supporters in the past.
>
> I discovered very quickly that running a city isn't as cut-and-dried as running an office-equipment company; that it is one thing to make campaign promises and quite another thing to harness a massive city-government machine to make the promises come true. I simply was not conversant with the urban political process, having had little or no worthwhile experience at it. I didn't know how to push the buttons to get things going. I didn't know how to manipulate the board of aldermen. I didn't understand the very basic theory that the public has to be fully informed about what the city is doing or planning to do—through the use of citizens' advisory committees or through useful manipulation of the press—before you can gain its support. I had not gained the instinctive feel you have to have to do the right thing at the right time without having to sit down and think it over. This is something that can only come with experience on the job.
>
> I got an inkling of what was in store for me on the night of the inauguration ceremonies when Louise and I drove up to the City Hall parking lot and were stopped by the attendant at the gate. "Buddy, I'm full up," he said. "Maybe you can find a place down there back of that church."[2]

By the end of his second year in office, Allen had modified his original approach to the job. He did not significantly alter his agenda setting pattern, but he did make changes in his patterns of network building and task accomplishing.

Before Hartsfield retired, he had succeeded in securing an appropriation from the state legislature for a chief administrative

[2]Allen (1971), abridged from pages 66, 67, 70, 71, 72.

officer, but he had not filled the post. In late 1963 Allen convinced Earl Landers, the city controller, to take this job. Landers, who had been a city employee for 28 years, had worked closely with all the department heads, many for more than two decades. He also was highly respected by the business community. He accepted the position with great reluctance, preferring a less visible and more secure office.

It became Lander's job to administer the bread-and-butter details of city government. He ran the city bureaucracy as he had almost been doing before as controller. The department heads reacted favorably to the new arrangement, since they were relieved that the man who occupied this new position of power was one they could trust. Allen's capacity to get things done at city hall increased significantly (cooption).

Allen's relationship with the board of aldermen was never bad. In his first year, however, it was not characterized by strong cooperation. Two incidents, in particular, seem to have led to an improved relationship.

Hartsfield had made it a policy for 22 years not to change any committee appointments. As one political pro observed, "This made for a better understanding between the mayor and the aldermen, since the aldermen had some security in their jobs." Allen continued this policy with one exception: he removed from office the chairman of the Police Committee, with whom he had had a "misunderstanding" concerning the allocation of liquor licenses.

Allen was known to be a powerful man in town, and he made it clear that he would use that power in the Police Committee incident. However, he wanted the aldermen to trust him and be friends; hence his appointment of Earl Landers as chief administrative officer. With these steps (coercion, cooption), Allen assured himself of a solid relationship with the aldermen.

Allen also began to devote more time to maintaining and nurturing the relationships he had created in his 1961 campaign. He spent time with people—charming them, listening to them, and discussing policy (personal and purposive appeals).

The most drastic change Allen made during this period involved his approach to the accomplishment of specific tasks. He moved more toward an entrepreneurial process, as in the case of the second bond election. He began this effort by going to Ed Smith, the head of the First National Bank, and convincing him to run the bond program. Together they strategically selected members of a bond committee.

One of the major opponents of the first bond election was on the committee (cooption), and he was also named to the Board of the Chamber of Commerce (discrete exchange). He changed his views.

Smith's committee held open hearings on the bond issue and gave everyone a chance to speak. Smith and Allen mobilized the Chamber and the newspapers into actively supporting the bond program. Allen worked closely with a number of black leaders. At a rally held at Wheat Street Church some of the younger, left-leaning blacks argued that there was not enough in the bond issue for blacks. They told the crowd that the mayor and the city really wanted segregation. When the situation began to look bad, the Reverend Borders broke in and said: "Well, wait a minute, Segregation isn't all bad." The crowd became quiet and stared at Borders.

> Look, you know you elected me to serve on the Council which meets yearly in Chicago. Every year I went down to the train station and asked for an upper berth, and paid my money. Every year they gave me a drawing room. In the past few years they've managed to integrate the train. This year I went to the station, asked for an upper berth, gave the man my money, and I'll be damned if he didn't give me an upper berth.[3]

Everyone laughed and Borders regained control. The bond issue passed easily.

Allen also altered the manner in which he used what we have called an individualistic process. As he became accustomed to the job, he gained a sense of timing and a feel for when and how to use this process—that is, when to act as an individual, not an executive or a public entrepreneur. The most dramatic use of this process in his early years as mayor came as a response to a tragedy.

> On a beautiful Sunday morning in June I was rummaging around our farm at Franklin, Georgia,

[3]Source: interview notes.

about seventy miles west of Atlanta near the Alabama line, when I was told that my wife had been trying to reach me by phone. I returned the call, and Louise said King Elliott, a newsman at WSB, had called with a fragmentary news report that a large number of Atlantans had been killed in the crash of a chartered jet plane at Orly Field in Paris. The news hit me like a Mack truck. Exactly a month earlier I had officially said goodbye to a group of 106 prominent Atlantans, most of them patrons of the arts who were visiting European art capitals under the sponsorship of the Atlanta Art Association. This was about the day they were supposed to return from Paris on Air France.

I immediately called Ann Moses [personal secretary] and told her to open the office and try to get something official, expecially the list of Atlanta passengers, from Air France. Still wearing the old khakis I had been wearing around the farm, I jumped into my car and pointed it toward City Hall. As I sped toward the city I listened to the radio reports, which were still incomplete. At one point it was announced that my good friend Jack Glenn was on the plane, but I had been with Jack only a few days earlier and I knew better. Yet there was enough solid information now to make me certain that this was the Atlanta Art Association charter flight that had crashed, killing 106 Atlantans.

By the time I reached City Hall, having driven the seventy miles in slightly more than one hour, my office was a madhouse. Phones were ringing off the hook. Distraught relatives of people who were supposed to be on the flight didn't know where to turn. The networks and wire services were already calling and preparing to send people down to Atlanta. Local reporters and photographers surged back and forth in the office, which they were using as a nerve center on the disaster story, wanting to know what the city government was going to do. Still unshaven and wearing my khaki work clothes, I told them we would take all of the courtesy actions possible—issue a proclamation of sorrow, lower the flag at City Hall, assure the relatives that the city would offer any assistance necessary—but I knew this wasn't enough.

Finally I reached Gene Patterson, the only executive of Atlanta Newspapers whom I could locate on a Sunday morning, and when he asked me what I planned to do I surprised both of us by blurting out, "I'm going straight to Paris." Exactly what I could do when I got there, I hadn't considered. "That's the right thing to do," Patterson said. "You can at least represent those families over there." Just how I could represent them, I didn't know. But my instincts told me I should go.

The instant the plane came to a stop on the ground at Orly Field, the door was opened and two French gendarmes boarded the plane. "No one will leave the plane until Mayor Allen and his party have departed," one of them said. It took no more for me to realize that the French, with their compassion for man and their love of art, were pouring out their hearts to Atlanta. As I stepped out of the cabin onto the steps leading from the plane I couldn't believe my eyes. Spread out below me at the foot of the steps wearing striped trousers and frock coats on a beautiful hot June morning in Paris, were more than two dozen members of the official French family: a personal representative of Charles de Gaulle, the head of French aviation, chairman of the board of Air France, et al. I realized how insignificant I was, but I knew I had to assume the posture of representing these families and, indeed, the entire city of Atlanta, Georgia. I knew nothing about protocol, foreign relations, aviation, international agreements, or any of the other details I might become involved in. I was nothing but the mayor of Atlanta and a friend and neighbor of 106 people who had been killed at this same airport only the day before. All I could think was, "At least you've got a good education and at least some training, what if Lester Maddox had become mayor instead of you?"

As I walked down the steps to meet this delegation I threw my shoulders back and sucked in my stomach and talked myself into summoning all of the dignity and restraint I could find. I would represent those families to the best of my ability.

I have never met with a more understanding and

sympathetic group. They were anxious to help in any way, and after the usual exchange of greetings and extensions of sympathy it was suggested that I hold a press conference. Instead of the half-dozen reporters I was accustomed to talking to at press conferences in Atlanta, or the thirty-five or forty who had met us in New York, there were about 150 at Orly—international press, local reporters, the wire services, photographers, television cameramen, and broadcasters—the largest contingent of newsmen I was to meet during my years in office. I spoke no French at all, and again I was being maneuvered into a position of indicting Air France for the crash, but somehow the press conference came off well. Then everybody moved to the scene of the accident.

The morning after the crash, we were being shown where the wheels had locked and skid marks had dug into the concrete for some eleven hundred feet. The fuselage looked like the burned-out skeleton of a whale, the ribbed tail section hovering over it like a vulture. And all over the area, scattered for hundreds of yards, there were the personal belongings of my friends. I recognized some of the pastel tulle dresses that Nancy Frederick, my first date, always wore and looked so beautiful in. I saw bottles of rare champagne, bought on the trip, which had miraculously survived when the baggage compartment was thrown clear. I picked up a West Point Rotary Club flag, which belonged to my friend Morgan Canty, and got permission to take it back with me and give it to the club. It was a gruesome task, having to walk through the wreckage and discover so many belongings of close friends, but I had to get a clear understanding of how the accident happened so that I could be prepared for the inevitable questions that heartbroken families and friends would ask me when I returned to Atlanta.

Then, after lunch in Paris, we had to go to the morgues to try to identify the bodies. The closest we came to making any identification was by a bracelet on one body and a checkbook in the pocket of another. We gratefully returned to our hotel and made some thirty transatlantic calls that night, to the press and to

> relatives of those who had been killed, trying in some way to console them and explain what had happened and assure them that Air France and the French government were doing everything possible as far as identification and return of the bodies was concerned.
>
> There wasn't much else for us to do in Paris. On Wednesday morning a magnificent memorial service, attended by hundreds of Americans and scores of Parisians, was held in the American Cathedral. Gene Patterson had arrived by this time for a newspaper publishers' convention, and he helped us make the final arrangements with Air France to send a delegation to Atlanta to explain about the crash and the plans for the transferral of the bodies.
>
> When we got back to Atlanta that night and were met by a large crowd of citizens and newsmen, it was only the beginning of long and sad hours of reconstructing everything we knew about the accident. There was no widespread anger toward Air France, only an empty sadness over the loss of so many of our finest leaders in one flaming instant. Atlanta did manage, however, to turn its adversity into success. That crash served as the catalyst for the building of the $13 million Atlanta Memorial Arts Center, a stunning memorial to the 106 Atlantans who went to Europe for knowledge and never came back.[4]

THE AGENDA SETTING PATTERN: 1963–1969

The process with which Allen set his intermediate and daily agendas for the bulk of his administration was similar to our #3 agenda setting process. Intermediate agendas were established with an eye to long-run objectives, considering current opportunities and difficulties, as well. The daily agenda reflected concern for the intermediate agenda and for network maintenance and daily problems.

Allen appears to have been very much in control of his agenda. *He* decided what would go on the long-run, intermediate, and short-run agendas, basing his decisions on a pragmatic assessment of the data.

[4]Allen, pp. 73–80.

Allen was by no means an "urban expert." He was a sharp man but not an intellectual.

The information brought to bear on decisions appears to have been fairly extensive, especially in the range of sources. Allen used his friends in the press to help him keep informed about a wide range of sentiment in Atlanta. He kept in close touch with business and black leaders. Besides his own formal staff, Allen had a "shadow" staff of young, bright people (often officially a part of the Chamber) who did policy studies for him. Although these groups sometimes strongly disagreed, they seldom, if ever, missed anything. That is, the breadth and depth of the information available rarely failed to identify a possible crisis or a clever alternative.

The long-run objectives in Allen's agenda shifted slightly during his administration (and, of course, some were removed by virtue of accomplishment). In particular, the objective dealing with schools broadened considerably and went up in priority, while the transit objective diminished. The process by which these basic changes occurred is an important one. In the case of the mass transit objective, it appears that Allen's inability to make headway forced him to assign to it a lower priority. That is, a constraint in his task accomplishment process altered his agenda. On the other hand, the growth in Allen's relationship with the black community seems to have been influential in slowly modifying the school agenda item until it became a strong equal rights objective. That is, incremental changes in the network building process produced incremental changes in the agenda. We can only speculate regarding Allen's modified relationship with the black community and the apparently related change in his agenda. One simplistic answer is that Allen was acting out of political expediency in a town with a large black population. This answer, however, does not fit the data: Allen risked his career by becoming the first important southerner to testify in Washington for the Public Accommodations bill in 1964. Equally simplistic is the suggestion that he was doing what he always knew to be morally correct; such motivation cannot realistically be attributed to a man who once wrote a serious proposal to the governor of Georgia that the blacks be shipped back to Africa.[5] We might better take into account that the mayor, like most people, was a complex human being operating in a complex environment. Clearly

[5]Source: interview with Ivan Allen, Jr.

his relationship with the black community became a source of personal pride that extended far beyond direct political benefits. The intensity of this relationship is seen in this statement by one of Atlanta's older black leaders: "Ivan's the greatest living man in the United States today."[6]

THE NETWORK BUILDING PATTERN: 1963–1969

The basic process of network building that Allen developed after his first year in office remained stable through the rest of his administration. Compared with his first year, he later spent considerably more time at this activity.

In particular, Allen daily nurtured his relationship with the local press. Allen had grown up with the editors and publishers of the city's two newspapers, the *Atlanta Constitution* and the *Atlanta Journal.* As mayor, he used to see them about once a week, discussing current issues very openly. He received the working press daily. He was very candid with them, too, and appears to have built up strong friendships and personal loyalties. As one reporter put it, "With his mild manner and sense of humor, and his good program, he had us all snowed."

In 1963–1964 it became increasingly clear to Allen that achieving his objectives in the areas of highway construction, urban renewal, and assistance to the poor depended on the large sums of money that were available in Washington. As a result, he once again used charm, purposive appeal, and cooption to create a positive link to the federal government.

> It was pretty simple, actually. The whole South was damning the federal government, expecially because of the race issue, so I just made speeches at appropriate times, saying how wonderful the federal government was. I praised them up and down. They liked that.
>
> In 1964 I hired Dan Sweat [a Community Action Program associate director] to be the director of government liaison. Dan was very knowledgeable

[6]Source: interview notes.

> about Washington, the federal programs, writing proposals, and all that.[7]

After Sweat had worked with Allen for a while, he became much more than a liaison with Washington. During the late 1960s Atlanta's black community was changing—becoming less cohesive, and spawning new, young leadership in some areas. Sweat encouraged Allen to start establishing new ties with the black community. From the U.S. Conference of Mayors, Sweat was assisted in funding a new $25,000 staff position. Johnny Robinson, a young black man from the Office of Economic Opportunity, was hired. His first task was to arrange housing for families displaced by urban renewal. Robinson became a good link with some black neighborhoods and young leaders. During 1966, 1967, and 1968, he developed an organization and a number of programs. At various times he had as many as 46 city service coordinators reporting to him, each acting as a one-man city hall in his area. Through Sweat and Robinson, Allen secured bonds of cooperation with a part of the black community with which he was not familiar.

The network building processes and the resulting network developed by Allen are graphically summarized in Figure 9-1. Clearly Allen used all nine network building processes, in varying degrees, and most of his relationships were based on multiple processes, which apparently strengthens a relationship and makes it more stable (less subject to fluctuation downward).

Two relationships appearing in Figure 9-1 have not been discussed. Allen's relationship with the heads of the county was based primarily on their friendship toward Landers, secondarily on specific negotiations concerning their future cooperation with the city, and finally on an axe Allen held over their heads—they were elected by almost the same voting population that elected the very popular Allen.

Allen's relationship with the state was hurt by the traditional big city–state government rift, but it was destroyed when Lester Maddox was elected governor. Allen's dislike for Maddox grew to a near-obsession that hindered his dealing with the state government.

Allen actively tried to mold his network in only one way: he created

[7]Interview notes.

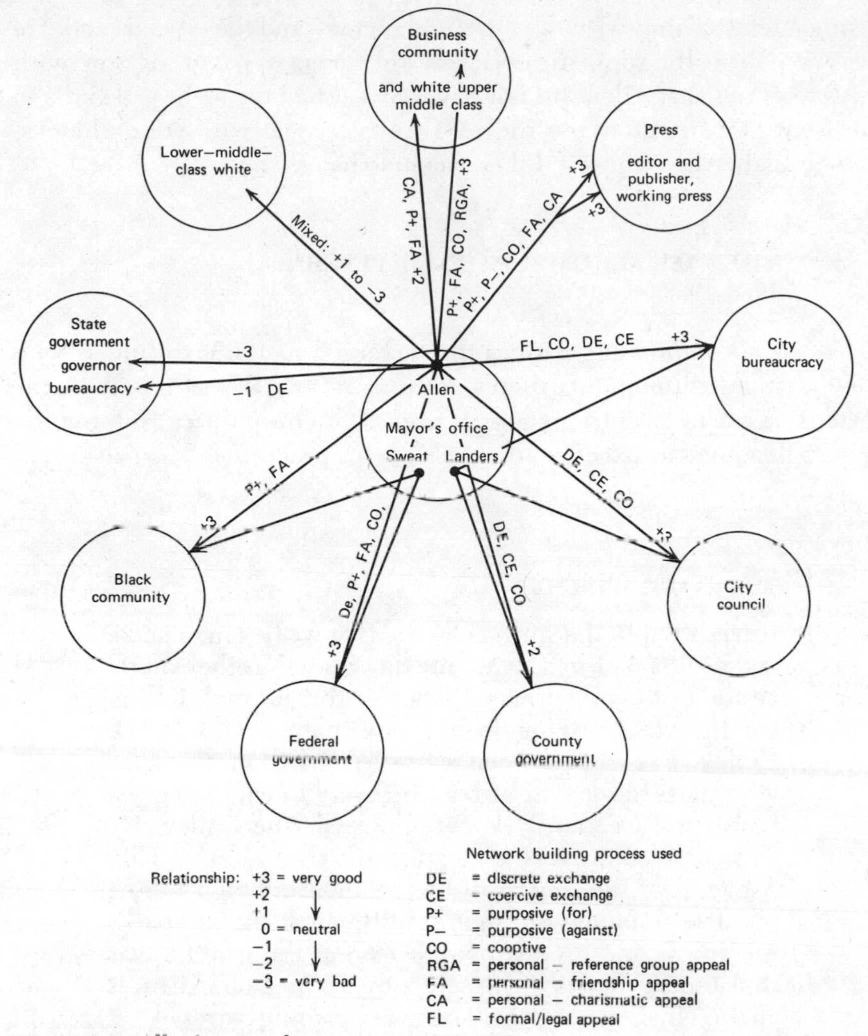

Figure 9-1 Allen's network.

a small but important mayor's office. He did not try to make substantial changes in the city bureaucracy, nor to mold the membership of the city council. He did not try to create a permanent political organization, and he did not try to organize or disorganize population groups. Instead, he simply hired Landers and Sweat, who played important roles in his administration—roles that Allen himself could not assume. Landers was central to Allen's creating, maintaining, and using a relationship with the city bureaucracy and the city council. He was a politically sophisticated and nurturing type of person with historical ties that Allen did not have. Sweat had the technical skills to deal with Washington and the sensitivity to deal with young blacks, which again Allen himself did not seem to have.

THE TASK ACCOMPLISHING PATTERN: 1963–1969

The task accomplishing pattern that emerged in 1963 continued with few changes throughout Allen's administration. It was based on the extensive use of an entrepreneurial process. In his political autobiography, Allen gives an excellent example of this process.

> **THE STADIUM INCIDENT**
>
> It wasn't until the spring of 1963 that we began to make any headway. I had a call one day from the other sports editor in town, Furman Bisher of the *Journal*, telling me he was bringing in a fellow named Charles O. Finley. I've always been a big baseball fan, the kind who starts his day off by reading every line in every box score, and I certainly knew about Charlie Finley. He was the controversial owner of the Kansas City Athletics of the American League, with not too solid a reputation among the staid traditionalists in baseball's hierarchy, and after a poor season at the gate he was threatening to move his club on to greener pastures again. Bisher said Finley was coming to look at possible stadium sites and that he might want to build one and move the Athletics to Atlanta. We had three basic sites in mind at this time, recommended after a survey financed by some of the philanthropic interests in the city, and Bisher said he would take Finley around and show him the sites.
>
> A day or two later, Bisher called again and said Finley wasn't interested in anything he had seen and was ready to go back home. "Can you think of anything else to show him?" he said. I happened to be facing a map

on my wall that outlined the urban-renewal areas in Atlanta, and my eyes fell on a large acreage adjoining the expressway interchange: what we referred to as the Washington–Rawson area, which was being cleared of its decaying slum houses and had no immediate plans for use. "I've got the greatest location in the world," I told Bisher (in pure desperation, since I wasn't sure what we could do with the area and knew little about how much land would be required for a stadium), and George Royal [aide] and I went to get Bisher and Finley so we could show them the area.

I had ridden over Washington–Rawson many times. At one time it had been one of Atlanta's nice neighborhoods with plenty of magnolias and beautiful old homes surrounded by stone walls, but it had deteriorated into one of our worst slums and now was being cleared under the urban renewal program. We rode to the top of the hill overlooking the expressways, got out of the car, and walked among some old magnolias and weeds. I let Finley take his time looking around, trying to picture in his mind how a stadium might fit in there, and finally said to him, "Mr. Finley, this is the finest site in America for a municipal stadium."

"What are those buildings down there?" he said.

"That's Five Points. Downtown Atlanta."

"What's all that construction over there?"

"Where four interstate highways come together."

"How big is the interchange?"

"Thirty-two lanes," I said. "Biggest interchange in the South."

To say the least, Finley was impressed. He said, "Mr. Mayor, I agree with you. This is the greatest site for a stadium that I've ever seen. I tell you what. If you'll build a stadium here, I'll guarantee you I'll bring the Athletics here just as soon as it's finished."

We thought we had reached an agreement with Finley, from the way he was talking. I took him by to talk with Mills Lane that afternoon, and when he left town the next day he again said he would bring the Athletics to Atlanta if we put up a stadium on the Washington–

Rawson site. As soon as he had left,I went by and got Mills Lane and drove him over to show him the area just as I had done with Finley. It didn't take Lane thirty seconds to say, "This is it."

"I don't know how we overlooked it all this time," I said.

"What do you want to do?"

"Build a stadium right here."

"How bad do you want this stadium, Ivan?"

"Bad."

"You've got it," he said. "Tell you what. If you'll recreate the old Stadium Authority and appoint the people I recommend, and make Arthur Montgomery chairman and me treasurer, I'll pledge the full credit of C&S Bank to build it. And if that's not enough to get it done, you and I can't get it done."[8]

THE PRO FOOTBALL INCIDENT

It was time for me to start looking around for help again, but I had just about exhausted my resources. I couldn't ask Mills Lane to extend himself any further, after his involvement in the stadium. I had run Arthur Montgomery's legs off, naming him chairman of the Stadium Authority. Robert Woodruff had let me know some time earlier that he simply couldn't take on major-league sports at his age; and after the support he had given the city in projects like the cultural center, I really didn't know where to turn until I suddenly thought of Leonard Reinsch at Cox Broadcasting, the group that ran WSB radio and television. Leonard, I knew, was one of the best salesmen in the country. He also had, at that very moment, strong business reasons for wanting to see Atlanta secure a pro fotball franchise. The NBC television network had been beaten to the punch by CBS in the bidding for pro football television rights: CBS won the contract with the NFL, and NBC had to settle for the weaker AFL. It would behoove NBC to put an AFL team into the

[8]Allen (1971), pp. 155–157.

South, sewing up this vast virgin territory and to some degree offsetting their loss of the NFL television contract. Since WSB was an NBC affiliate, Leonard Reinsch was the logical man for helping me to land an AFL team for Atlanta.

Reinsch and I must have been thinking on the same wavelength, because the day after I started working on this idea I had a visit from Ray Moore and Don Elliott Heald of WSB. They were proposing that Atlanta go after an AFL franchise. "Look," I said, "why don't *you* do it? You've got more leverage than the city of Atlanta does on this thing." They lit up and shot out of my office and thirty minutes later Leonard Reinsch was calling me. "I'm going to go to work on it," he told me, and when he tells you that he means it. He would call me from Dallas on his way to Denver, and then he would call from Denver that night as he was leaving for Washington. Then he'd see Foss [Joe Foss, then the commissioner of the American Football League] in New York and come by to give me a report on his way to Oakland. He almost bought the Denver Broncos, almost got the San Diego Chargers, nearly came up with a deal in Philadelphia. But it couldn't be done. The only thing we could do, he finally told me, was get an expansion team. Atlanta could get the franchise if somebody could get to New York Jets owner Sonny Werblin and talk him into supporting Atlanta instead of Philadelphia when it came to a vote. That brought me full circle, back to Robert Woodruff. There were few men Sonny Werblin admired more than Robert Woodruff of Coca-Cola, and if anybody could sway him it would be Woodruff. I went to see him immediately; he said he would call Werblin, and within forty-eight hours the American Football League was meeting and awarding an expansion team to Atlanta.

Leonard Reinsch came plowing back into Atlanta and called me at 11:30 that night. "Ivan, I've got the contract and I'm coming over to your house," he said, like a kid on Christmas. He showed up at midnight with a signed contract from the AFL, turning over a

> franchise to Atlanta for $7.5 million. That was too much for an AFL franchise, but Reinsch was willing to pay it. "Have you signed up the Stadium Authority?" I asked him. "They've got to come to me," he said. "I've got the franchise and Atlanta's got to have it." What he didn't know was that Pete Rozelle of the NFL had gotten wind of the deal with the AFL, and he was headed for Atlanta himself.
>
> Before we could even get with the Stadium Authority the next morning, Rozelle was already in town looking for somebody to take an NFL expansion team. For several months we had been flying around the country with hat in hand, begging for a pro football team, and now all of a sudden we were being courted by both of the major pro leagues. The city was in a stew. We had about resigned ourselves to waiting two or three years for pro football, but now we could take our pick of which league we wanted. There was really no doubt which one we would take, because at that point the AFL was still the weak sister of the two. If we had taken the AFL franchise we would have been run out of town. So I got a call from a wealthy young insurance man named Rankin Smith who had been recommended to Rozelle by Carl Sanders [Pete Rozelle, Commissioner of the National Football League, Carl Sanders, Governor of Georgia], and when he said, "Do you have any objections to my bringing NFL football here?" I gave him my blessings. Poor Leonard Reinsch had done all of the legwork and had been the catalyst, but had lost out to a man who didn't have to lift a finger to get the franchise.[9]

Allen used the same type of process in pursuing almost all the items on his agenda. To accomplish his urban renewal goals for which he needed money and expertise, Allen worked especially with local businessmen, Washington, and the black community. Using Sweat's expertise and his own good relations with Washington, Allen secured important financial resources. He called on business friends to help

[9]Allen (1971), pp. 155–157.

with real estate transactions, on the black community to cooperate with the short-run inconveniences, and on the city's bureaucracy and the city council to help with the legal and operational details. Juggling four or five balls at a time, he pushed the program in the direction of his desired goal.

To accomplish his economic development objectives, Allen worked closely with the Chamber in pursuing the Forward Atlanta program he had started in 1960 as Chamber president.

> More than a million and a half dollars were donated by private businesses to get it going. The Chamber staff was reorganized and expanded. Four primary objectives were set: national advertising, public relations, creation of a reasearch and marketing staff to provide data on Atlanta, and a beefed-up development effort. What we were doing was selling our city like a product. For the first four years the staff included a full-time traveling representative who spent half of his time on the road, calling on industrial and business prospects in major American cities, and the other half back home servicing those he had talked into moving their firm or a branch of it to Atlanta. We began sponsoring *Atlanta* magazine, a slick monthly publication that presented the story of Atlanta to business executives all over the country and quickly began winning awards as one of America's finest city magazines. Every month there were appealing ads in journals like *Business Week* and *The New York Times* and *Newsweek*, telling about Atlanta. At the end of the first three-year phase of Forward Atlanta, there was a unanimous vote from the two dozen or so top sponsors that they wanted to continue. When it came time to develop Phase III, the last three years of the sixties, Forward Atlanta's goals showed that we had raised our sights considerably beyond merely trying to attract new industry. Now we were shooting for national headquarters operations and planning to take on the problems the earlier Forward Atlanta programs had brought: traffic congestion, housing, mass public transportation, and pollution. Forward Atlanta was the leading program of its type in

> America, and during the sixties some 150 cities sent delegations to Atlanta to talk with the Chamber of Commerce officials about how they could get the same thing going.[10]

Allen used the bureaucratic type of process less than the entreprenurial one, primarily because Landers headed the city bureaucracy on a day-to-day basis. Allen used this process when dealing with his own staff, and when dealing with the city bureaucracy directly, but seldom under other circumstances.

Those close to the mayor agreed almost unanimously that he was an excellent executive and administrator;

> He was good at delegating. He was an efficient organizer of his work. He was good at soliciting information and making judgments. Once he understood the city government, he was good at pushing the proper buttons at the right times.[11]

After the 1962 period, Allen tended to use an individualistic process to deal with two particularly sensitive types of tasks—short-run racial problems, and major crises and tragedies such as the crash at Orly. His style in these matters was always the same.

> I was learning that the best way for me to handle a racial problem was by barging into it myself, since somebody would always wind up throwing it right back into my lap anyway, and there seemed to be no satisfactory intermediaries.[12]

[10]Allen (1971), pp. 149–150.
[11]Source: interview notes.
[12]Allen (1971), p. 185.

In his 8 years in office, Allen "refereed" hundreds of meetings between white and black leaders who were trying to resolve problems.

In crisis situations, Allen's style was to instantly move toward the center of the incident, as he had done following the airline disaster. When Atlanta had a disturbance in the Summerhill area in 1968, Allen rushed to the scene and walked into the center of a small riot. In still another incident, on the night of Thursday, April 4, 1968, he recalled

> . . . Louise and I were in our bedroom at home watching television and reading the newspaper when a bulletin flashed on the screen: *MARTIN LUTHER KING, JR., SHOT IN MEMPHIS.* The second I saw it I jumped to my feet and said "Good God, won't they ever learn? First Kennedy, now King!" It is hard to describe the feeling I had. I suppose millions of others all over the world had the same feeling of shock and anger at that same second. Dr. King had been in Memphis during a sanitation workers' strike and was just getting ready to go out to dinner with some of the other SCLC workers when a shot rang out and dropped him on the balcony of the Lorraine Motel. Instinctively, I called Ann Mosses and got the Kings' home telephone number from her and dialed it. Mrs. King answered. I had moved so fast I didn't know whether she had even been told of the shooting yet.
>
> "Have you heard about Dr. King?" I said.
>
> She seemed composed. "I just talked to Memphis."
>
> "What do you want to do?"
>
> "I'm going up there right now."
>
> "Is there anything I can do for you?"
>
> "There's a plane leaving in about fifty minutes, and I would appreciate your help in getting me on it." I told her I would send a police car after her, and that I would be there myself as soon as I could, and we hung up. At this point all of my responses were as a friend of the King family rather than as mayor of Atlanta. From my brief conversation with Mrs. King, I gathered that her husband was not in serious condition because she had just talked to someone in Memphis and seemed steady.

> Even so, she needed friends with her and her children. I arranged to have a police car rushed to the King home and quickly put on a shirt and tie.[13]

THE 8 YEARS IN PERSPECTIVE

Six months after Allen first became mayor, his system resembled that depicted in Figure 9-2. The mayor–agenda, mayor–city, agenda–city, and mayor–network relationships were close to being aligned. His agenda–network and network–city relationships, however, were considerably out of alignment. Allen's very ambitious agenda called for a stronger network than he was maintaining, and his complex and varied domain needed a network with a differentiated implementation capacity—not just a highly structured, uniform city bureaucracy.

These nonalignments caused a number of disturbances during Allen's first year in office, which he describes as one in which nothing significant was accomplished. The mayor's popularity dropped, and he felt terrible.

Allen, or some adaptive part of him, reacted to the unfavorable first-year situation by altering his network building and task accomplishing processes. He spent more time at network building and used more of the network building processes. He augmented his mayor's office with some critical resources. He changed from a predominently bureaucratic task accomplishment process to a predominantly entrepreneurial one. We have called the pattern of such a revised set of processes the "Program Entrepreneur."

As a result of these changes, Allen created a system with no major nonalignments and with enough power in his network to survive the next election. This stability continued for nearly 6 years.

The overall effects of Allen's coaligned system are somewhat difficult to determine, although on the surface they seem to be very positive. By 1969 Allen had effectively accomplished all his objectives except one (mass transit). In the 1966 reelection campaign he polled more than 70% of the vote. The eight experts queried in this study unanimously agreed that Atlanta, of all the cities they rated, was the finest example of a healthy city getting healthier. Nevertheless, Allen is

[13]Allen (1971), p. 196.

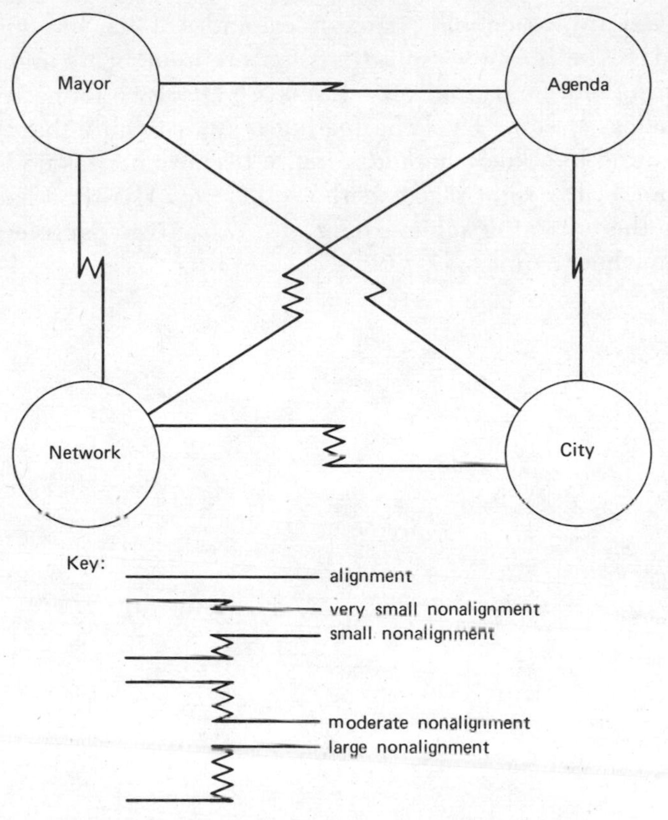

Figure 9-2 Allen's system 6 months after his first election.

not without his critics, who point out that he developed no successors, that he did not encourage the political development of the black community, and that he made life miserable for some lower-middle-class whites.

RETIREMENT

Ivan Allen, Jr., retired from politics in 1969. For a man who had been the center of activity for 8 years, this was undoubtedly a painful move. Readjustment to a "normal" life after being a successful mayor of a large city is not easy.

Atlanta changed during Allen's administration; in its sociopolitical structure and in its physical aspect. The New Frontier had given way to the Nixon doctrine and Nixonomics, and Atlanta, like most cities, reflected this shift. The reasons for Allen's retirement are numerous: he was getting old, he had promised to retire after two terms, and so on. Nevertheless at some level the feeling is unavoidable that Allen and those around him knew he *had* to retire because he was no longer the right man, at the right place, at the right time. His time had passed. Perhaps the crowning achievement of a proactive-adaptive person is knowing when to quit.

Being a mayor is like walking on a moving belt while juggling. Right off you've got to walk pretty fast to stay even. After you've been in office a short time people start throwing wads of paper at you. So now you've got to walk, juggle, and duck too. Then the belt starts to move faster, and people start to throw wooden blocks at you. About the time you're running like mad, juggling and ducking stones, someone sets one end of the belt on fire. Now if you can keep the things you are juggling in the air, stay on the belt, put out the fire, and not get seriuosly injured, you've found the secret to the job. You have managed to put it all together into something that works.

FORMER MAYOR ERIK JONSSON OF DALLAS[1]

CHAPTER 10

SUCCESSFUL AND UNSUCCESSFUL COALIGNMENT BEHAVIOR

The foregoing metaphorical description of a mayor's behavior might well be applied to the administration of Ivan Allen, Jr. In our terminology, such a mayor actively tries to maintain a coalignment (juggling) while dealing with short-run constraints (stones, fire, the strain of juggling, etc.). From now on, we refer to behavior that seems to represent an attempt to move a system toward a state of coalignment as "coalignment behavior." In this model, coalignment behavior consists of:

- using some pattern of behavior in the three mayoral processes
- within a system of short-run constraints
- to produce impacts on the four contextual variables
- which will either move the system toward or maintain it near

[1]Source: interview notes

- a state in which all six relationships among the contextual variables are aligned.

Allen, for one, very clearly exhibited coalignment behavior.

THE MAYOR'S NEEDS, DRIVES, VALUES, AND ASPIRATIONS

A mayor's reasons for displaying coalignment behavior can be understood in terms of the model we have developed. As long as a person has predominant needs, drives, aspirations, or values related to "making something work" (perhaps a competence motive, an achievement-power motive, success-oriented or pragmatic values), one would expect him to exhibit coalignment behavior as mayor. A coaligned system would produce the type of success that would satisfy such a person.

If, on the other hand, the overriding need or aspiration of a mayor is a single future goal state (e.g., desegregation or racial equality), one would not expect him to exhibit coalignment behavior. On the contrary, he might totally ignore coalignment in pursuit of his value or goal, behaving like a "martyr." That is, he would hold his agenda setting process and his agenda *fixed* (on his goal) even if such a course created very large and numerous nonalignments that "destroyed" him.

If a mayor has very strong needs for personal wealth and fairly flexible values, he might ignore coalignment in favor of acquiring that wealth, legally and illegally. We generally call such a person a thief.

If a person has no strong "making it work" or "wealth" or "goal state" needs and values as mayor, he may very well "drop out" if he encounters a difficult situation. That is, if he is faced with a situation that is not satisfying him, and if behaving like a martyr or a coaligner would not satisfy him either, he may react by withdrawing. Confronting a large uncomfortable crisis, such a mayor might simply head for the Bahamas.

There are undoubtedly other types of behavior that might be expected, given different needs, drives, values, and aspirations. It is not necessary to compile an exhaustive list.

In Chapter 8 we noted that the 20 mayors in this study varied considerably in the coalignment they did or did not achieve while in office. Of course these discrepancies may be due to the different needs, drives, values, and aspirations among the mayors. For example, perhaps the mayors with strong "making it work" motives or values exhibited coalignment behavior that helped them achieve a state closer to coalignment than the mayors with other needs, drives, values, and aspirations. Such an explanation is implicit when we judge a person's capacity for a mayoral position by questioning his motives and goals.

The data from this study suggest strongly that the foregoing superficial explanation is inadequate. One or two mayors exhibited considerable withdrawal behavior at the very end of their tenure. A few mayors behaved like martyrs, but only briefly. One or two mayors have been charged with illegal behavior, convicted, and jailed. Nevertheless, *over all, all our mayors exhibited coalignment behavior almost all the time.* It would appear that each of the 20 mayors had fairly strong "making it work" values or motives relative to the other types we identified (e.g., having needs for personal wealth or having one strong goal).

We are left now with a very intriguing question. If most of the mayors in the study were trying to move their systems toward coalignment most of the time, why were some much more successful than others? Why were Ivan Allen's efforts to achieve a coalignment quite successful and Ralph Locher's efforts quite unsuccessful? This very important question is of the type that is usually ignored (as in the Public Entrepreneur and Policy Expert models outlined in Chapter 2), and we devote the rest of this chapter to exploring it.

UNSUCCESSFUL COALIGNMENT BEHAVIOR

The case of Chester Kowal in Buffalo, New York, is one of our clearest cases of unsuccessful coalignment. Kowal, a Polish Republican, worked for the city for much of his life, holding a number of posts, including that of city comptroller. Most people described him as a friendly man with some abilities. Although his personality was not very broad and flexible, it did to a degree bridge the gap between the ethnic groups in the city and the Anglo-Saxon groups. Kowal campaigned for mayor in 1960 with an agenda that included midrange items relating to police reform and urban renewal. In a three-way race he won the election with 38% of the vote. The city council was dominated by the Democratic party, as was the city bureaucracy, and when Kowal took office, the alignments in his "system" could be represented as in Figure 10-1. One relationship was significantly out of alignment—that between agenda and network. Kowal's network was

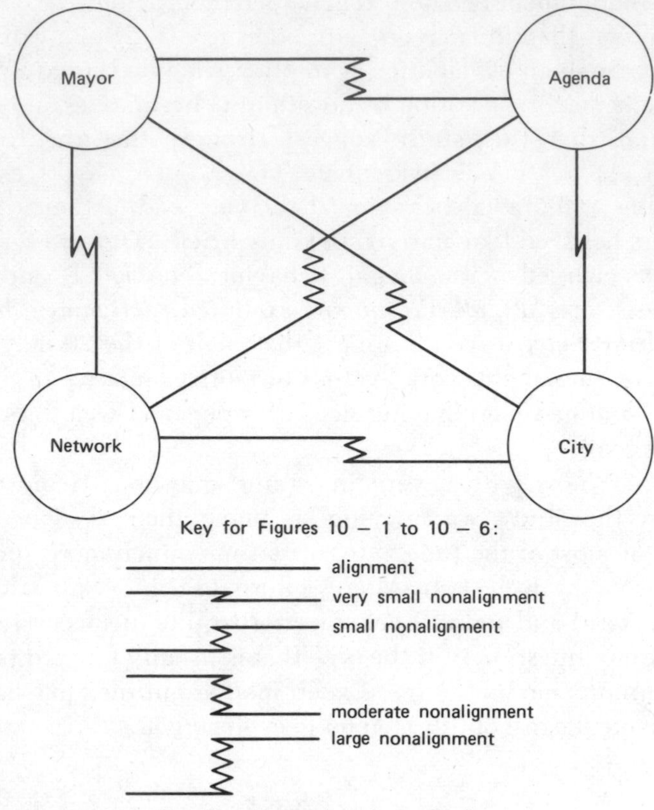

Figure 10-1 Kowal's system when he took office.

very weak, yet his agenda included the rather ambitious items of police reform and urban renewal. The mayor–agenda, mayor–network, and mayor–city relationships were somewhat out of alignment also. Kowal's technician orientation was somewhat out of line with heterogeneous, changing Buffalo (mayor–city relationship). Despite his ethnic background, he was not extremely effective at speaking the lower-middle-class language in the city (mayor–network). The agenda called for strong power brokerage skills, which Kowal apparently lacked, as well (mayor–agenda).

In his first year in office, Kowal's efforts to pursue his agenda were frustrated again and again. His actions were blocked and delayed, and he reacted by trying to build positive, cooperative relationships in his network. Fully recognizing that he was in an unfavorable position, he apparently reasoned that he should be careful not to antagonize even more people; thus he proceeded cautiously in all matters. A combination of factors—the mayor's reluctance to take risks, his limited abilities, and a strong Democratic opposition—determined that Kowal was quite unsuccessful in his network-building efforts.

Aware that one large nonalignment still existed after a year or so, Kowal slowly abandoned the more ambitious projects in his agenda and switched from a #2 to a #1 agenda setting process. As a result, his agenda and network came more and more into line with each other. At the same time, however, the alignment between his agenda and the city became worse and worse (see Figure 10-2).

During the middle of his term, Kowal apparently devoted a good deal of his energy to a fight within his own party, perhaps hoping to win the fight and use his new position of power to arrange for a nonmunicipal nomination when his mayor's term ran out. By then it was no doubt clear to him that continuing as mayor could only bring him problems. He lost the intraparty battle, however, leaving his already weak network still weaker.

By Kowal's third year in office, the network members who were cooperating with him because of his police reform and redevelopment

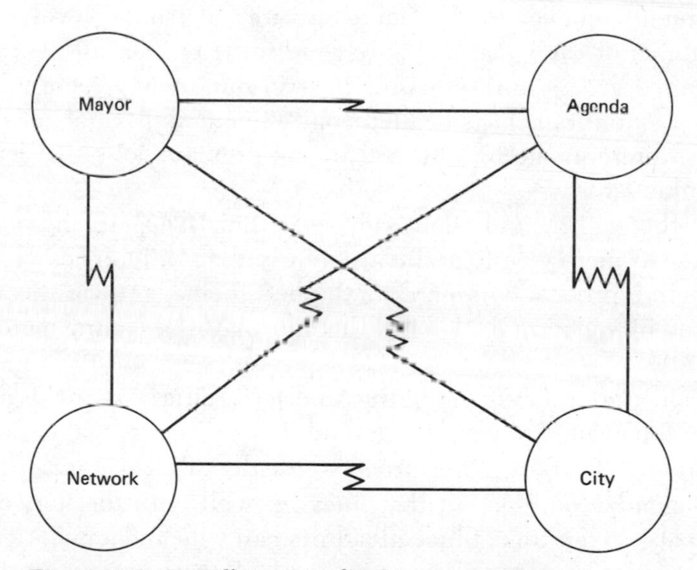

Figure 10-2 Kowal's system after 2½ years in office.

goals fully realized not only that his efforts were ineffective but that he had abandoned these objectives. As a result, relationships with most of the press, some of the business community, and some of the white middle class began to deteriorate badly.

By his fourth year in office, Kowal was under indictment, and he had no chance for reelection. He retired instead of running again and died shortly afterward.

COALIGNMENT PROBLEMS

An intriguing question at this point is why was Kowel plagued by large nonalignments in his system? More generally, why are some mayors much more successful coaligners than others? Are there some common characteristics among the situations in which the mayors we studied were unsuccessful at coalignment?

It is tempting to simplify the issue by saying that some people are better coaligners than others. That is, producing coalignment might be a personal, human skill. Mayors who are well equipped with this "skill" would be expected to achieve a better coalignment than their less gifted colleagues. To a limited degree, the data appear to support such an assertion: the mayors who were more successful at coalignment tended to be more aware, at some level, of the implications of the situations they were in. However, all people who have gained access to responsible jobs in our society seem to have a moderate amount of this so-called coalignment skill. Such a "skill" is usually a prerequisite for survival in the previous jobs that lead to a high-ranking post.

Two themes in our data address the issue of unsuccessful coalignment more clearly and consistently than differences in "skill." The election process dominates in the first theme, and various natural processes of social and physical change play the central part in the second.

The election process in most American cities is "designed" to produce fairly good alignments among the four contextual variables in our model. That is, the process ideally finds a mayor or a mayor–agenda combination that lines up well with the network and the city at a given time. Since all adults can vote and a majority rules, candidates are encouraged who can speak all the languages in the city (mayor–network). The voter today is socialized by our culture into believing that he should select a candidate who is qualified and understands the city (mayor–city); who has a sensible program, given the current state of the city (agenda–city); and who has the capabilities to fulfill his promises (mayor–agenda), given the resources available and other constraints (network–agenda, network–city). If the winning candidate fails to deliver, he can be replaced in 2 to 4 years.

Unfortunately, the election process deviates from the form just described for thousands of reasons. Not all people vote. Those who vote do so based on limited information that has been analyzed by them for a limited time. It costs money to send information, and money is not evenly distributed in the community. The socialization process we spoke of is not the same for everyone in a typical city.

Thus a mayor can face one or more very large nonalignments the moment he takes office. Such was the case for Chester Kowal. We cannot assert that the nonalignments Kowal faced were so pervasive that no amount of hard work and skill could have overcome them, but evidence suggests this gloomy conclusion. At best, a mayor in Kowal's position can make changes to reduce some nonalignments; but in the process he will probably create others (as indeed Kowal did).

The second theme relates to natural changes in the city and its population. Of the four contextual variables in our model, the mayor is the most stable, between elections at least. An adult's personality, his orientation to the world, and his values and skills change very slowly if at all. A mayor's network, on the other hand, *can* change over time. The population can shift, people's expectations can change, important individuals can come or go, organizations can grow or die, and the makeup of state and national governmental organizations can shift drastically. The city itself, perhaps to a lesser degree, can also change over fairly short periods. It can grow older in some areas, while developing new ones. It can explode into a crisis involving transportation, health, or taxes. Insofar as the mayor does not change while his city and network do, large mayor-network and mayor-city nonalignment can be created.

We have no evidence, however, that a city or network can change enough in 4 years to take the mayor's system from a state of coalignment to a state of serious nonalignment. Instead, changes in networks or cities that lead to nonalignment tend merely to amplify a situation already characterized by alignment problems, probably because of an election. The case of W. Ralston Westlake in Columbus, Ohio, seems to typify this issue.

Westlake was elected mayor by a very small margin, in an election which had a poor voter turnout. Three days before the election the city's major newspaper ran a front-page story about an alleged scandal in Westlake's opponent's police department.

In the 4 years before Westlake's election, and during his administration, the sociopolitical structure of Columbus was undergoing important changes. During the 1930s and 1940s one dominant family had owned the city's major newspaper, a bank, and a factory, among other things. Together and separately, this family and a strong local Republican organization controlled much of what happened in Columbus. In 1952 the elder member of the dominant family died. New to the city, a few large national corporations (like GM) had brought in a group of professional managers who had no ties to the area's past. Annexation after World War II had increased the city's population, and its growth attracted a number of aggressive new entrepreneurs. Its percentages of blue collar families and nonwhites increased considerably. As a result, when Westlake was elected, the city was undergoing a shift in the mayor's network, especially in the "business community." The one-family leadership was diminishing, and leadership initiatives were arising from other parts of the community. Although not yet organized when Westlake was elected, some of the new leaders were coalescing in such organizations as the Metropolitan Committee, the Redevelopment Committee, the Downtown Area Committee, and the Chamber of Commerce.

Westlake was elected with a network that had two predominant, strongly positive relationships—one with the Republican party and one with the town's prominent old family—and apparently he spoke their language fluently. He did not, however, relate well to the emerging leadership in Columbus (mayor-network).

Westlake, who had been a small businessman and a city councilor, understood routine city business fairly well. However, the issues surrounding urban renewal and other large problem areas seem to have been largely outside his vision (mayor-city).

When Westlake began his term as mayor, he faced the system represented in Figure 10-3. There were moderate nonalignments between the mayor and his network, and between the mayor and the city. As Columbus continued to change during Westlake's administration, these nonalignments grew.

During his first 18 months in office, all was rather quiet in

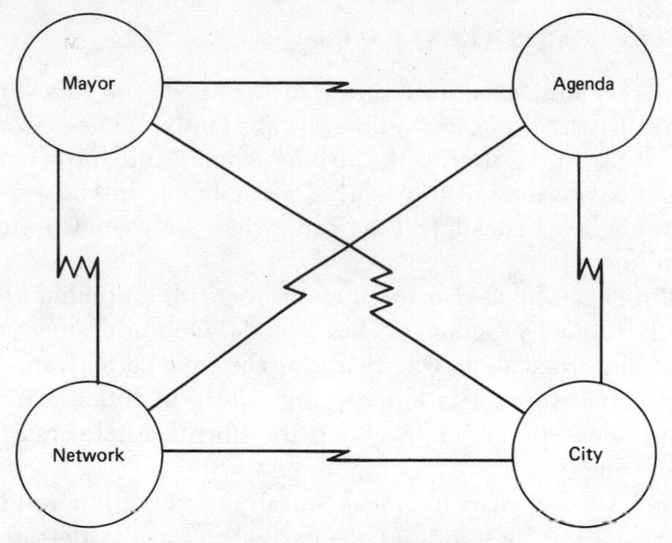

Figure 10-3 Westlake's system in 1961–1962.

Columbus. Westlake seemed to enjoy the mayor's ceremonial activities and performed them well. The city bureaucracy continued its service, although probably with some slippage in efficiency.

However, by the middle of his administration the volume of conflict within the business community increased. The new groups began initiating proposals for renewal and growth which the once-leading family tended to block, feeling they were bad for the city. Westlake usually relied on the advice he received from the inner circle of the prominent family, and when his actions prevented the state government from building an $80 million office complex in Columbus, the second newspaper in the city and most of the new leaders in the business community cried out in horror.

Like many mayors, Westlake assembled a very homogeneous group of staff members and advisors. Their links were with the Republican organization and the once-leading family. Thus it is entirely possible that Westlake was not aware of the changes occurring around him.

As in the case of Chester Kowal, after 4 years (one term in office) Westlake was not reelected. He was soundly defeated by people who felt that he had wasted resources and opportunities in a way that hurt Columbus.

THE "IN-BETWEEN" CASES

As Figure 8-7 indicates, only a few of the mayors in this study were quite unsuccessful at coalignment, and only a few were quite successful. Arthur Naftalin, the urban scholar and former mayor of Minneapolis, was not unsuccessful at coalignment, but he was not very successful either. Instead, he falls somewhere between Chester Kowal and Ivan Allen, Jr.

Naftalin began his 8-year reign as mayor with a number of projects and partly formed programs in his agenda. One midrange project he was very concerned about was changing the city charter from a weak to a strong mayor form. His longer-range ideas included a number of ambitious social programs in which the liberal, intellectual Naftalin believed strongly.

During his first 2 years in office, Naftalin tried hard to build support for his strong mayor proposal. Nevertheless, it was defeated at the polls. Those we interviewed in Minneapolis unanimously agreed that the charter change was defeated primarily because of Naftalin's inability to get specific tasks done. Naftalin's ability to understand what was happening in his city was very good; he was better in this respect than perhaps any other mayor in the study. His skills at execution, on the other hand, appear to have been very limited.

After the charter defeat Naftalin changed from a #3 to a #2 agenda setting process and gradually abandoned some of his more ambitious long-term agenda items. He learned to take advantage of short-run opportunities for smaller but real gains. He did not change his network building (based on purposive and personal appeal) or task accomplishing (highly individualistic) processes, however. Naftalin continued with this Personality/Individualistic pattern until his retirement.

Naftalin began his term as mayor with a coalignment situation like that depicted in Figure 10-4. There was one moderate nonalignment—between the mayor and his agenda. Naftalin's initial agenda was ambitious and required execution skills that apparently were far beyond those the mayor possessed. The first sign of this nonalignment was the charter defeat. Naftalin's reaction to the charter defeat —switching from a #3 to a #2 agenda setting process—eventually brought his agenda more in line with his own skills. His system then contained no major nonalignments (see Figure 10-5), but there were a number of small nonalignments.

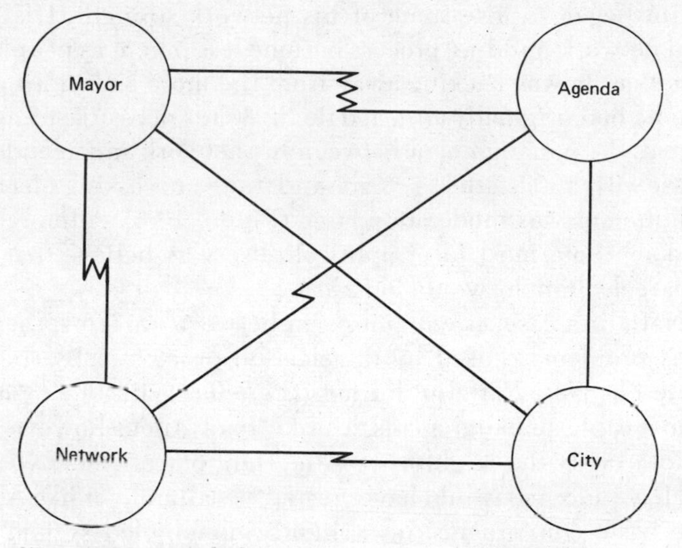

Figure 10-4 Naftalin's alignment at beginning of term.

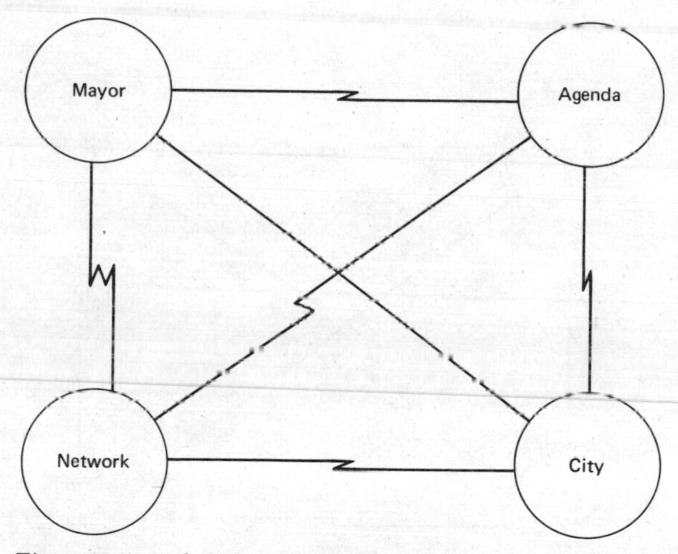

Figure 10-5 Naftalin's alignment after 2 years.

One important consequence of changing his agenda was that Naftalin began to lose some of his network strength. His purposive appeal network building process became less potent as people began to realize that he was backing away from the more ambitious goals with which he had originally attracted them. As his network strength slowly declined, the nonalignment between his network and agenda began to increase. By 1969, after 8 years and four successful elections, this nonalignment was moderately large (Figure 10-6). Although Naftalin retired in 1969, most local political observers believe that if he had sought reelection, he would have lost.

In Naftalin's case, as with most "in-between" mayors, there were no serious problems caused by the election process or by social-demographic changes. Naftalin did not take office with one or more large unmanageable nonalignments. Unlike Ivan Allen, however, Naftalin was not exactly the "right man at the right place. . . ." No pattern he could have adopted would have created a coalignment like Allen's.

The basic consequence of a slightly nonaligned system is a slow deterioration in the system. Maintaining that state of no large nonalignments becomes progressively more difficult over time. The mayor's support begins to very slowly decay. Unlike the mayor who is

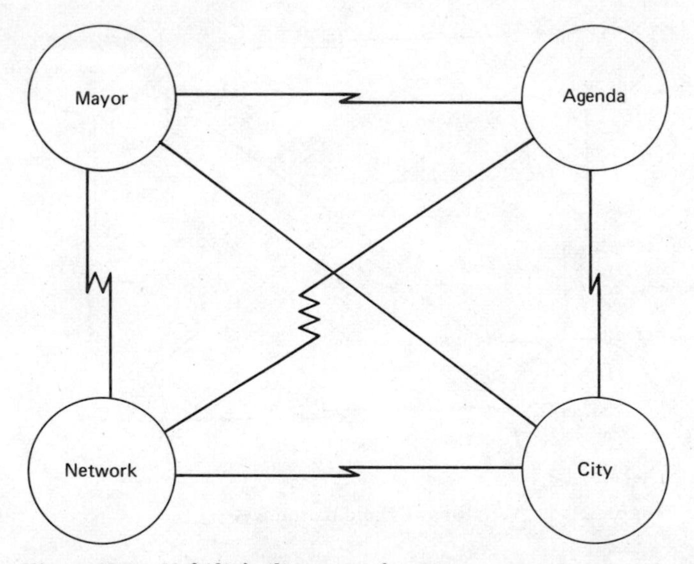

Figure 10-6 Naftalin's alignment after 8 years.

very unsuccessful at coalignment, the in-between mayor does not find himself confronting a major emergency after a few years. Unlike the mayor who is very successful at coalignment, the in-between mayor has no system that "rejuvenates" itself. Instead, it slowly seems to run down over time.

SUMMARY

"Coalignment behavior" is any behavioral pattern in which the actor tries to move a system toward, or keep it near, a state of coalignment. Although only a few of the mayors in this study were relatively successful at coalignment, most exhibited coalignment behavior most of the time. The unsuccessful coaligners tended to face one or more large and simply unmanageable nonalignments.

Such nonalignments were created by rapid urban changes and by election processes that did not work as they were designed. The democratic election process in most cities is intended to create, initially, a state of coalignment in a mayor's system. In some cases, however, it operates very poorly, creating for the new mayor one or more large nonalignments. The city itself, and the mayor's network, can change fairly rapidly while a mayor is in office. Since a mayor's characteristics tend to remain stable, or to change very slowly, alignments between mayor and city and mayor and network can become nonalignments under conditions of rapid change. If these relationships are already somewhat nonaligned, change can create very large and unmanageable nonalignments.

CHAPTER 11

PATTERN EMERGENCE

With the aid of the model we have been developing and exploring, we can now provide some answers to the question of pattern emergence. Why is it, for example, that a Caretaker pattern developed in Cleveland in the early 1960s and an Executive pattern in Louisville? Why did a Program Entrepreneur pattern develop in Atlanta and a Ceremonial pattern in Cincinnati? Why have we found those five mayoral types? Why not five others? As a matter of fact, why did we find five types instead of one or two dozen?

THE MODEL'S DESCRIPTION

According to our model, the mayoral behavior pattern that emerges in a particular situation is a function of:

1. The exact nature of the four contextual variables—the mayor, the city, the network, and the agenda.
2. The dynamic relationships among the three processes we have identified and the four contextual variables. In a sense, these relationships limit the number of feasible patterns in the short run.
3. The nature of the relationships among the four contextual variables: in a sense, these relationships dictate what behavior patterns are stable in the long run.

4. The mayor's proactive element, which in most cases tries to move his system toward coalignment instead of away from it.

It is now easy to see why we had difficulty with the question of pattern emergence earlier. Pattern emergence is far from a simple cause-and-effect process. Nor is it a deterministic process in which one set of initial states always leads to one set of final states. Things are not that simple.

In the case of Ivan Allen, for example, the Program Entrepreneur pattern developed slowly over a period of at least 2 years (one before and one after the election). Allen's fairly good alignment with his city and his network facilitated the information flow and interaction that led to the creation of the Chamber Goals—the basis of his agenda. Consciously or intuitively, the mayor undoubtedly realized that his initial agenda, he himself, his network, and Atlanta, combined to eliminate some patterns as feasible alternatives. The Ceremonial mayor would obviously make no progress on Allen's agenda. The Caretaker mayor would have to depend heavily on a discrete exchange network building process, which was unacceptable to Allen's rather strict sense of right and wrong. Because Allen was more familiar with an Executive pattern (as president of the family business), he adopted something resembling it early in his administration. When he recognized that it was not working, however, noting the presence of two fairly large nonalignments (agenda–network and network–city), he changed to another feasible pattern. The Program Entrepreneur pattern created something close to a coalignment, and it remained stable.

In a similar way our model can help "explain" (after the fact) why a particular pattern emerged in each of the 20 cases we studied. Its capacity to predict which pattern will emerge before the fact, given initial condition data, is still untested but is probably much smaller. Such is the complex and nondeterministic nature of the emergence process. Nevertheless, the model yields a number of rules of thumb that can be useful for predictive purposes. For example, it says that if a pattern that creates a coalignment is feasible, it probably will eventually emerge.

Although the contextual variables do not influence pattern emergence in a directly causal fashion, examining the types of cities and agendas and mayors that are associated with different patterns in this study may disclose some more rules of thumb for predictive purposes. We explore this avenue next.

PATTERN AND CONTEXTUAL VARIABLE ASSOCIATIONS

Before looking for associations, we need to clarify an important aspect of the four contextual variables. Our four variables deal with different types of abstractions at different levels of abstraction; more important, they are neither mutually dependent nor independent. The city and network change slowly over time. The mayor and agenda can change abruptly after an election. Because of elections, the city and network variables are, in a sense, more "independent" than the mayor and agenda variables. For example, although the following causal sequence is not strictly accurate over time, it does have some validity: the city influences the network members who choose the mayor who constructs an agenda, which guides his behavior, which may have an impact, which modifies the city. Thus, we should expect the agenda and mayor variables to have a more obvious and stronger association with the five behavior patterns than the city and network variables. This is precisely what we have found.

The relationship of the agenda to the five patterns is very clear and straightforward (see Table 11-1). Each pattern is associated with a different type of agenda. There are almost no exceptions to this rule in

Table 11-1 Agendas Associated with the Five Mayoral Patterns

Mayoral Behavior Pattern	Agenda
#1—Ceremonial	Limited in scope. Contains short-run agendas.
#2—Caretaker	Fairly large in scope but limited to short-run agendas.
#3—Personality/Individualist	Moderate in scope with short-run and midrange agendas. Includes some "projects."
#4—Executive	Fairly large in scope with short-run and midrange agendas. Includes some "projects."
#5—Program Entrepreneur	Very large in scope with short-, medium-, and long-range agendas.

our data. The associations in Table 11-1 are certainly not surprising. We have discussed them indirectly at length in Chapters 4 and 7. The Ceremonial and Caretaker mayors have short-run agendas and a #1 agenda setting process. The Personality/Individualist and Executive mayors have short-run and midrange agendas and a #2 agenda setting process. The Program Entrepreneur has short-, medium-, and long-run agendas set with a #3 process. Furthermore, the agenda of the Ceremonial mayor is very limited in scope; the Personality/Individualist has an agenda with a moderate scope; the Caretaker and Executive have fairly broad agendas, and the Program Entrepreneur has one with a very large scope.

The relationship of the mayor to the five patterns is not nearly as straightforward, although there are a number of apparent associations (see Table 11-2). The mayors within each type of pattern have certain qualities in common. The Ceremonial mayors tend to be very gregarious, if limited men; their backgrounds include service on the city council and in small organizations. Caretaker mayors, as a rule, are dedicated "nice guys" with a background of extensive governmental service often in a city bureaucratic position. Personality/Individualist mayors seem to have strong, somewhat unique personalities, along with varied backgrounds, usually not in local government. Most Executive mayors are fairly aggressive individuals with managerial backgrounds. Finally, the Program Entrepreneurs tend to be very proactive and to have numerous observable "talents"; as a rule, they have been conspicuously successful in several areas.

The number of exceptions within each category is moderate. As opposed to the agenda, there is no universally appearing, clear-cut association between the mayor and his pattern. Nevertheless, it is fair to say that each pattern is associated with a general personality. In addition, the personality type associated with a pattern is always the one we would logically expect, given the pattern. A person of somewhat limited capabilities, for example, is associated with an undemanding pattern.

The association between the network and the mayoral patterns is still less clear, although it has some identifiable aspects. The formal, legal relationship between the mayor and his network members, especially the city bureaucracy, seems to be related to different mayoral patterns (see Table 11-3). All four of the Ceremonial mayors officiated in cities with city manager charters, whereas all five of the

Table 11-2 Personal Characteristics of the Mayors Associated with the Five Behavioral Patterns

Mayor	Description (Typical comments from Interviews)	Background
#1—Ceremonial		
Bachrach (Cincinnati)	"Nice guy of limited ability"	City council and small family business (restaurant)
McCann (Fort Worth)	"Big, good-looking personable guy"	Son of mayor; president of small company, ambassador, and city councilor
Curran (San Diego)	"Dedicated, honest, hard-working, earthy man of limited abilities"	Manager of a fraternal lodge and city councilman
Lamb (Rochester)	"Friendly, outgoing, decent man of limited abilities"	Membership official at YMCA and city councilman; father was mayor
#2—Caretaker		
Locher (Cleveland)	"A nice, honest, decent, dedicated public servant"	In "politics" (groomed by very successful politician)
Westlake (Columbus)	"A handsome, placid man who tended not to make enemies"	Councilman and small businessman; son of local official
Kowal (Buffalo)	"A nice guy of limited abilities"	City comptroller and head of local American Legion
Addonizio (Newark)	"A nice guy with some political skill"	14 years in Congress; former war hero and football player
Schiro (New Orleans)	"A dedicated, hard-working, nice guy"	Insurance salesman (built small business); president of city council
#3 Personality/Individualist		
Bartle (Kansas City)	"A lovable, dedicated, hard-working man with strong oratory skills and weak administrative skills"	Lawyer, investor, and national official in the Boy Scouts
Martin (Norfolk)	"A strong-willed, honest, straightforward, outspoken man"	President of small business and city councilman.
Naftalin (Minneapolis)	"A very intelligent student of government who was often too high and mighty"	Professor, state government official, and assistant to a mayor
#4—Executive		
Cowger (Louisville)	"An attractive, talented, ambitious young man"	Small businessman active in civic affairs

Mayor	Description (Typical comments from Interviews)	Background
Christopher (San Francisco)	"Strong, determined, honest, aggressive, straitlaced individual"	Built dairy company from nothing, served as president of Board of Supervisors
Boswell (Indianapolis)	"Honest, intelligent, articulate, well-organized, conservative person"	In city government (managerial positions)
Whelan (Jersey City)	"Fairly gregarious, businessman type"	Councilman and minor manager for telephone company
Welch (Houston)	"Aggressive, pragmatic, intellegent guy"	In city government
#5—Program Entrepreneur		
Allen (Atlanta)	"A sharp, hustling, efficient, courageous, gregarious, honest leader"	President of business equipment company, president of Chamber of Commerce, various state government jobs
Lee (New Haven)	"A dynamic, charming, honest, courageous, talented administrator and showman"	Newspaper reporter, councilor, assistant secretary at Chamber of Commerce, manager of Yale news bureau
Jonsson (Dallas)	"A very capable, sharp, impatient man of vision"	Self-made multimillionaire; built and ran Texas Instruments Inc.

Caretaker mayors lived in strong mayor charter cities. Most of the Personality/Individualist mayors were elected in city manager cities, and most of the Executive mayors reigned in cities with strong mayor charters. Only the Program Entrepreneur pattern has no apparent relationship to the city charter.

It is certainly not surprising to find the city manager charter associated with the patterns connected with agendas of small and moderate scope. Significantly, absolutely no relationship appears to exist between the charter and the Program Entrepreneurial pattern. The most obvious explanation is that this pattern generates so much power that the formal power arrangements eventually amount to no

Table 11-3 City Charters Associated with Each of the Five Behavioral Patterns

Type of Mayor	Type of Charter
#1—Ceremonial	• 4 City manager
#2—Caretaker	• 5 Strong mayor
#3—Personality/Individualist	• 2 City manager
	1 Weak mayor
#4—Executive	• 4 Strong mayor
	1 Weak mayor
#5—Program Entrepreneur	• 1 Strong mayor
	1 Weak mayor
	1 City manager

more than a small part of the total. Thus charter type is somewhat irrelevant.

If we divide the networks into three categories—ethnic predominance, white middle-class predominance, and other—we find the association revealed in Table 11-4. In general, the Ceremonial, Personality/Individualist, and Executive patterns seem to be associated with white middle-class-dominated cities, whereas the Caretaker pattern is usually found among ethnic communities. As before, the Program Entrepreneur pattern is not associated with anything.

Table 11-4 Population Type Associated with Each of the Five Behavioral Patterns

Mayoral Pattern	City's Population
#1—Ceremonial	• 4 White middle-class predominance
#2—Caretaker	• 3 Ethnic predominance
	1 White middle-class predominance
	1 Other
#3—Personality/Individualist	• 2 White middle-class predominance
	1 Other
#4—Executive	• 3 White middle-class predominance
	1 Ethnic predominance
	1 Other
#5—Program Entrepreneur	• 1 Ethnic predominance
	1 White middle-class predominance
	1 Other

The first, third, and fourth patterns tend to be associated with similar city charters and city populations. If we take one more step and look at the pattern of the city managers in cities whose mayor had a #1 or #3 pattern, we find the associations given in Table 11-5. In general, mayors who used a #1 pattern had a different type of city manager from mayors who used a #3 pattern. In some ways, the city managers of #1 type mayors had a pattern like #3 mayors, and the city managers of #3 mayors had a pattern like that of #1 mayors. Moreover, if we "add up" the patterns of the mayor and the city manager in each case, we find similar "total" patterns that look very much like a somewhat restricted #4 Executive pattern.

White-middle class (Anglo-Saxon) cities appear to be associated with a type of city government that comes in three forms—the Executive mayor, the Ceremonial mayor and an aggressive city manager, and the

Table 11-5 City Manager Types Associated with #1 and #3 Mayoral Types

Mayor's Pattern	City Manager's Pattern
#1 (Bachrach, Cincinnati)	Somewhat restricted #2 agenda setting process, some use of all network building processes. Heavy bureaucratic TA[a] process with some use of the other two.
#1 (McCann, Fort Worth)	First term: restricted #1 agenda setting, no network building, bureaucratic TA. Second term: restricted #2 agenda setting, limited network building, bureaucratic TA.
#1 (Lamb, Rochester)	Restricted #2 agenda setting, some use of all network building and TA processes, but heavy on bureaucratic.
#1 (Curran, San Diego)	Restricted #2 agenda setting, limited use of all network building and TA processes, but heavy on bureaucratic.
#3 (Bartle, Kansas City)	First term: restricted #2 agenda setting, limited network building, bureaucratic TA. Second term: #1 agenda setting, no network building, some bureaucratic TA.
#3 (Martin, Norfolk)	#1 agenda setting, no network building, bureaucratic TA process.
#3 (Naftalin, Minneapolis	No city manager, but a coordinator who used #1 agenda setting, no network building, and bureaucratic TA.

[a]Task accomplishment.

Personality/Individualist mayor and a passive city manager. The ethnic (lower-middle-class immigrant) cities, on the other hand, tend to prefer a type of government that basically has one form—the Caretaker mayor.[1]

The association between the city and the five mayoral patterns is the most elusive of all. While the impact on a city that is apparently due to a mayor's actions bears a very clear relationship to the five patterns (see Chapter 12, Pattern Impact), the relationship between more general city indices and the five patterns is much less clear. On many dimensions, the cities in which different patterns were found appear to be alike or randomly different. In the case of a few variables, however, the differences do not seem to be random. We have listed these in Table 11-6.

Cities in which we found patterns #1 (Ceremonial) and #3 (Personality/Individualist) are very similar. If we treat those cities as one group #1–#3, they are seen to differ from pattern #4 (Executive) cities and from pattern #2 (Caretaker) cities in a very systematic way. On all ten dimensions shown in Table 11-6, ignoring pattern #5 cities, pattern #1–#3 cities have one extreme value, pattern #2 cities the other extreme value, and pattern #4 cities a value in between.

Pattern #1–#3 cities tend to be the youngest, the smallest, the least dense, and the fastest growing. They tend to have the most highly educated population, the most white collar workers, the most "sound" housing, and the highest retail sales per capita. During 1950–1960, they experienced the least growth in their nonwhite populations. They tend to have the smallest number of city employees per capita.

On the other extreme, pattern #2 cities are the oldest, biggest, slowest-growing, and most dense of our cities. They experienced the largest increase in their nonwhite population during the 1950s. They have the least educated population, the fewest white collar employees, the lowest retail sales per capita, and the most "unsound" housing. Finally, they tend to have more municipal employees per capita than the other cities.

Pattern #4 cities fall between these extremes, although on most dimensions they are most like #1–#3 cities. The exceptions are in size and density, in which they are more like #2 cities.

[1]The political ethos of the immigrant and the political ethos of the white Anglo-Saxon are discussed in Banfield and Wilson (1967). The authors do a good job of explaining the origin of the various ethos and how they manifest themselves in a local government.

Table 11-6 Description of Cities Associated with Each of the Five Behavioral Patterns

	Mean Value for Cities with Each Mayoral Pattern				
City Data	#2 (N=5)	#4 (N=5)	#1 (N=4)	#3 (N=3)	#5 (N=3)
Date of Incorporation	1828	1840	1844	1853	1825
			(1848)		
1960 Population	600,000	560,000	450,000	420,000	420,000
			(438,000)		
1960 Population/ 10,000 square mile	10,000	5,000	6,000	5,000	
			(5,400)		
Population change, 1950–1960	+3%	+12%	+23%	+13%	+32%
			(+17%)		
1950–1960 change in nonwhite population	+10%	+4%	+4%	+1%	+5%
			(+2.7%)		
Years of school attended by those over age 25, 1960	9.7	10.8	10.8	11.3	10.8
			(11.0)		
Percentage employed in white collar jobs, 1960	39%	45%	46%	50%	45%
			(48%)		
Percentage of homes with sound plumbing, 1960	74%	78%	81%	82%	77%
			(81%)		
Retail sales per capita, 1963	$1,400	$1,200	$1,200	$1,200	$1,800
			($1,200)		
City employees as percentage of population	1.8%	1.5%	1.4%	1.5%	1.6%
			(1.44%)		

In general these findings are very consistent with the last ones concerning networks. We normally expect an ethnic population to live in an older, bigger, denser, poorer, manufacturing-oriented city, whereas a white middle-class population usually lives in the younger, smaller, white collar cities. Interestingly, the older, bigger, and denser white middle-class cities tend to be associated with the Executive pattern and the younger, smaller ones with the #1 and #3 patterns.

As Table 11-6 suggests, pattern #5 cities do not vary systematically on our chosen city dimensions. As in the case of the network variable, the city does not seem to have any clear association with the Program Entrepreneur pattern. Drawing conclusions based on only three mayors of this type is dangerous. Nevertheless, it is tempting to speculate that this pattern is not associated with any particular type of city or network.

FIVE PATTERNS

It is now fairly apparent why we found five patterns instead of one or twenty. The model we have created describes a complex, interdependent system. Its parts are connected in numerous ways, involving a far from unorganized set of variables. Although, theoretically the different processes we identified in Chapters 4, 5, and 6 could combine into hundreds or thousands of mayoral patterns, in reality this is impossible because of the connectedness of our system. The model we have created contains so many interdependent relationships that the total system can take on relatively few configurations.

For example, of all the theoretically possible patterns, around 30 of them include a #4 agenda setting process with a task accomplishment process that is only moderately individualistic. It is impossible to imagine a setting in which these patterns could remain stable for more than a very short time.

We cannot determine precisely how many patterns are feasible. Certainly far fewer than the maximum number are feasible. At the same time, it is clear that more than five are feasible. Why then did we find only five?

The answer lies in the differences and similarities of the contextual variables. At first glance our 20 study situations seem to represent a fairly broad range: from a small, old city (New Haven) to a large, new city (Houston); from a mayor who was an insurance salesman to a mayor who had been a small town politician to the former chairman of the board of a large corporation.

If we look beyond these surface differences and consider *all* possible types of mayors, networks, cities, and agendas, today or in the past, in the United States or in Europe, we find that our 20 situations represent a *very small* sample of the total variety. That is, compared with Denver in 1850 or London in 1800, all our 20 situations look remarkably alike. Our cities were all equipped with mid-twentieth-century technology. The networks all reflect contemporary social, economic, and legal development. All had one very important network member in common—the federal government, which during the 1960s was not a passive institution. All our mayors were white males who grew up in this country in the first half of the twentieth century. We have noted before that there were relatively few different agenda types.

An obvious but nevertheless important implication can be drawn from this discussion. *There are undoubtedly more than five fundamentally different types of mayors.* Exactly how many types are possible (how many configurations the system can take) is unknown. We would expect, for example, that if we had data about a set of 20 cities during the 1920s, we would find at least one or two more mayoral patterns. Likewise, we would expect to see a few new patterns in the coming decades. Even today, most people can probably think of a mayor who does not fit the five patterns we have identified. Perhaps the most obvious example is the machine boss of the early 1900s. It is very important to keep this point in mind that it is highly unlikely that we have exhaustively catalogued all mayoral types. Hopefully, however, we have found a general model that accounts for the emergence of all mayoral patterns.

SUMMARY

A number of types of behavior patterns are observable among American mayors. We have identified five in this study, but there are undoubtedly more. The process by which these patterns emerge in a particular situation is not at all a random one. Our model of the process includes the following important elements:

- The different possible configurations of behavior patterns in the form of three mayoral processes.
- Four contextual variables: the agenda, mayor, network, and city.
- A set of dynamic short-run relationships between the mayoral processes and the contextual variables.
- A set of long-run relationships among the contextual variables.
- A natural tendency in most mayors to push toward a coalignment of the contextual variables.

We can generalize cautiously about pattern emergence beyond describing the rather complex and dynamic process. Certain types of agendas tend to be associated with certain mayoral patterns, as do certain types of mayoral personalities, certain types of networks, and certain types of cities. Since these are not simple cause and effect relationships, associations described do not hold in all situations. Nevertheless they provide rules of thumb to help us predict what type of pattern might emerge in a particular situation.

CHAPTER 12

PATTERN IMPACT: RATING THE MAYOR'S PERFORMANCE

When we began this inquiry, we planned to "evaluate" and "rank" each mayor's performance after we had finished the field work. That is, we assumed we would rank the 20 mayors on their positive impact on their respective cities. We thought this would be possible for three very straightforward reasons.

1. We assumed that some core values are held by almost all twentieth-century Americans. These values, for example, attach a positive valence to health, sufficient food, shelter, and educational and occupational opportunities.
2. We assumed that we could get a number of reasonable "judgments" about the effect, if any, the mayor in question had on dimensions that are relevant to those core values. At least one of these assessments would be analytic, one would be based on the evaluations of the people in the city, and one would be based on the judgments of urban "experts."
3. If the separate judgments did *not* drastically diverge, we would take an average for the final effectiveness rating.

We recognized that our ratings would be approximations, but nevertheless useful approximations.

Either explicit or implicit in most of the current mayoral models we examined in Chapter 2 was a relationship between a pattern of behavior and a single final result variable. Such a relationship is implicit in all statements that begin: "A good mayor. . . ." We had assumed that we might find some relationships or correlations between positive and negative impacts and different types of behavior patterns. That is, we assumed we might learn that an X-type mayor constantly outperforms the rest or that a Y-type mayor outperforms the others under certain circumstances.

At the end of the first phase of the field work, we still had enough confidence in our original assumptions to state a number of generalizations in the following form: "The more effective mayor is/has/does the following things: . . . ."

By the end of the second phase of the field work, our belief that we could talk about one useful final result variable (effectiveness or health) had diminished considerably. That is, we concluded that talking about the "good" or "effective" or "best" type of mayor was misleading and not useful. To explain how we reached this conclusion, we must first present the process in which we were involved.

THE RESEARCH PROCESS

Over a long period of time we went about gathering the data that we planned to use eventually to rate each of the mayors. We did not examine the lot until after the completion of the field work.

The first set of judgments we collected neither confirmed nor refuted our original assumptions. We requested top-notch "urban experts" to rate on a questionnaire the situations with which they were acquainted, telling us how the "net health" of certain cities had changed during specific administrations.[1] We gave them three choices—positive, neutral, negative. Eight of the "experts" rated the 48 mayors on our questionnaire. In the cases of 10 of the 48 mayors, only

[1]The details of why certain administrations were included in the questionnaire while others were not, how we selected our "urban experts," of how we polled them, and so on, are included in Chapter 1.

two of the eight respondents felt well enough acquainted with the administrations to rate them. Of the 38 other cases, the experts unanimously agreed in 6 cases, and strongly disagreed in 9 other cases (at least one rated the mayor's impact positive and one negative). For the majority of the cases, 20 to be exact, they tended to basically agree (see Appendix B).

We collected a second set of judgments that consisted of the opinions of the local populations. That is, we used the mayor's record at the polls as an indication of how the citizens rated his performance. In the first field study of six mayors, these judgments coincided exactly with those of the experts. In the second field study of 14 mayors, these two ratings did not match nearly as well. In trying to explain why the two sets of ratings differed, we found ourselves posing some hard questions. For example:

1. Some mayors were elected in years of national elections; others were not. Among other things, this difference seemed to strongly affect voter turnout at local elections. How do we take into account the fact that some election statistics are based on 25% of the voting population and some are based on 80%? What about the effect of national landslides? Could not an effective Republican mayor have gotten 48% of the vote in 1964 in one city, while a very ineffective Democratic mayor have gotten 52% of the vote somewhere else?
2. Some mayors faced very strong opposition, and others faced none. Clearly, election statistics reflect the population's judgment concerning not one person, but two. Is it not possible for a very effective mayor to get 60% of the vote against a formidable opponent while a mediocre mayor gets 65% of the vote against a fool?
3. Since for most mayors we have the results of more than one election, how should they be combined and turned into a simple rating? Which of the mayors below is better?

    mayor A—60% (4 years, could not succeed himself)
    mayor B—52%, 57% (8 years total)
    mayor C—55%, 65%, 57%, 55% (8 years).

These and other issues raised serious questions in our mind concerning the usability of such data for our purposes.

The third set of data we collected was to be statistical. We had identified 10 areas that coincided with 10 basic values we believed that most people hold. The areas were: health, education, housing, income, employment, business sales and profits, cultural activities, recreational activities, civil rights, and environmental quality. We had planned to collect data that would give us a measure of the change that a city underwent on these dimensions while a particular mayor was in office.

For the person who has spent most of his life studying business organizations and working in an environment in which hard data are highly valued, our next discovery is an enormous shock. Hard data on these, the most basic measures of the quality of life in our cities, are relatively nonexistent.

After spending countless hours hunting for the data we needed on our 20 cities, we learned the following things:

1. The data that do exist are seldom yearly data; often we must use data collected every 10 years. Therefore, it is impossible to compare conditions when most mayors were elected and when they left office. For example, the performance of the mayor whose term ran from 1964 to 1972 would have to be measured with 1960 and 1970 data.
2. Data are very spotty for more than half the mayors whose cities were smaller than the 18 largest metropolitan areas. That is, for 60% of the cities in our study, little data exist.
3. *Most* data are for a "metropolitan area," *not* a city. Usually well over half the population and considerably more than half the geographic area in a metropolitan region is outside the core city. In some cases, two core cities are included in one metropolitan area (Oakland/San Francisco). It is not at all certain that data for an entire metropolitan area accurately reflect changes in a core city.
4. When a number of statistics are available, there is often no obvious right choice. For example, available housing statistics include the cost for a family of four, the percentage of homes lacking some or all plumbing, and the percentage of homes with 1.01 or more persons per room. Which of these three statistics should we use, or how should we combine them?
5. As with all statistics, it is not too difficult to challenge the validity of the method by which they were created.
6. Even if we could obtain the desired statistical data, how could we reduce the data on our 10 indices to a single rating? Consider the following hypothetical data summaries of changes in two cities while two different mayors were in office:

Variable	Mayor 1, City 1	Mayor 2, City 2
Housing	0	+
Health	–	=
Education	+	0
Unemployment	+	++
Crime	=	–
Income	+	+
Business profit and sales	++	0
Environmental quality	=	+
Racial equality	–	+
Cost of living	+	=
Poverty	0	+

Key: ++ health much better
+ health better
0 little change
– health worse
= health much worse

Certain subgroups within our society most certainly would rank these mayors differently.

Given the circumstances and insights just outlined, we realized that finding and then using statistical data in accordance with our original plan was impossible.

We could continue for pages to describe problems we encountered in rating the 20 mayors from this study. However, it would already be apparent that our difficulties have at least three interrelated sources.

UNDERLYING PROBLEMS

First, although it still seems safe to assume that most contemporary Americans share some core values, it appears that various people and groups within our society attach different priorities to these values in the short run. That is, given a choice of tradeoffs between changes in core value areas people will often disagree. Is a plus (+) on racial equality and a minus (–) on crime better than a minus (–) on racial equality and a plus (+) on crime? How about a minus (–) on health and plus (+) on income?

Because of our different backgrounds, we all have different ways of looking at the world, different needs, different aspirations for the future. Despite our remarkable homogeneity as a culture, many differences appear among us when we begin to consider details. For example, most businessmen would rate a (+) on business sales and profits and a (–) on unemployment as good, but most members of the lower middle class would rate such conditions as bad.

Some people would say that the tradeoff questions we have raised constitute not a value issue but a technical issue—that is, one *can* evaluate a (+) on A and (–) on B versus a (–) on A and a (+) on B by using technical expertise. Technical expertise, they would argue, can tell us how values A and B are interrelated, what their relationships are to the other values in our system (unemployment, environmental quality, etc.), and how all the values are related to net system health. This knowledge might take the form of a complex, sophisticated urban model, or it might be divided into hundreds of rules of thumb about cause-and-effect relationships in the system of interest; for example: "A drop in the unemployment rate by 1% or more is almost always followed within a year by an increase in the cost of living by 2 to 4%."

This brings us to the second apparent source of our difficulties. Our current understanding of cause-and-effect relationships in the physical and social sciences varies a great deal across different domains. In some restricted domains, current knowledge is quite extensive. In other areas we know almost nothing.

In the past decade many people have written books about cause-and-effect relationships in urban systems. Some of these works contain valuable insights. Unfortunately, however, the authors tend to disagree on almost all fundamental points. All are woefully lacking in substantive data that can allow us to properly understand the problems with which they deal and to resolve disagreements.

The type of urban model that would reduce this problem to a "technical issue" not only does not exist today, it is not even close to existence. Cities are very open systems whose complexity can only crudely be approximated by current models. That is not to deny that we have made progress in the past decade in understanding our cities. We have. To say that we have a reasonably good understanding of our urban areas, however, is quite inaccurate.

Indeed, a fair generalization about our knowledge of things is that the larger the system is, the less we know about it. Although we may not be able to understand much about the enormously complex cause-and-effect relationships in a city of a million inhabitants, we know infinitely less about a continent populated by 300 million people.

The final "root cause" of our problem is a partial consequence of this restricted understanding of cause and effect. The better a phenomenon is understood, the easier it is to gather and create relevant indicator data; and the better it is understood, the more data become available.

The amount of "indicator" data currently available on cities is extraordinarily small and difficult to find. Some progress has been made recently by the Urban Institute in gathering what data there are and presenting them in usable form,[2] but there is still a great gap between what is available and what we would have liked for this study. It is probably correct to say that the executives at General Motors collect, analyze, and use more data on their "system" each year than the leaders of the city of Detroit do in a decade or more.

IMPACT GENERALIZATIONS

Therefore, because of the factors just discussed—lack of indicator data, our currently limited understanding of cause and effect in cities, and the absence of a value tradeoff consensus in our culture—it has not been possible for us to rate the 20 mayors in this study along one effective–ineffective dimension in a meaningful or logical manner.

Furthermore, for the same reasons, we cannot rate the 20 mayors with our original procedure on multiple end-result criteria. Such an attempt was an obvious next step, and one that is becoming more common in the applied social sciences. By doing so, one allows a reader to "add things up" with his own values and beliefs and to make his own final judgment. Although one therefore does not need value tradeoff consensus to rate a situation on multiple end-result dimensions, one does need indicator data and some understanding of cause and effect. Unfortunately, we have neither.

Nevertheless, even given these constraints and problems, we can make some generalization about the overall impact of the different mayors on their cities. Indeed, we have already implicitly and explicitly done so. Such statements are not based on the type of systematic measurement that we had originally envisioned using, but

[2]Flax (1972).

they are important and meaningful generalizations.

For example, the data from this study suggest that each of the five mayoral types we identified has a different overall impact on his city. Specifically:

> ***Impact Generalization #1.*** Different mayoral patterns are associated with different overall impacts in scope and direction (see Figure 12-1). In general, the impact will be of the type we intuitively expect given the pattern of the three key processes. That is:
>
> (a) the Ceremonial mayor has a small positive impact on his city, one that is not directed toward change. Insofar as people are made unhappy by what does not happen, he is subject to criticism for having a negative impact in some areas by not acting.
>
> (b) the Caretaker mayor has a reasonably large positive impact on his city in discrete ways that are usually focused on maintenance. Since he does not deal with the long run or with the city as a whole, he is subject to criticism for not "looking to the future and tackling our large important problems."
>
> (c) the Personality/Individualist mayor has a moderately positive impact on his city in the form of changes in certain aspects of the city as a whole. The mayor is subject to praise that the changes were good, and criticism that they were not good.
>
> (d) the Executive mayor has a fairly large impact on his city both in the form of discrete maintenance and in terms of changes in certain aspects of the city as a whole. He is subject to criticism for doing too much or too little, and for doing the wrong things.
>
> (e) the Program Entrepreneur has a very large positive impact on his city as a whole in the middle and long run. The city will noticeably change as a result of this mayor's administration. He is subject to criticism for making some poor long-run decisions and for having a negative impact in the short run.

When we asked our respondents in each city for the major accomplishments and failures of the mayor in question, we found that the same types of mayor tended to elicit the same type of response. The people in Cleveland and New Orleans (both Caretaker mayors) did not

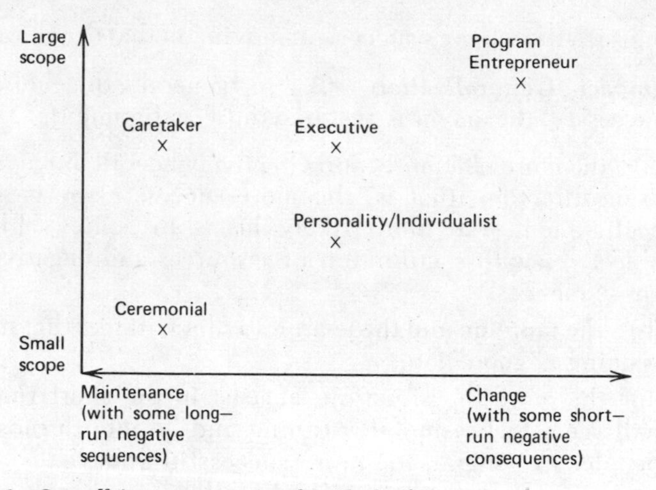

Figure 12-1 Overall impacts associated with the five mayoral types.

mention the same items for accomplishments and failures, but they gave the same type of response. That is, people in both cities listed numerous discrete maintenance-oriented items under accomplishments and few large long-run items under failures. Those interviewed in Ceremonial mayor cities classified very few items under accomplishments or failures. They often noted that the mayor conducted himself well on the job, that he treated people well, or that he projected a good image. Under failures, it was not unusual to hear that the mayor "didn't do much of anything." Personality/Individualist mayors were praised for specific projects, such as building a convention hall downtown, bringing in a professional football team, or securing the passage of important legislation. They were criticized for a wide variety of reasons—poor decisions on their projects, not doing more, not doing less, and so on. Executive mayors were often praised for a number of specific projects and for running the city well. Like the Personality/Individualists, they were criticized in various ways. Those interviewed in Program Entrepreneur cities tended to list a small number of very large long-run accomplishments (rebuilding the downtown area, significantly increasing harmony between the races, etc.) and a moderate number of fairly small, shorter-run failures (ignoring one part of the community, not finding a successor, etc.).

The first generalization thus tells us something about the "direction" the mayor took, and we can make a second impact generalization relating more to the mayor's success in moving in that direction.

> ***Impact Generalization #2.*** In general, the more successful the mayor is at achieving a coalignment,
>
> (a) the more efficiently and effectively he will move in some direction; that is, the more successful he is at coalignment, the more likely he is to achieve his objectives with a minimum of resources and negative consequences;
>
> (b) the more he and those around him will feel that he is doing a "good" job;
>
> (c) the more the situation, at least in the short run, will seem to be smooth running and "right" to most people. In general, the more successful a mayor is at coalignment, the more popular he will be.

Our interview responses clearly indicated that the impact of mayors who were fairly successful at coalignment was perceived differently from that of mayors who were fairly unsuccessful. In general, interviewees listed significantly more impact "successes" and significantly fewer "failures" for mayors who were successful coaligners. Even the close friends of mayors who were fairly unsuccessful at coalignment tended to admit that the official in question "wasn't a very good mayor," even while insisting that he was a very talented and good individual.

The difference between successful and unsuccessful coaligners was particularly striking in our first field study. Three of the mayors were fairly successful at coalignment and three were fairly unsuccessful. The nature of our respondents' comments about their former mayors' impact were very similar within the two sets of three mayors and very different between sets. There were consistently more signs of crises, wasted resources, angry people, and missed opportunities among the mayors who were not successful coaligners.

Table 12-1 displays the overall impact of the 20 mayors in this study along the three dimensions inherent in the #1 and #2 impact generalizations—scope of impact, change or maintenance oriented, and coalignment results. The reader can decide for himself which were the better and which were the worse mayors in this study, in the light of the importance he attaches to these three dimensions.

In concluding this discussion of pattern impact, we must raise one

Table 12-1 Overall Impact of Each of the 20 Mayors

Mayor	Scope of Impact	Orientation	Coalignment Results
Allen (Atlanta)	Large	Change	Very successful
Kowal (Buffalo)	Moderately large	Maintenance	Very unsuccessful
Bachrach (Cincinnati)	Small	Maintenance	Successful
Locher (Cleveland)	Moderately large	Maintenance	Very unsuccessful
Westlake (Columbus)	Moderately large	Maintenance	Very unsuccessful
Jonsson (Dallas)	Large	Change	Successful
McCann (Fort Worth)	Small	Maintenance	Unsuccessful
Welch (Houston)	Moderately large	Change and maintenance	Successful
Boswell (Indianapolis)	Moderately large	Maintenance and change	Somewhat successful
Whelan (Jersey City)	Moderately large	Maintenance and change	Unsuccessful
Bartle (Kansas City)	Moderately small	Maintenance and change	Unsuccessful
Cowger (Louisville)	Moderately large	Change and maintenance	Successful
Naftalin (Minneapolis)	Moderate	Change and maintenance	Somewhat successful
Lee (New Haven)	Large	Change	Very successful
Schiro (New Orleans)	Moderately large	Maintenance	Unsuccessful
Addonizio (Newark)	Moderately large	Maintenance (some change)	Unsuccessful
Martin (Norfolk)	Moderately small	Change and maintenance	Successful
Lamb (Rochester)	Small	Maintenance	Somewhat unsuccessful
Curran (San Diego)	Small	Maintenance (some change)	Somewhat unsuccessful
Christopher (San Francisco)	Moderately large	Change and maintenance	Somewhat successful

last issue. A close examination of Table 12-1 shows that some *types* of mayor were, on the average, much more successful at coalignment than others. That is, Program Entrepreneurs tended to be the most successful coaligners, the Executives second, the Personality/Individualists third, the Ceremonial mayors fourth, and the Caretakers fifth. While it is possible that different types (patterns) do better than others at coalignment, we strongly suspect that with a large sample of mayors this conclusion would not stand up.

Instead, we believe that one situational factor, which was common to all 20 mayors, played a large role in producing this particular pattern–coalignment association. All 20 mayors in the study held office during a very turbulent and proactive era in history. The patterns that were completely maintenance oriented (Caretaker and Ceremonial) were clearly out of step with that period. Thus we would expect that mayors adopting those patterns would have some difficulty with coalignment.

A second factor common to all 20 situations could also be influencing the pattern–coalignment association we have found. All 20 cities in the study were reasonably large. Only one was under a quarter-million in 1960 population. It could well be that after cities reach a certain size, they become so complex and demanding that patterns having a small scope cannot realistically expect to achieve successful coalignments.

SUMMARY

In this chapter we have drawn two broad generalizations about pattern impact: (1) that each of the five mayoral types we have identified tends to have a different type of impact; (2) that a mayor's success at coalignment, or lack of it, influences his effectiveness and efficiency in achieving this type of impact.

We have rated the overall impact of the 20 mayors in the study along three dimensions—scope of impact, change or maintenance orientation, and coalignment results. We were not able, however, to identify and justify a method by which we could rate the mayors' performances along a single end-result dimension (effective–ineffective).

CHAPTER 13

IMPLICATIONS FOR SOCIAL SCIENTISTS: A COALIGNMENT MODEL OF ADMINISTRATION

A MODEL OF THE ADMINISTRATIVE PROCESS

James Thompson, from whom we have borrowed the term "coalignment," has argued that the coalignment function is the very essence of administration.

> Perpetuation of the complex organization rests on an appropriate coalignment in time and space not simply of human individuals but of streams of institutionalized action. Survival rests on the coalignment of technology and task environment with a viable domain, and of organization design and structure appropriate to that domain.
>
> The coalignment we assert to be the basic administrative function is not a simple combination of static components. Each of the elements involved in the

> coalignment has its own dynamics. Each behaves at its own rate, governed by forces external to the organization. Technology, for example, is embedded in the cause/effect belief systems of a wider environment. The rate of obsolescence and the direction of innovation in that wider environment may be predictable, but the organization can neither prevent nor command innovation or obsolescence.
>
> Now if the elements necessary to the coalignment are in part influenced by powerful forces in the organization's environment, then organization survival requires *adaptive* as well as *directive* action in those areas where the organization maintains discretion. Since each of the necessary streams of institutional action moves at its own rate, the timing of both adaptive and directive action is a crucial administrative matter.
>
> Thus, in our view, the central function of administration is to keep the organization at the *nexus* of several necessary streams of action; and because the several streams are variable and moving, the nexus is not only moving but sometimes quite difficult to fathom.
>
> We must emphasize that organizations are not simply determined by their environments, [nor are they] independent. The configuration necessary for survival comes neither from yielding to any and all pressures nor from manipulating all variables, but from finding the *strategic variables*—those which are available to the organization and can be manipulated in such a way that interaction with other elements will result in a viable coalignment.[1]

Following Thompson's lead, if we state the model developed in this study in a more generalized form, we would have the following:

[1]James Thompson, *Organization in Action* (New York: McGraw-Hill, 1967), pp. 147–148. Copyright © by McGraw Hill, Inc, 1967. Used with permission of McGraw-Hill Book Company.

> That which most people would describe as successful administration is a behavioral pattern of a particular set of processes that is feasible and stable in the short run; this set of processes, moreover, has a desired impact on a number of key variables, serving to create or maintain a simultaneous alignment among those variables.

Before we proceed, let us examine this statement closely. First, it equates what "most people" would describe as "successful" administration with successful coalignment behavior. It does not say that this type of behavior is right or good in an abstract sense. Nor does it say *all* people. Some would rate as successful the administrator whose relentless pursuit of a goal causes the creation of a major nonalignment, if they believe very strongly in that goal (as compared with all other possible goals). The statement simply suggests that most people who are acquainted with administration today would label successful coalignment behavior as successful administration.

The statement next mentions "a particular set of processes." The administrator, it says, like the mayor, can set his agenda, manage his resources, and get tasks done in a number of different ways. There is no one correct way. The administrator has a choice.

The statement also indicates that any set of processes that would typify a "successful" situation would be both feasible and stable in the short run. That is, the successful administrator is sensitive to the short-run constraints in the system which make some processes unworkable, ineffective, or inefficient. The "successful" administrator who is failing to complete 80% of his tasks will not maintain a #4 agenda setting process (in the short run) because such a process *requires* effective execution of most, if not all, tasks.

Successful administration has the "desired impact on a number of key variables." For example, the "successful" administrator who has no charisma does not try to maintain his resources with a charismatic cooperation building process, which he recognizes would not work.

The "key variables" to which our statement refers are the equivalent of the network, city, mayor, and agenda in this study. The statement does not specify those key variables simply because it is not yet clear that there is a universal set of key variables, applicable to all administrative situations. At this point, we suspect that different settings require slightly different key variables.

Finally, the statement talks of creating "simultaneous alignment among those variables"—a coalignment. As in this study, we doubt that a perfect coalignment is ever achieved by an administrator. Instead, successful administration realizes something fairly close to a coalignment.

ADVANTAGES OF A COALIGNMENT MODEL

We find this model to be of more than casual interest for a number of reasons, a few of them very simple and straightforward. First, the model fits our own experiences with administration, not only in this study but in everyday life. Second, it even seems to fit nicely with the metaphors our culture has developed to describe administration. The administrator is often depicted as a person juggling. Such a visual representation is the essence of coalignment.

The model itself seems to have a number of advantages over other administrative models for at least three reasons: it avoids simple cause-and-effect dynamics, it focuses on both structure and process, and it does not rely on such mystical forces as those which produce "equilibrium."

Most social scientists today agree that a simple cause-and-effect model cannot adequately describe complex social phenomena. Nevertheless, it is very awkward to talk about, write about, or create models that do not explicitly or implicitly lean heavily on cause-and-effect dynamics. As a result, most of the current administrative models are constructed in terms of dependent and independent variables. The coalignment model is not completely free of such language, but we think it has gone a long way in the right direction. Instead of talking about which variables determine which other variables, it conceptualizes variables as streams moving through time in mutual interaction with other streams or flows.

The time-honored distinction between structure and process has been useful to the social sciences, but it has caused problems also. Much of today's research on administration tends to fall into one of these two camps. Sociologists often create models focusing on personality structure, social structure, formal organizational structure, technological structure, and environmental structure. Social psychologists often create models focusing on decision-making processes, planned change processes, goal-setting processes, problem-solving processes, and resource management processes. Critics of administrative theory complain that relating these two types of research is very difficult and quite confusing.

Our coalignment model combines structure and process. It does not focus on *all* processes and structures, but only on the structures that are a part of the key alignments and only on the processes that offer strategic levers to the administrator(s). It suggests that each affects the others in a mutually interactive and dynamic way. Processes change or help maintain the structure in a short-run dynamic. Structures can change or help maintain processes in a longer-run dynamic.

Another widely discussed problem in social theory is that many, if not most, of our models have a somewhat inappropriate basis in the physical or biological sciences. Implicitly or explicitly, numerous models assume a kind of mystical tendency toward "equilibrium" or "homeostasis." These key concepts are borrowed, of course, from physics and biology. As a number of people have very articulately pointed out,[2] social phenomena are different from physical and biological phenomena along certain extremely important dimensions.

The coalignment model, unlike most existing models of administration, is a morphogenic general systems model. Unlike physical science models, it does not assume the existence of a mystical force toward equilibrium. The relationships among its parts are complex, not simple. Unlike an atom or other passive elements, some of the parts of the coalignment model are alive. They can grow and change by themselves, independent of the rest of the system. Whereas biological models include a regulating mechanism that keeps certain key parameters within set limits (homeostasis), the coalignment model has deviation-amplifying characteristics. Atlanta was not governed by homeostasis during the 1960s. Some significant changes occurred in its social and physical structures. Mayor Allen did not dampen these changes or trends. To the contrary, his coaligned administration amplified some of them. That is, by creating something close to a coalignment in his system, Allen allowed some changes to occur faster and with fewer short-run negative consequences.

Finally, perhaps our most important reason for favoring the

[2]See Buckley (1967).

coalignment model is that it seems to usefully integrate some of the most important current trends in administrative research (both structural and process). This point is important enough to merit detailed exploration.

ALIGNMENT RESEARCH

Some of the most interesting work focusing on organization–administrative phenomena in the last 10 to 15 years belongs to a somewhat new type, which we call "alignment research." Either explicitly or implicitly, these efforts have similar basic formats. They identify two main variables or constructs, explore the relationship between the two variables, and consider the consequences of different states of the two variables. Very often the researcher concludes that when the two variables "fit" or "matched" or were "congruent" or "consistent," the consequences of their relationship were "good" for the system (in terms of effectiveness, health, etc.). When the two variables were "mismatched" or "inconsistent" or "not congruent," the consequences of their relationship were "bad."

In our terminology, these researchers are identifying key variables and describing what constitutes an alignment. Sometimes they do this fairly explicitly, often they do not. *In all cases, however, they seem to be working on different pieces of a coalignment model.* A few examples of the better alignment research will help to clarify this point.

Woodward: Technology and Organization

In 1954 Joan Woodward and her colleagues began a study that was designed to see "how far theories implicit in [our] teaching were applied in practice locally, and whether such application was linked in any way with . . . commercial success."[3] They collected considerable data in 100 firms in the South Essex area of England. To their initial surprise they found that the firms that adhered to the classical principles of management were no more successful economically than those which did not.

Continuing to examine their data, the researchers eventually discovered that if they segregated the data according to two

[3]Woodward (1965).

variables—management practices (formal organization) and production system complexity (technology)—some patterns became very clear. Specifically, certain organization–technology combinations tended to be associated with economic success, but others did not. For example, successful firms with a small batch or unit production technology tended to have three levels in their management hierarchy, whereas successful large batch and mass production companies tended to have four levels, and process or continuous production companies had six levels.

After almost 10 years of work, Woodward concluded that "commercially successful firms seemed to be those in which function (technology) and form (organization) were complementary."[4]

Argyris: Personality and Organization

Written from a psychological point of view, Chris Argyris's early statement of the conflict between formal organizations and people has become a classic.[5] As the title of his book suggests, Argyris focuses on two macro concepts: personality and organization. He describes at length one type of human personality and one type of formal organization. He then argues convincingly, that the two are "incongruent."

The type of personality Argyris describes is similar to Maslow's self-actualizing person—active, aware, and independent; having a broad repertoire of behavior, a fairly long time perspective, and some deep, complex interests; and being capable of self-control. The type of organization he describes is a classically structural one, inflexible and centralized. It is characterized by a high degree of task specialization, a clear chain of command, and centralization of decision making at the top. In such an organization, employees will tend to work in an environment in which:

1. they have minimal control over their workaday world;
2. they are expected to be passive, dependent, and subordinate;
3. they are expected to have a short time perspective; and
4. they are induced to perfect and value the frequent use of skin-surface, shallow abilities.

[4]Woodward (1965), p. vi.
[5]Argyris (1957).

Thus, that type of organization and that type of individual are "incongruent," and this results in individuals who feel frustrated and conflicted. The way individuals adapt to this situation is complex and definitely "impedes integration with the formal organization." Therefore, Argyris argues, the consequences of the incongruencies are not good for either party. Argyris concludes his essay by suggesting that a different type of formal organization—one that was more decentralized and flexible—might be congruent with the type of personality he has described.

Chandler: Strategy and Organizational Structure

Alfred Chandler's historical study of a few giant American corporations is clearly one of the most important pieces of business and organizational research completed in the past two decades.[6] Although he focuses on a wide variety of variables and phenomena, Chandler especially deals with two macro concepts. The first, strategy, is defined as the determination of the basic long-term goals and objectives of the enterprise and the adoption of courses of action and the allocation of resources necessary for carrying out those goals. The second, structure, is defined as the design of organization through which the enterprise is administered.

In exploring the relationship between strategy and structure, Chandler concludes that for economic efficiency, a firm's strategy and structure must be compatible. That is, there are many "sound" strategies and many "legitimate" organizational structures which are incompatible and could lead to organizational failure if used together.

In the successful cases Chandler studied, the corporations tended to make changes in their strategies to take advantage of environmental changes and to follow with appropriate changes in structure: "A new strategy required a new or at least a refashioned structure if the enlarged enterprise was to be operated efficiently. The failure to develop a new internal structure . . . can lead only to economic inefficiency."[7]

Tavistock: Technology and the Social System

A research team from the Tavistock Institute in England (Trist,

[6]Chandler (1962).
[7]*Ibid.*, pp. 15–16.

Higgen, Murray, Pollock, and others) studied mining operations during the mid-1950s and developed the now well-known notion of a sociotechnical system. They concentrated on two macro variables—the technology and the social system at work—and studied the relationship between the two during a time of change.

The mining company under study, which was feeling competitive pressure due primarily to advances in technology, decided to make some sweeping changes in its technological operation. Over a fairly short period, it ceased to be a craft technology in which almost everyone did the same job, becoming a machine technology in which there was heavy job specialization. Worker unrest soon produced an explosive situation. A second set of technological job design changes was finally introduced with the aid of a Tavistock research group, and after a while these proved to be satisfactory.

Within the researchers' conceptual scheme, the problem in this case was caused by an incompatibility between the first new technical system and the workers' social system. The old craft technology meshed well with the workers' culture, which was characterized by high interpersonal interaction and egalitarian–cooperative norms. The machine technology demanded a very different social system—one characterized by status stratification and low interpersonal interaction. The second set of changes stabilized the situation by modifying both the social and technological systems, once again producing a near-alignment.

Among other things, the research group concluded: "It is the goodness of fit between the human work organization (social system at work), and the technological requirements that ultimately determines the efficiency of the whole system."[8]

Lawrence and Lorsch: Organization and Environment

In a comparative study (in three industries) of 10 organizations with different levels of economic performance, Lawrence and Lorsch found that the more successful ones were organized differently but in ways that seemed to fit the demands of their respective environments. They developed two concepts to aid in the analysis of their data. The first, differentiation, is defined as the differences in cognitive and emotional orientations among managers in different functional departments and

[8]Trist, Higgin, Murray, Pollock (1963), p. 294.

the difference in formal structure among those departments. The second, integration, was the quality of the state of collaboration existing among the departments that are required to achieve unity of effort by the environment. They concluded that "the state of differentiation in the effective organization was consistent with the diversity of the parts of the environment, while the state of the integration was consistent with the environmental demand for interdependence."[9]

In other words, the researchers found that when three internal characteristics of organizations (formal structure, orientations of managers, state of interdepartmental collaboration) matched or fit environmental characteristics, the organizations seemed to be more effective than those not achieving this alignment.

Etzioni: Strategy and Network

In a brilliant theoretical essay, Etzioni argues that compliance relations serve as a good base for the comparative study of organizations.[10] He identifies three types of involvement that people or groups can have with an organization, each one being based on a different kind of power and compliance. The three types of compliance are coercive, utilitarian, and normative. The first relies on the application or threat of application of negative sanctions, the second on the control of material resources, and the third on the allocation and manipulation of symbolic rewards. A prisoner's relationship to a prison is usually based on coercive compliance, a plant worker's to his plant on utilitarian compliance, and that of a professional to his professional society on normative compliance. In the terminology developed in this study, Etzioni is saying that a "network member" can be bound to a focal organization in one of three ways. His compliance with the focal organization can be dependent on threats, money, or symbols and abstractions.

According to Etzioni, each type of compliance elicits different behavior from the network member. Indeed prisoners, office workers, and APA members do behave differently with respect to their organizations.

After noting that organizations can have different types of goals (or

[9]Lawrence and Lorsch (1967), p. 157.
[10]Etzioni (1971).

agendas or strategies), Etzioni asserts that certain types of goals and compliance patterns are more congruent than others. He suggests that order goals are congruent with coercive compliance, economic goals with utilitarian compliance, and cultural goals with normative compliance. "Certain combinations of compliance and goals are more effective than others."[11]

This Study: Extensions of Perrow and Simon

In the current study we have extended the work of a number of people to suggest a strategy–environment alignment and an individual–environment alignment. These alignment statements, outlined in Chapter 8, have their roots on the individual side in the work of Herbert Simon and other cognitive theorists and cognitive psychologists. Simon was one of the first to argue explicitly that it was useful to view man as an information processor.[12] Our conceptualization of an individual's cognitive orientation in Chapter 8 is derived from the evolution of some of Simon's research, now being conducted by McKenney and Keen.[13]

On the environmental side, the alignment statements we made are easily traced to the work of Charles Perrow,[14] who makes explicit technology–organization alignment statements. We have extended his work to make environment–individual and environment–agenda (strategy) statements.

Others

There are numerous other examples of alignment research; we list only a few here. Thompson and McEwen[15] have explored the relationship between an organization's goals (or agenda or strategy) and its network. Burns and Stalker's[16] study of the organization–environment relationship was an important antecedent to Lawrence and Lorsch's work. A variety of economists and business policy experts have researched the strategy–domain relationship. Likewise, many organi-

[11]*Ibid.*, p. 71.
[12]March and Simon (1958).
[13]Keen and McKenney (1973).
[14]Perrow (1970).
[15]Thompson and McEwen (1958), pp. 23–31.
[16]Burns and Stalker (1961).

zational and social psychologists, especially Rensis Likert and his colleagues,[17] have explored the individual–social system relationship within an organizational context. Fred Fiedler[18] pioneered in the study of the relationship between leadership styles and their situations. Kotter[19] borrowed Argyris's, Levinson's,[20] and Schein's[21] concept of the psychological contract and has explored the relationship between an individual's expectations and those of his organization. Fouraker,[22] an economist, has studied the organization–environment relationship, drawing conclusions similar to those of Lawrence and Lorsch. In a study of 150 nonindustrial societies, Udy[23] has formed ideas about the relationship between technology and organization structure. In his now-famous communication studies, Hal Leavitt[24] focused on the organizational–task relationship. Finally, Vroom[25] has explored the relationships between "participative" management and the individual (personality variables).

PROCESS RESEARCH

The alignment research we have mentioned fits predominantly into the "structural" camp. During the past decade, a number of interesting new models that are basically process oriented have also been developed.

There appear to have been two promising trends in the development of process research. First, new forms of administrative process are being identified and modeled—as opposed to merely elaborating or changing previously defined forms. Second, there is a growing tendency to consider administrative processes as contingent phenomena. We examine these trends separately.

The men who first proposed modern administrative models a half-century ago—Fred Taylor, Luther Gulick, Lyndall Urwick, and their followers—tended to describe just *one* administrative pattern. This pattern more often than not ignored what we have called the

[17]Likert (1961).
[18]Fiedler (1967).
[19]Kotter (1973).
[20]Levinson et al. (1962).
[21]Schein (1965).
[22]Fouraker, unpublished manuscript.
[23]Udy (1959).
[24]Leavitt (1962).
[25]Vroom (1960).

agenda setting process, describing instead a very simple utilitarian network building process (money exchanged for labor) and something close to what we have called a bureaucratic task accomplishment process.

Beginning probably with Mayo and Roethlisberger, social scientists and administrative theorists began to identify, describe, and prescribe new administrative patterns. The so-called human relations theorists identified and prescribed something resembling what we have called a personal appeal network building process. Others, the "participative management theorists," described what we have called cooptive and purposive appeal network building processes. Researchers interested in project management and temporary task management produced models similar to our entrepreneurial task accomplishment process. Still others identified agenda setting as an important administrative process and described a form of it somewhat like our #4 process (rational deductive ideal).

In the past decade, researchers have continued to identify new forms of the basic administrative processes. One of the finest examples of this research is Joseph Bower's study of the resource allocation process.[26] Bower spent 2 years examining the strategic investment planning process in a giant corporation. He found that the current models of that process (rational, economic, and financial models) were not at all adequate for describing what he was observing. Instead, he noted a number of processes occurring at different levels of management and at different points in time. At crucial points he found managers sometimes making decisions for seemingly irrelevant, often "political" reasons.

Although the complex process Bower discovered seems at first to be irrational, the author shows that it is quite logical. He points out that unlike the assumptions made in the economic and financial models, the world in which that corporation had to operate was characterized by many uncertainties. Generating information was expensive and time-consuming. The knowledge necessary to process information was dispersed among specialists. Coordination of that knowledge was difficult, and costly in terms of money and time. However, this successful corporation had developed a somewhat odd looking, but apparently effective, means of dealing with these realities.

The second trend in process research is closely related to the first.

[26]Bower (1970).

Much of the so-called administrative process research between 1920 and 1950 was directed at better describing one "correct" administrative pattern. Not until the late 1960s did many people begin to consider seriously that different processes could *all* be appropriate or correct under different circumstances. Guided by the theoretical and empirical work of Lawrence and Lorsch (1967), in the last decade increasing numbers of administrative theorists have been accepting the notions of conditionality or contingency.[27] That is, many people are beginning to believe that there is no one best pattern of administration. Instead, the most appropriate set of processes from the administration point of view is contingent on various situational factors.

An interesting example of contingency process research is the work of Fred Fiedler, who identified two forms of the leadership process. Behavior associated with a "task-oriented" style focused on accomplishing a specific task, whereas "relationship-oriented" behavior focused on maintaining relationships with others. Based on an enormous amount of research, Fiedler concluded that these two forms of leadership led to higher group performance under different conditions. He identified three situational variables: (1) the simplicity or complexity of the task, (2) the prior positive or negative feelings between leader and group, and (3) the amount of traditional power at the disposal of the leader. When conditions were very favorable or very unfavorable for a leader (extreme values on all three situational variables), the task-oriented process worked best. When conditions were in between the extremes, the relationship-oriented process worked best.[28]

Overall, then, these two process research trends seem to be aimed in a direction that is quite consistent with out coalignment model. Like the coalignment model itself, such trends are indicating that there are a number of different forms of administrative process and that from the administrator's point of view, the appropriateness of any form is contingent on the situation in which the administrator finds himself.

IMPLICATIONS FOR FUTURE RESEARCH

The coalignment model suggests a number of interesting courses for

[27]See Kast and Rosenzweig (1973).
[28]Fieldler (1967).

future research on administration, and we conclude our discussion of this model by examining a few of its implications.

First, a coalignment theory suggests that the debate now surfacing in the professional literature over whose alignment theory is correct, is a waste of time and resources. A coalignment theory says that there is certainly more than one key alignment that is relevant to administration—perhaps there are many. Although debates over which variables and relationships are more useful or important than others can be profitable, arguments about which two variables and one relationship (technology–organization, strategy–structure, organization–environment) hold *the* answer are not very useful.

Second, our coalignment model suggests that process researchers might profitably attempt to identify new forms of administrative processes and to clarify the conditions under which these and other forms emerge or work well. It seems to us that this route could be much more enlightening than a path that uses resources to make one process 5% clearer or to "prove" that another process is always the best.

Third, the model suggests the network concept is at least one useful focus for structural researchers. Of all the contextual variables discussed in this chapter and elsewhere in the book, the one that has had the least attention from alignment theorists is the "network." Indeed, interorganizational phenomena have received little attention outside of economics, most of it in the past decade.[29]

[29]Economic models can be useful, but they are clearly limited for our purposes. The more interesting noneconomic efforts to date include:
Aldrich (1971).
Assael (1969).
Clark (1968).
Emery and Trist (1965).
Evan (1966).
Guetzkow (1966).
Heskett, Stern, and Beier (1970).
Kotter and Allen (1971).
Levine and White (1961).
Litwak and Hylton (1962).
Ridgeway (1957).
Selznick (1949).
Terreberry (1968).
Thompson and McEwen (1958).

The questions network researchers ask should include:

- What different types of networks can public and private organizations have?
- What is the relationship between different types of networks and organizational strategy?
- Between different types of networks and different organizational forms?
- Between different types of networks and different task environments?
- What processes do organizations use to build and maintain networks?

Finally, in pursuing this research, the methodology we were not able to fully develop here may be of significant use. The pattern recognition idea still seems valid to us. Since we are trying to identify large, complex social patterns, instead of exploring them piecemeal, we can capitalize on the pattern recognition capacity which some individuals clearly have. In general, such a methodology would be utilized by way of the following steps:

1. Identify people who have complex pattern recognition capabilities, a history of "seeing" the phenomenon in question, and a willingness to cooperate.
2. Work with a subgroup of these people clinically, to identify the range of patterns in question.
3. Develop brief descriptions of the patterns.
4. For each situation of interest, allow a different subgroup to examine the pattern statements and identify the one that was descriptive of that situation.

Certain inherent problems notwithstanding, it seems to us that this procedure could be very useful.

Turk (1970).
Warren (1967).
Litwak and Meyer (1966).

CHAPTER 14

IMPLICATIONS FOR MAYORS

A number of findings from this research have practical relevance to mayors. Seven implications seem to be particularly important, yet none is currently an accepted part of "conventional wisdom."

> ***Lesson #1.*** There are *at least* five approaches to the mayor's job. We have called these types the Ceremonial mayor, the Caretaker, the Executive, the Personality/Individualist, and the Program Entrepreneur.

A detailed description of the five types of mayor we have identified appears in Chapter 7. The Ceremonial mayor's behavior is the least complex. He attends council meetings regularly and ceremonial activities on request. He maintains a network of friendships in his city. The Caretaker mayor assumes a much larger role, primarily geared for maintenance, not change or innovation. He achieves a reasonably powerful position for himself and spends much time "politicking." The Executive mayor's role is even larger; it includes some "projects," and the Executive is considerably more proactive than the Ceremonial or the Caretaker mayor. The Personality/Individualist is also somewhat proactive and usually has some "projects." Unlike the Executive, however, he takes on a much smaller role that includes much less managing (he does things himself) and politicking. Finally, the Program Entrepreneur has the largest role of all and generates the most power, using a variety of appeals. He tends to establish an overall "program" for his administration and relies heavily on an entrepreneurial "hustling" approach to accomplish many tasks.

It was surprising (to us) how many of our respondents explicitly or implicitly believed that there is only one type of mayor, or perhaps two. A number of the mayors in the study began their tenure knowing only "one way" to be a mayor. If their background was political, the "one way" conformed to the tutoring they had received from older politicians. If their background was commercial, the "one way" was that which had worked for them as businessmen. Not more than one or two of the mayors in the study had any sense of the range of possible approaches to the job.

Having a sense of the alternative ways a mayor can approach his job can be a lifesaver to an urban officeholder. Several mayors in this study experienced serious difficulty because they knew of only one approach to their job, and unfortunately that approach worked poorly under the circumstances. We found the following pattern in a number of cases. A young man works for or with a very successful mayor. After years of apprenticeship he "absorbs" the mayor's style and approach and learns to use it effectively. Eventually he himself is elected mayor, and he uses the only approach to the job he knows. Unfortunately, in the 10- to 20-year period since his successful tutor was mayor, a great deal has changed. The city is facing very different problems. The city's population is significantly different. The country and its mood have changed. What had worked well 20 years ago produces poor results today. The mayor recognizes that something is wrong, but he never seriously considers altering his overall approach to the job because he does not understand the alternatives (or recognize that there are alternatives). He desperately tries the remedies that happen to be a part of his familiar approach. They sometimes produce short-run relief, but eventually a crisis occurs, and the protege-type mayor is defeated at the next election.

The lessons here for a mayor require little elaboration. First, there are a number of basic approaches to the job. Second, it is clearly in the mayor's best interest to understand what these approaches are and how he might use them.

> ***Lesson #2.*** The notion that one approach to the mayor's job is best (given any definition of "best") is a

> fallacy. The same approach, under different conditions, can lead to very different results.

Many of the people we interviewed believed that there must be one best way to be mayor, regardless of the circumstances. "It is essential that a mayor always build a strong positive link to his city's business community," said one person. "If the mayor is not willing to put in a 70-hour week, there is no way that he's going to be successful," said another. The data from the study do not support such statements.

A number of our mayors approached their jobs in almost identical fashion, only to find themselves in very different situations, with very different results after 2 or 4 or 6 years. Differences between cities, their populations, the issues of importance, and the mayors themselves all interact with similar approaches to produce different results.

Both Tom McCann (Fort Worth) and Walton Bachrach (Cincinnati), for example, adopted the job approach we have called Ceremonial. Bachrach eventually retired, undefeated. Even today his tenure is regarded as a "good time for the city" by most people in Cincinnati, and Bachrach is still popular. McCann, on the other hand, was voted out of office by his city council. When the city charter was changed to allow direct popular election of the mayor, he ran again but was soundly defeated. Most Fort Worth residents look back on his tenure and on McCann himself with either bad or neutral feelings. Both mayors had a limited impact on their cities (a characteristic of the Ceremonial approach) but, by almost all standards, Bachrach's impact was more positive.

It is not difficult to understand this case or others like it. The situations these two men faced were similar in many ways (e.g., the towns were about the same size and age, and the two men had somewhat similar personalities and backgrounds). But they were also different along some important dimensions. Bachrach was blessed with a very competent city manager and city bureaucracy, a reasonably prosperous city economy, and a good relationship with a fairly well-organized and powerful business community. McCann faced a shifting and somewhat unorganized power structure, a period of economic downturn, and a very weak city bureaucracy. Under these rather unfavorable conditions in Fort Worth, the minimal Ceremonial approach was simply unworkable.

Similarly, the Executive approach worked much better for William

Cowger (Louisville) than it did for Tom Whelan (Jersey City). The Personality/Individualist approach served Roy Martin (Norfolk) much better than Roe Bartle (Kansas City). The Caretaker approach worked better for Victor Schiro (New Orleans) than for Ralph Locher (Cleveland), although both mayors had some difficulties. The Program Entrepreneur approach worked better for Ivan Allen (Atlanta) than for Erik Jonsson (Dallas), even though both administrations were relatively "successful."

The lesson for mayors is again a simple but important one. Just as it is wrong to think that there is only one approach to the mayor's job, it is also a mistake to think that only one approach works or is best. Circumstances can change and situations can differ. What worked for one mayor may well be disastrous for another.

> ***Lesson #3.*** A mayor engages in three key processes daily: deciding what tasks to undertake (agenda setting), establishing and maintaining a network of cooperative relationships (network building), and undertaking tasks (task accomplishment). There are a variety of ways of performing or behaving in each process. As we would expect from lesson #2, the same approach to any one of these processes, used under different conditions, can lead to very different results. This finding contradicts *all* schools of politics, management, and planning according to which there is one "best" way to perform these processes regardless of the conditions.

In our field work we found a variety of agenda setting processes being used by the mayors (see Chapter 4 for details). These processes could be described as points along a continuum. At one extreme, agenda setting is reactive, short-run oriented, part oriented, continuous, and disjointed ("muddling through"). At the other extreme it is proactive, long-run oriented, holistic, periodic, and logically interconnected ("rational planning"). Approximately eight of the mayors in this study exhibited an agenda setting pattern in the first part of the continuum (#1, near the "muddling through" end), nine in the second, three in the third, and none in the fourth (#4, near the "rational planning" end).

The mayors in this study used nine distinctly different processes to establish cooperative relationships with the groups and organizations (network members) that possessed valued resources (see Chapter 5). These include a process of discrete exchange (I give you, you give me), a coercive process (you give me, or else), two purposive appeal processes (for a superordinate goal or against something), a cooptive process (absorbing elements of a group into a mayor's policy-forming effort), a reference group appeal process, a friendship appeal process, a charismatic appeal process, and an appeal to formal/legal authority.

Mayors not only used each of these processes in different proportions, they actively tried to alter the members of their network in various degrees. Some worked within the status quo; others aggressively tried to alter the makeup and structure of the city bureaucracy, their party, or the city council, to make the job of establishing solid ties to resources easier or more feasible. Some mayors gathered important resources close to them in a "mayor's office," but most did not.

The mayors in this study also relied on three distinctly different processes to achieve specific tasks (see Chapter 6). We identified a bureaucratic management process, which is characteristic of the behavior of an executive in a formal organization; an entrepreneurial process, which is similar to hustling; and an individualistic process, which is simply the behavior of one who needs only his personal resources to work on a task. The mayors in this study relied on the bureaucratic and individualistic processes the most.

Again and again we encountered the belief that some of the ways of behaving in these processes are "right" and some are "wrong." People argue that the best way to build support is with personal appeals. Others say that the best way is to play power broker—investing your favors, patronage, and money wisely. Planners insist that long-range plans are an essential part of agenda setting. According to others, one needs to be flexible and responsive, and plans get in the way. Businessmen often argue that the only way to accomplish tasks is with a well-organized executive approach—delegation, communication, control, evaluation. Others say that a mayor lacks the authority or control to act that way; thus he is obliged to rely on himself or his powers of persuasion.

The important lesson here is that the data from this study do not support any "best way" ideas. The critical point is the mayor's full understanding of the context in which he is operating. The same methods under different conditions can lead to very different results.

> ***Lesson #4.*** If a mayor ignores any of the three key processes, he may find himself facing numerous sources of annoyance. That is, the mayor who focuses almost exclusively on "politics" or "policy" or "execution" will probably create some severe problems.

Several of the mayors in this study tended to focus on one of the three key processes to the exclusion of the others. A person with a political background often concentrated on network building. A business background seemed to lead to high priorities for task accomplishment. A mayor with an "urban expert" background (professor, former staffer) focused on agenda setting. As a result of such narrowness of focus, many mayors made injudicious decisions relating to the other processes (e.g., ignoring situational constraints and trying to make a program work without the proper resources). Since all three processes are highly interdependent, these mistakes eventually produced problems elsewhere, which came to the mayor's attention in magnified form.

One mayor in this study was so concerned with the task accomplishment process that he established a poor process of selecting "what to do" (agenda setting). He did get a good deal done, but he accumulated a great deal of criticism about what he had accomplished ("what an ugly building"). Another mayor concentrated so hard on building and maintaining his power (network building) that he failed to accomplish anything that required more than momentum from the past. Again, this eventually brought more and more critics ("my God, he's been in office 2 years and he hasn't done anything"), along with a few unnecessary crises. Still another mayor focused so heavily on making policy decisions to guide his administration that he was almost defeated after his first 2-year term, even though most people who knew of his decisions approved. He made little effort to maintain the relationships that originally had helped secure his election. This oversight almost took away his chance to make sure his policy decisions were implemented.

The lesson here is simple, but the trap is also very seductive—especially when a mayor's prior successes naturally lead him to focus primarily on only one key process.

> ***Lesson #5.*** A carefully selected staff or circle of advisors can go a long way in making up for a mayor's

weaknesses in creating effective agenda setting, network building, and task accomplishment processes.

As a city grows in size, and as the magnitude of the mayor's role increases, it becomes even more difficult for the incumbent to "go it alone." As a result, staff and other close help become particularly important. Whenever a job demands more time than there are hours in the day, a staff is needed to act as extensions of the person in charge—to make his reach broader, longer, words louder, his day larger. However, in situations that are also complex and difficult, a staff can serve another more important function. Staff members can provide skills that the mayor does not have. Instead of merely extending him, they can help compensate for his weaknesses and give him wider and more flexible skills.

The case related in Chapter 9 is most instructive here. Ivan Allen (Atlanta) relied on two key staff personnel plus a number of informal advisors (shadow staff). His shadow staff of bright young men, along with one or two old political professionals, were invaluable aids in agenda setting. His two staff members gave the mayor one or two key "connections" that Allen himself did not have. One provided and maintained (network building), then used (task accomplishment), a relationship with the city bureaucracy and the county government. The other did the same with the federal government and part of the black community. Between Allen and his staff, all three key processes were handled very competently.

As anyone who has been mayor for a period of time probably recognizes, some problems and risks are associated with using staff as Allen did. A mayor almost never has as much control over the situation as he would like, and the uncertainty can make life very unpleasant for him. Thus it is *very* tempting to select a staff based primarily on loyalty, not skills, thereby removing at least one source of uncertainty. This rule is written in capital letters in most political bibles.

We are not suggesting that a staff that is not completely controllable cannot be a problem. Instead, our lesson relates to risk. As any good gambler knows, if you take only a small risk, the best you can get is a small return. If you take a larger risk, you have a chance at a much bigger return. Our data suggest that a staff that complements and adds to a mayor with respect to the three key processes can produce a very large return, indeed. The mayors in this study who took the risk and won (none really lost) received considerable benefit.

> ***Lesson #6.*** Some mayors in this study were reelected by wide margins, were (and still are) praised by many people, retired undefeated, and now, by most standards, appear to have had a positive impact on their cities; that is, they were "conspicuously successful." The key explanatory factor for the conspicuous success of some mayors, but not the majority, seems to be success at coalignment.

Like a skilled juggler, a conspicuously successful mayor kept a number of key elements in his situation properly aligned, or compatible. He managed to maintain a certain fit among them.

In some ways this is the most important lesson of all, as well as the most subtle. Its full presentation (in Chapters 8, 9, and 10) cannot be paraphrased here; nor can we restate the complicated dynamics behind our findings. Instead we focus almost entirely on the implications of this material for the best interests of a mayor and his staff.

First, a mayor must make sure that he thoroughly understands the current state of four key elements in his situation. He needs to ask himself:

- What is the nature of my current relationships with my network—the people, population groups, and organizations with which I must interact? Which are good, which are bad, and on what are the relationships based?
- What problems and opportunities face my city? Is any matter at or nearing the crisis point? Which of these fits within the area I have defined as my domain?
- What does my agenda look like these days? Explicitly or implicitly, what plans or actions or goals have I committed myself to tomorrow, next week, next year?
- Finally, what are my own current assets and liabilities? What are my skills and my limitations? What needs and aspirations do I have and how strong are they?

Any mayor will be able to answer parts of each of these questions immediately. However, it has been our experience that many mayors are hard put to answer one or two of the questions well. Often the mayor who has been in politics all his life can give an extraordinarily precise picture of his network, but he finds it much more difficult to describe his city's problems and opportunities. Sometimes the executive-turned-mayor can describe his agenda in great detail, but not his network. Many mayors, especially those who have never held a post of major responsibility before, have difficulty in accurately describing their own assets, liabilities, and needs.

Having carefully identified the current state of these four elements, the mayor must look next for incompatiblities (nonalignments) among them. He needs to ask himself:

- Are the resources that are accessible to me in my network of the right kind and amount to pursue the tasks on my agenda?
- Is the amount of future planning I have in my agenda in line with the feasibility and payoff of planning in my domain? Am I planning too little or too much?
- Are my own thinking and perceptive abilities adequate to the task of sensing and understanding the major events in my domain? In the city as a whole? Does my orientation to the world leave me with blind spots that make it difficult for me to understand or sense conditions of certain types?
- Are the implementation resources in my network appropriately organized and structured, given the nature of my domain?
- Do I have the interpersonal ability to handle all the "languages" spoken in my city? How good am I at speaking the language of the most powerful groups?
- Finally, do I have the cognitive and interpersonal skills that my agenda either explicitly or implicitly demands? Can I really accomplish the tasks I have defined?

Data from this study suggest strongly that unless a mayor is able to reconcile any large incompatibilities that appear in the answers to these questions, he will eventually encounter serious difficulties. A large nonalignment sooner or later leads to a crisis situation for the mayor and is almost always responsible for his defeat in the next election. No less than 8 of the 20 mayors in this study suffered these consequences.

The lesson here is a powerful one. If the mayor cannot create a minimum alignment among all four key elements, he had better be prepared for a terribly difficult and painful situation.

> ***Lesson #7.*** As mayor, one should be prepared for the possibility of many disappointments and no higher political position afterward.

Overall, the 20 mayors in this study found their jobs to be rewarding but often difficult, unpleasant, and even dangerous. Until one becomes mayor, it is probably impossible to realize what are the high points and the low points associated with that role. Without experiencing them, it is very difficult to appreciate their intensity.

Many of the mayors in this study found the period after they retired from the mayor's role to be much more unpleasant than they had expected. We devote the final chapter to a discussion of this issue and its implications.

CHAPTER 15

THE FUTURE: SOME DISTURBING TRENDS

AN ODE TO FORMER MAYORS

We have said almost nothing about what happened to the mayors in this study after they left office, yet their postmayoral histories are quite interesting.

Not surprisingly, most of our subjects had political ambitions beyond the mayor's office. At least 17 wanted to move on to the senate, the governor's mansion, or a cabinet post. One seriously planned to run for President. In general the men were very energetic and ambitious and wanted these positions dearly, *but not one achieved his postmayoral objective!*

In most cases, our former mayors did not lose elections to higher offices, they lost the fight for nomination. Many even failed to get into the nomination ring. They were just ignored. To the almost unbelievable frustration of some of the men in this study, the mayoralty turned out to be a "dead-end" job. No matter where they wanted to go, it was impossible to get there from the mayor's office.

Two of our subjects are dead today. Both died relatively young—one following an unsuccessful bid for senatorial nomination, the second shortly after indictments were brought against him. At least six of the others are not in good health, and their friends claim that they aged very quickly while they held office. At least three of the former mayors had their lives seriously threatened while in office. Two are in jail today, serving sentences for diverting and stealing public funds.

With a few exceptions, the mayors in this study made significant financial sacrifices. The difference between a mayor's salary (in the 1960's) and that of a good lawyer or businessman is considerable.

Most subjects seem to have some bitter feelings about their time as mayor. Sometimes these are subtle, but quite visible. The attitude is expressed as follows: "I made some very real sacrifices as mayor. I worked hard and, under the circumstances, did well. Instead of praise and respect, I'm often criticized and ignored. It's not fair."

Obvious difficulties in passing judgment notwithstanding, it appears from our interviews that only three of our former mayors are happy with who they are and what they are doing today. Some are still looking for that opportunity to serve again. Some are bitter, some are cynical and angry, others are just tired. Overall, the postmayoral histories are quite depressing.

These results raise a number of interesting questions. Is this the normal plight of mayors? Are there some trends in the data that suggest disturbing implications for the future of mayors and cities? Can a leadership role with the drawbacks we have noted attract enough talented people in the long run? We explore these questions and others in this final chapter.

HISTORICAL TRENDS

The mayor's role, at least in this century, has never been an established part of any clear-cut and viable career path in the American social system. To be mayor, a nonpolitician must abandon his career or take a "leave of absence." Politicians have found that the mayor's role does not fit well into state or national political careers. State legislator–mayor–governor or congressman–mayor–senator career paths seem to be very rare. Only one of our Presidents to date has been a mayor. In a study of the period immediately preceding this study (1940–1960), it was found that about 10% of the mayors were subsequently elected to a higher office.[1] A reader of that article, published in 1963, probably would not have thought that the situation could worsen. Possibly it

[1] Gittell (1963).

has, however. In this study, 0% of our mayors were subsequently elected *or* appointed to a higher office.

The prestige of the mayor's role has at times been quite high in this century. In a poll conducted in 1947, out of 90 different jobs, people listed the mayoralty (of a large city) as sixth highest in prestige.[2] When the same poll was taken again in 1963, the mayor's role ranked eighteenth.[3] In a more broadly defined opinion poll reported in 1972, people ranked "politicians" nineteenth in a field of 20 professions with regard to prestige.[4] In the last three decades, it appears that the prestige associated with the mayor's job has been dropping.

The difficulty of the mayor's role seems to have increased since the beginning of this century. The average mayor of a large city has to deal with a significantly larger city than he did 50, 40, or even 10 years ago. The expectations of our urban population with regard to "adequate" performance have gone up too, especially during the 1960s. The promises of advanced technology, increasing affluence, and the Great Society have all fueled this trend.

Finally, there seems to be a downswing in the financial rewards of the mayoralty. In 1940 a typical mayor of a large city made $10,000, or about 13 times the current United States per capita income. By 1973 the mayor's income was $27,000, but this figure is only 5 times the 1973 per capita income. Although a mayor's income has gone up, it has not increased proportional to the growth of an average person's income. Relatively speaking, a mayor receives less financial reward today than 50 years ago.

Although we have little data to back our conclusions, it seems that the trends just mentioned have made the mayor's job a less appealing one over the past half-century. This conclusion is also supported by the limited anecdotal literature on early twentieth-century mayors. The depressing picture outlined at the beginning of this chapter is not found in that literature.

IMPLICATIONS FOR THE FUTURE

It seems reasonable to assume that clear-cut career paths, prestige, job

[2]Hodge, Siegel, and Rossi, Eds. (1966).
[3]*Ibid.*
[4]Undated personal document.

difficulty, and financial rewards would all affect the attractiveness of the mayor's role and, subsequently, the number of people who would seek it. It also seems reasonable to assume that this effect would have some time delay in it; that is, if the current negative information about the mayor's role discourages young people from directing their careers toward this role, the consequences will not become evident until sometime in the future. So if one believes that increased competition for a job increases the quality of the people who eventually serve in it, then unless some trends change, we may end up with some fairly low-quality mayors in our cities in the future.

This somewhat bleak prospect looks even worse if one also extrapolates current trends affecting our cities and their populations. Over the past twenty years, racial tensions, physical decay, relative erosion of the property tax base, the flight to the suburbs, and the attendant economic downturns have all enormously complicated the problems of governance in large cities. The major federal programs which were designed to deal with these matters—federal housing projects, urban renewal, model cities, OEO projects—appear to have left many city dwellers cynical and alienated from government at all levels. These aspects of the urban scene have been well documented.

How can we expect these various factors to play themselves out if we insert them into the model that we have been developing throughout this volume? In terms of our model, general apathy and cynicism among the population will seriously weaken the network that any mayor could create. Gaining cooperation from alienated people is extremely difficult for even the most capable politician. If at the same time the quality of mayors continues to decrease, then it is likely that most of them will wind up with very weak networks.

If concurrently the problems of our cities continue to increase in scope, then there will be virtually no possible agendas that a mayor could develop which could achieve an alignment with both his network and his city. An ambitious agenda created by a #3 or #4 agenda setting process in a large domain will be completely out of alignment with a weak network. A modest agenda created by a #1 agenda setting process in a small domain will create a large nonalignment with a problem-filled city.

As a result, our model would predict that Caretaker mayors will be damned as "do-nothing." At the other extreme, Program Entrepreneurs will discover that they cannot muster the resources to complete their projects and achieve their goals. In between, other types of mayors will suffer both problems to some degree. Irate and disappointed constituencies will continue to vote incumbents out. It would be rare for a mayor to survive more than one term in office.

Such a turnover of mayors can only make the job even less attractive. Constantly nonaligned systems will aggravate rather than reduce urban ills. In other words, the situation could continue to make itself even worse.

> *Unless subsequent events change or alter these trends, our model predicts an urban crisis of unparalleled size and scope.*

POSITIVE SIGNS

Any number of events could change the foregoing trends, and it is hoped that they will. A few, presently weak influences already beginning to go to work could in time counteract this grim picture. Current disillusionment with the effectiveness of federal intervention is often drawing public attention back to more direct citizen involvement at the local level. Proposals are being circulated and sometimes seriously considered for structural reforms that go well beyond the limited number of charter options available to our cities in the 1960s (strong or weak mayor or city manager).[5] Such structural changes, however, can be made no faster than the growth of an underlying base of educated public support. Even in this all-important aspect, some stirring is occurring. Young people in particular are becoming more sensitive to the potential for action at the local government level. And as citizens of all ages become active and concerned, they are, in effect, dropping the role of passive resident for that of a potential resource in a mayoral network. One of the encouraging consequences of the federal urban programs of the 1960s is the development of a cadre of neighborhood leaders with political know-how and motivation for action. New gifted urban leadership might emerge fairly quickly from these ranks. Many of these leaders will probably be black. Perhaps fresh leadership can draw the latent interest of citizens into a stronger network with an ideology that

[5]Committee for Economic Development (1970).

emphasizes community values. Such a network and such leadership could then evolve an agenda more in alignment with the true needs of the city.

Jane Jacobs has written that throughout man's civilized history his major cities have always tottered on the brink of chaos and collapse, but, at the same time, these cities have consistently been the birthplace of each new step forward in the evolution of our civilization. As we approach the end of the twentieth century, this dual hazard and promise acutely characterize our urban scene. Neither benign neglect nor expensive panaceas will change the disturbing trends we have identified. Our best hope for the future lies in realistically confronting, examining, and accepting (not denying) the true situation in our cities. Only then will we recognize the great gap between the present urban conditions and the requirements of wise governance. Only by this process can we spark the public concern and the fresh leadership that is required for our cities' continuing renewal.

APPENDIX A

EXHIBIT I INTERVIEW WITH MAYOR

(Phase I Interview Guide)

I. Introduction and small talk.

II. We'd like to begin by getting some idea as to how you saw ________(city) when you took office in ________ (year).

(a) What were the various population groups in the city?

- Where did they live?
- Approximately how big were each?
- What were they like? (Probe for value differences.)
- Did this change during your tenure?
- Why?

(b) What was the quality and quantity of community leadership? (For each of the groups listed below ask the following questions.)

- How well organized was the group?
- Who were its leaders?
- How good were they?
- How did this change?

Business
Labor

Education
Religion
Press
City bureaucracy
Minority groups
Health and medical organizations
Political parties
Charity organizations

(c) How much power did the city charter officially give you? Has this changed? What was the makeup of the city council when you took office (friendly, unfriendly)? Change? How strong were the two political parties? Change?

(d) I have some figures here that I'd like you to help me interpret . . . (ask him questions about the financial and economic data that have been compiled).

III. We'd now like to get some feeling for how you approached your job.

(a) Did you have any particular thing in mind that you wanted to do? (Probe for goals; if he gives more than one, get him to assign priorities to them.)

(b) How did you plan on getting these things done? (Probe for plans, reasons behind them.)

(c) How did you decide to focus on these areas (goals)? How did you create the plans (if he had any)?

(d) How did this change over time?

(e) In retrospect, do you think that your goals were the right ones to pursue?

IV. We'd now like to get a picture of your daily operations as mayor.

(a) How many people did you have on your staff?

- What were their names?
- What did each do?

- How did this change over time?

(b) What did you do? What was a typical day like?

V. We'd like now to get some feeling for the relationship between the mayor's office and the primary groups in the city.

(a) Did you have any special relationship with each of the groups below? How did this develop or change? (Probe to make sure that if there was, you have the following elements of the relationship— who in the mayor's office was connected to whom and why and where this other person fit into his own organization.)

- Business
- Labor
- City bureaucracy
- State government
- Federal government
- Education
- Medical and health organizations
- Religion
- Minority groups
- Charities
- Political parties
- Press

(b) Could you give us an example or two of a successful or an unsuccessful project in which you or your office worked with a number of those groups?

VI. We'd like to get some feeling briefly for how you thought about your job.

(a) If someone who didn't know what a "mayor" was asked you what was your job, how would you reply?

(b) Did you ever think of yourself in any of these ways?

- Administration head
- Legislator
- Fund raiser
- Leader of the people

- Project coordinator
- Power broker

(c) Where did you actually spend your time, on the average? That is, what percentage of your time was spent in these tasks? Where else was it spent?

VII. We'd like to know a little bit about your own background.

(a) Can you briefly outline your own life history?

(b) • Where, or in what place, groups, or organizations would you say that you had close friends or contacts when you took office?
- Why did you want to be mayor?
- What were your personal goals in ________(year)?
- Who supported you when you ran for office?
- Why were you elected?
- Did you ever consider holding another office?

VIII. Finally, we just have some general questions about urban problems that we'd like your opinion on.

(a) From a mayor's point of view, what does it take to move a city ahead?

(b) Why do mayors have problems?

(c) What enables a mayor to do something important to help a city?

EXHIBIT II INTERVIEW GUIDE, STAFF

(Phase I Interview Guide)

I. Introduction and small talk.

II. We'd like to begin by getting some information about ______________(city) in ________(year) when ________ ________(mayor) took office (go over these questions fairly quickly with an eye toward validating what the mayor said).

(a) What were the various population groups in the city?

- Where did they live?
- Approximately how big were each?
- What were they like? (Probe for value differences.)
- Did this change during the mayor's tenure?
- Why?

(b) What was the quality and quantity of community leadership? (For each of the groups listed below ask the following questions.)

- How well organized was the group?
- Who were its leaders?
- How good were they?
- How did this change?

Business
Labor
Education
Religion
Press
City bureaucracy
Minority groups
Health and medical organizations
Political parties
Charity organizations

(c) How much power did the city charter officially give the mayor? Has this changed? What was the makeup of the city council when he took office? (friendly or not) Change? How strong were the two political parties? Change?

(d) I have some figures here that I would like you to help me interpret (ask him questions about the financial and economic data that have been compiled).

III. Now we'd like to ask you some questions about the mayor's office.

- How many people were on his staff?

- What were their names?
- What did they do?
- Who did each person report to?
- Who did each person work or interact with frequently?
- Who on the staff were close friends?
- How much time did each spend with the mayor?

IV. We'd like to get a feeling now for how the mayor approached his job.

(a) What did the mayor want to do when he was elected? Did he have an explicit set of goals, plans, or strategies? (Start with this, let him take off, and then probe for the following.)

- How explicit was the strategy?
- What were the goals?
- What was the order of the goals?
- What was the plan to accomplish each?
- How did he create this plan?
- How did this change over time?

(b) In retrospect, do you think his goals were the right ones to meet the city's needs?

V. Now we'd like to get some information about the mayor, his background, and what he did as mayor.

(a)
- Before coming into office, where were the mayor's contacts and friends and how extensive were they?
- How wealthy was he when he was elected?
- Did he have any trouble raising campaign money?
- Approximately how much did he spend on his campaign?
- Who supported him?
- Why do you think he was elected?
- Why did he want to be mayor?
- What were his personal goals?
- Did he ever want to hold other offices?

(b) There are two predominant leadership styles that people use which we call task oriented or social oriented. (Explain each.) While he was working in the following settings, on the average, which style did he use? (Allow staff person to pick on a continuum between the two.)

Mayor's office
City bureaucracy
People at large
City council
Business
Labor
State government
Federal government
Education
Medical and health organizations
Religion
Minority groups
Charities
Press
Political parties

- How friendly or unfriendly was each of these settings? That is, how easy or difficult was it (for the mayor) to work with them?
- From your experience—try to be as objective as possible but fair—what were the mayor's real strengths and weaknesses?

(c) How did the mayor think about his job? Did he see himself as an administrative head, legislator, fund raiser, leader of the people, project coordinator, or power broker?

- Where did he actually spend his time on the average? (Get percentage for each role and for other areas that don't fit into the above list.)

VI. (a) What does it take for an administration to really help a city?

(b) If you were mayor now, what would you do?

EXHIBIT III INTERVIEW GUIDE, SUBSYSTEM PERSON

(Phase I Interview Guide)

I. Introduction and small talk.

II. We'd like to know a little bit about _______________(his subsystem).

(a)
- How well organized is it? Change?
- Are there subgroups?
- Who are the leaders of the subgroups? Change?
- What is this group like (orientation)? How is it different from other groups?
- What was _______________(subsystem's) relationship to the mayor's office? (Probe to establish who, to whom, and why.)
- Did you have any particularly important relationships with any other major group?

(b) Can you give us an example or two of successful or unsuccessful interactions you've had, or projects you've been involved in, with the mayor's office?

III. What did the mayor want to do when he was elected? Did he have a strategy, a set of goals, or plans? (From this start probe to find the following.)

- How explicit was the strategy?
- What were the goals?
- What was the order of the goals?
- What was his plan to accomplish each?
- How did he create the plan?
- How did this change over time?

(a) What were the city's short-run (long-run) needs and problems in _________(year)?

(b) Do you think that the mayor's goals were good ones in light of these needs?

IV. We'd like now to get some feeling for your impression of the mayor. (Go over the section fairly quickly, with an eye toward validation.)

(a) What was he like in his approach to the job and as a person?

- When working with the mayor was his orientation basically a task or social one? (Explain.)
- Frankly, from your experience, what were the mayor's basic strengths and weaknesses?

(b) Before coming into office, where were the mayor's contacts and friends and how extensive were these?

- How wealthy was he when he was elected?
- Did he have any trouble raising campaign money?
- Approximately how much did he spend on his campaign?
- Who supported him?
- Why was he elected?
- Why did he want to be mayor?
- What were his personal goals?
- Did he ever want to hold other offices?

V. Very briefly, we'd like to see if our picture of what the city was like at the beginning of and during his tenure is correct.

(a) Go over the responses that you have already.

(b) See if he agrees.

(c) Do it quickly.

VI. What do you think differentiates those administrations that are helpful to a city from those that aren't?

EXHIBIT IV "EXPERTS'" INQUIRY SHEET

Instructions: Please put each mayor's administration on the list in one of four categories (check). The categories are:

Category 1. During this administration many of the city's short-run problems were solved and the health of the city was improved. The outlook for the future was more optimistic at the end of the administration.

Category 2. This category is reserved for all cities and administrations that fall between categories 1 and 3.

Category 3. During this administration the situation in the city remained the same or got worse. The short-run problems were not solved and the city's health has declined. The outlook for the future was bad or worse at the end.

Don't Know: This category is reserved for those situations in which one does not have enough information to make a judgment.

Special note: We have included only mayors with tenures of 4 years or more, and we occasionally may have missed someone important. If you feel that some other mayor who served in the 1960s fits into categories 1 or 3, please write in his name.

___

City	Predominant Mayor in the 1960s	Category 1	2	3	D.K.
Akron, Ohio	Edward Erickson	___	___	___	___
Atlanta, Georgia	Ivan Allen, Jr.	___	___	___	___
Baltimore, Maryland	J. Harold Grady	___	___	___	___
	Theodore McKeldin	___	___	___	___
Birmingham, Alabama	Albert Boutwell	___	___	___	___
Boston, Massachusetts	John Collins	___	___	___	___
Buffalo, New York	Chester Kowal	___	___	___	___
Cincinnati, Ohio	Walton H. Bachrach	___	___	___	___
Cleveland, Ohio	Ralph Locher	___	___	___	___
Columbus, Ohio	W. Ralston Westlake	___	___	___	___
Dallas, Texas	Erik Jonsson	___	___	___	___
Dayton, Ohio	R. William Patterson	___	___	___	___
Denver, Colorado	Thomas G. Currigan	___	___	___	___
Detroit, Michigan	Jerome P. Cavanagh	___	___	___	___
Fort Worth, Texas	Thomas A. McCann	___	___	___	___
El Paso, Texas	Judson F. Williams	___	___	___	___
Honolulu, Hawaii	Neil S. Blaisdell	___	___	___	___
Houston, Texas	Louis Welch	___	___	___	___
Indianapolis, Indiana	Charles H. Boswell	___	___	___	___
Jersey City, New Jersey	Thomas J. Whelan	___	___	___	___
Kansas City, Missouri	H. Roe Bartle	___	___	___	___

City	Predominant Mayor in the 1960s	Category 1	2	3	D.K.
Long Beach, California	Edwin W. Wade	____	____	____	____
Louisville, Kentucky	William O. Cowger	____	____	____	____
Memphis, Tennessee	William B. Ingram, Jr.	____	____	____	____
Milwaukee, Wisconsin	Henry W. Maier	____	____	____	____
Minneapolis, Minnesota	Arthur Naftalin	____	____	____	____
New Haven, Connecticut	Richard Lee	____	____	____	____
New Orleans, Louisiana	Victor H. Schiro	____	____	____	____
Newark, New Jersey	Hugh Addonizio	____	____	____	____
Norfolk, Virginia	Roy B. Martin, Jr.	____	____	____	____
Oakland, California	John C. Houlihan	____	____	____	____
Oklahoma City, Oklahoma	James Norick	____	____	____	____
Omaha, Nebraska	J. Rosenblatt	____	____	____	____
	James Dworak	____	____	____	____
	A. V. Sorenson	____	____	____	____
Phoenix, Arizona	Milton Graham	____	____	____	____
Pittsburgh, Pennsylvania	Joseph Barr	____	____	____	____
Portland, Oregon	Terry D. Schrunk	____	____	____	____
Rochester, New York	Peter Barry	____	____	____	____
	Frank T. Lamb	____	____	____	____
St. Louis, Missouri	Raymond R. Tucker	____	____	____	____
St. Paul, Minnesota	George J. Vavoulis	____	____	____	____
San Antonio, Texas	Walter W. McAllister	____	____	____	____
San Diego, California	Frank E. Curran	____	____	____	____
San Francisco, California	George Christopher	____	____	____	____
Seattle, Washington	Gordon S. Clinton	____	____	____	____
Tampa, Florida	Nick Nuccio	____	____	____	____
Toledo, Ohio	John W. Potter	____	____	____	____
Tulsa, Oklahoma	James M. Hewgley	____	____	____	____

EXHIBIT V PATTERN QUESTIONS

(Phase II Interview Guide)

1. City's History and Current Situation

A. Founded (date).
B. Reasons.
C. Population growth over the years.
D. Reasons.
E. Important facts about the city's history and growth.
F. When the mayor was in office, what was this period like in the city? (Circle one.)

1	2	3	4	5
A period of calm and no major changes				A period with some major changes

G. List below your impression of the more important problems and opportunities that the city faced while he was mayor.

(1)
(2)
(3)
(4)
(5)
(6)
(7)
(8)
(9)
(10)

H. Generalizing now, how would you describe the city's problems in this period. (Circle one number on the scale.)

1 Typical municipal problems—sewage, roads, police, and so on.
2
3 About 50% typical and 50% new or nonroutine problems.
4
5 Very unusual or new problems, or ones that had not been focused on before—pollution, poverty, race relations, and so on.

I. Again generalizing about the problems—

1 Very large in size—that is, the problems were difficult to solve and required a large supply of resources.
2
3 Moderate in size—requiring a moderate outlay of time and resources.
4
5 Fairly small—relatively easy to solve.

J. Generalizing about the opportunities available to the city during this period—

1 Very large in size.
2
3 Moderate in size.
4
5 Fairly small in size.

2. The Formal Organization

A. Describe the present city *charter*, when it was adopted, and why. What was the city council makeup when the mayor was elected?

B. What was the organization of and the effectiveness of the city *bureaucracy* when the mayor took office?

C. Which party was in power at the county, state, and federal levels when the mayor was in office, and historically what has been the city's relationship with these other governments?

3. Sociopolitical Structure

A. Describe the sociopolitical structure of the community. Note the various groups that have some impact on public decisions, their size, the cohesion, the nature of the organization, the quality of their leadership, the values or other distinguishing characteristics, and the nature and size of their power. (If the community does not meaningfully break down in 15 or fewer groups, describe its sociopolitical organization in other terms.) Remember: *size, cohesion, nature of organization, leadership, values, nature and size of power, historical notes* (why it is this way):

(1)
(2)
(3)
(4)
(5)
(6)
(7)
(8)

(9)
(10)
(11)

4. The Mayor

A. What is the mayor's background?

B. How did he get into politics? Why did he win his elections?

C. General comments about the mayor.

D. Choose and circle one number of the scale.

1 The mayor, in a sense, had a personality that was the very personification of his city. He could talk easily and comfortably with all or almost all of the major groups that made up the city. He was able to speak all the "languages" spoken in the city.

2

3 The mayor had a personality that was able to communicate with and was attractive to many, but not all the main population and interest groups in the city. Groups representing from 20 to 50% of the city's population found him somewhat difficult to talk to, to understand, and to trust.

4

5 In a sense, the mayor's personality was the archetype of just one particular group in his town. He had some difficulty relating to other groups that made up perhaps one half of the population or even more. A few of the population groups found his particular personality and style extremely unappealing.

E. Did his "style," or manner of talking to people, vary much depending on whom he was talking to? (Check one.)

Yes, a great deal _____ Some _____ Little or none _____

F. If there was one *very* powerful group in town, how good was the mayor at talking their language? (Check one.)

Excellent ____ Good ____ Fair ____ Poor ____

G. Circle one of the five numbers on the scale.

1 The mayor was an extremely proactive person. He literally was the type of man who stands on the bow of the ship and points the way. He had a tendency to always establish missions and goals. He tried to lead others toward his vision of the future.

2

3 The mayor displayed a tendency toward, and a skill at, proactive or mission setting leadership. He was a somewhat proactive person. He tended to point the way and to actually lead people.

4

5 The mayor was somewhat reactive. He tended to take things as they came at him. He was not the type of person one could describe as being "up front." He tended not to establish a mission or create goals.

H. Circle one of the numbers.

1 The mayor displayed a rather extreme tendency toward what might be called managerial leadership. Given some purpose or goal, he was very skilled at organizing and managing an effort. He had a very strong tendency toward, and skill at, "getting things done" by organizing and managing complex activities.

2

3 The mayor displayed some tendency toward managerial leadership. He had both a tendency and some skill at organizing and managing efforts. He got things done, at least some of the time.

4

5 The mayor did not seem to have much of a managerial or organizational tendency at all. He didn't seem to have a tendency to organize people and resources to get things done. He displayed few, if any, administrative and managerial skills.

I. Again, circle one of the numbers.

1 The mayor was not particularly good with people. He sometimes got impatient with them and had trouble drawing

them together and getting their support. He was sometimes uncomfortable with groups. His political and social skills were not very sharp.

2

3 The mayor was reasonably good with people. He was more comfortable and more skilled at dealing with some types than with others. To a point he enjoyed being with and working with lots of people. He clearly had some social and political skills.

4

5 The mayor displayed extremely sharp social and political skills. He was very good and talented with people. He had a tendency to be with people and to spend time with them without any immediate reason or task. He was very comfortable with people and tended to gain their trust and support quite easily.

J. Circle one number.

1 The mayor's mind was oriented in such a way that he seemed to be able to grasp the complexities and to understand those critical problems and opportunities that faced the city while he was in office.

2

3 The mayor's mind was oriented in such a way that he seemed to have difficulty understanding some of the major problems and opportunities that faced the city while he was in office.

K.

1 The mayor's own conception of his job seemed to be an appropriate definition, given the nature of his city and the problems it faced while he was in office.

2

3 The mayor's own conception of his job seemed to be inappropriate, given the nature of his city and the problems it faced while he was in office.

What was that conception?

L.

1 The mayor's particular orientation with respect to time meshed well with the problems and opportunities he faced while in office. For example, perhaps the major urban issues that arose

were of the short-run crisis nature (a riot), and perhaps the mayor tended to be oriented toward the short run.

2

3 The mayor's particular time orientation did not mesh with the problems and opportunities he faced in office. For example, perhaps he tended to think in terms of operating problems and issues (middle time ranges), but the city faced a great number of long-run problems (rebuilding a ghetto) and short-run crises (a flood).

Comments:

5. Mayor's Role

Briefly, what did the mayor do? What role did he assume? Where did he allocate his time?

6. Direction (Mission Setting Leadership)

A. Did the mayor really try to *lead* the city in some direction?

Yes ________ (go to C)

No ________ (go to B)

Comments:

B. If the mayor provided little or no leadership himself, did he

______(1) Cooperate with major leadership initiatives elsewhere? If yes, who was providing initiatives?

______(2) Ignore or resist mayor leadership efforts elsewhere? If yes, who was providing initiatives?

______(3) Do neither of the above because there were no longer leadership thrusts in the city. The community was "drifting" or static. If you answer yes to this alternative, go next to G.

C. What was it that guided the leadership initiative? (Circle one.)

1 A detailed plan with goals of assigned priorities and methods for accomplishing the goals.

2 An "agenda," or a set of items in order of priority earmarked to change, perhaps surrounded by some theme.
3 Nothing—the initiative was simply the sum of daily decisions.
4 None of the above.

D. Please characterize, as best you can, the plan or agenda or campaign promises or whatever guided the effort.

E. By what process was this particular thrust developed? Describe this in as much detail as possible.

F. Did this thrust change while the mayor was in office? That is, were projects or priorities abandoned or changed in big or small ways? Why did things change, if they did?

G. Did this direction or thrust (or lack of it) ignore any really critical problems that faced the city during this time? Important but not critical problems? Did it ignore any *major* opportunities? (Circle one.)

Really critical problems	Yes	No	If yes, which ones?
Important problems	Yes	No	
Major opportunities	Yes	No	If yes, which ones?

7. Mayor's Staff

A. How could you characterize the mayor's staff? (Check one.)

_____ Because of the structure of the city charter, the mayor did not really have an office or staff.

_____ The mayor's immediate circle of staff and advisors (which could range from 1 to 50 people) could best be described as a "loyal" group. This group, or his "office," as it is sometimes called, was composed of people who in many ways were much like the mayor. While probably not outstanding in any way, they were trustworthy, and some at least worked very hard for him.

_____ The mayor's office contained one or more people who were very talented and important to the mayor. They provided some contacts or skills that the mayor could not really provide by himself. That is, they complemented the mayor in ways that were clearly important to his effectiveness.

______ (Other) __________________________________

B. Describe his staff in more detail.

C. Why did he end up with this staff? (Give reasons or forces.)
(1)
(2)
(3)
(4)
(5)

8. Network

A. (1) Write the names of each of the groups you have identified earlier in the spaces provided on the left-hand side of the table below.
(2) For each of the groups that you have identified and for the six other organizations already on the list, characterize their relationship with the mayor's office in question.
(3) Next characterize the basis of those relationships.
(4) Next characterize how the mayor's office used those relationships.
(5) Finally, note whether anyone on the mayor's staff was particularly central in forming, maintaining, or using each of these relationships.

Group	Relationship to Mayor's Office	Basis of Relationship	Use of Relationship	Mayor's Staff
	Excellent	A = Favors, patronage, financial incentives	A = Financial resources	Was someone in the mayor's office very central in establishing or using the ties with this group?
	Good		B = Information	
	Neutral	B = Charm, friendship, etc.	C = Support at polls	
	Poor	C = Superordinate goals	D = Manpower skills, organization	
	Terrible	D = Coercion		
		E = Results or other	E = Not block project	Yes? No? Who?

Group	Relationship to Mayor's Office	Basis of Relationship	Use of Relationship	Mayor's Staff
City bureaucracy				
City council				
County government				
The press				
State government				
Federal government				

B. Please characterize any changes in the relationships the mayor and his staff had with the various groups that you have previously listed.

1 These relationships became much more favorable for the mayor while he was in office (changed for the better).

2

3 The nature of these relationships overall did not change much while he was in office.

4

5 These relationships overall became much less favorable for the mayor while he was in office (changed for the worse).

C. Did this network of relationships provide the mayor with *access* to sufficient financial resources to deal with the problems and opportunities that the city faced while he was mayor?

Yes 1 2 3 4 5 No

D. Did the mayor have a positive relationship with the "power centers" who could block any attempt to deal with the critical problems and opportunities faced by the city?

Yes 1 2 3 4 5 No

E. Did the mayor's network of relationships provide him with access to the people, talent, organizations, machinery, and so on, that one might need to deal with the major problems and opportunities faced by the city?

Yes 1 2 3 4 5 No

9. Information & Decision Process

A. How would you characterize the process by which the mayor made daily decisions?

B. For each of the groups listed in Section 8, how well was the mayor "plugged into" their thinking, feeling, and so on? How good was the information flow to him? How did he keep in touch?
(1)
(2)
(3)
(4)
(5)
(6)
(7)
(8)
(9)

C. Did the mayor have a key set of advisors that he particularly listened to? Who were they?

10. Cooperation Building Processes

Think for a moment about how the mayor's office formed and maintained positive relationships with the various groups and organizations in and out of the city. For example, they may have used:

A Favors, patronage, financial incentives, (I give you something, you give me support).

B Friendships charm, their pleasant personalities (personal appeal for whatever reason—"nice guy," "he's one of us," etc.).

C An appeal to superordinate goals (such as harmony between the races or a better highway system).

D Coercion and threats (the use of subtle and unsubtle force).

E The results of his administration's actions ("he gets things done").

A. Please rank the five processes described above or others according to how often or how much the mayor and his staff relied on each to create and maintain their favorable relationships.

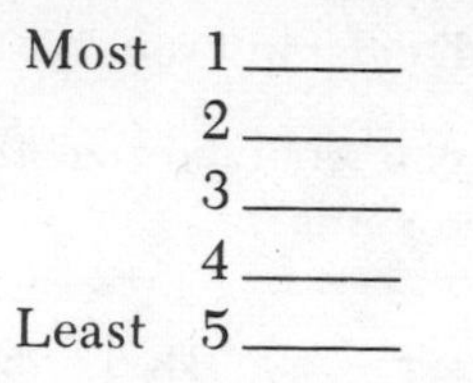

B. Comments (descriptions of how he maintained ties).

C. Why did the mayor establish this particular pattern? List reasons, or forces pushing him toward it.
(1)
(2)
(3)
(4)
(5)
(6)

11. Task Accomplishment

A. Which of the following statements best describe the manner in which the mayor and his staff accomplished large tasks and solved major problems? (Note what percentage of the time the mayor relied on each type).

_____% (a) The mayor relied heavily on the city bureaucracy and on its problem-solving capacities. In many ways he behaved like a manager in a large bureaucratic organization.

_____% (b) The mayor and his staff behaved something like entrepreneurs. Faced with a particular task or problem, they would identify resources and bring them to bear on that task. They called on and utilized a wide variety of groups and organizations, in and out of the city, as well as the city bureaucracy. There was a rather dynamic hustling orientation in the mayor and some of his staff.

_____% (c) The mayor and his staff often tended *not* to act on major tasks and problems. There seemed to be a reluctance on their part to confront problems or to make demands on various people or institutions, or to use their resources.

_____% (d) (Other) ______________________________

B. Comments and *examples* of task accomplishment.

C. Why is it that the mayor established this pattern? (List reasons or forces.)
(1)
(2)
(3)
(4)
(5)

12. Results

A. List the administration's predominant "successes."
(1)
(2)
(3)
(4)
(5)
(6)
(7)
(8)

B. List the administration's predominant "failures."
(1)
(2)
(3)
(4)

(5)
(6)
(7)
(8)

C. Please note how the following aspects of the city changed while the mayor was in office.

(1) The quality of the environment and the physical beauty of the city.

	Low quality				High quality
Before Mayor	1	2	3	4	5
	Very unattractive				Very beautiful
	Low quality				High quality
After Mayor	1	2	3	4	5
	Very unattractive				Very beautiful

(2) The climate of freedom and justice.

	Freedom and justice for few or none				Freedom and justice for all
Before Mayor	1	2	3	4	5
	Freedom and justice for few or none				Freedom and justice for all
After Mayor	1	2	3	4	5

(3) Entertainment opportunities (cultural opportunities and simple amusements such as nightclubs and sports events).

	Few				Many
Before Mayor	1	2	3	4	5
	Few				Many
After Mayor	1	2	3	4	5

APPENDIX B

EXHIBIT I ELECTION RESULTS

1. Atlanta—Ivan Allen, Jr.

1961	(Runoff)
	Allen, 38,820
	Maddox, 20,903 (approx.)
1966	Allen, 53,233
	Smith, 21,907

2. Buffalo—Chester Kowal

1961	Kowal, 70,447
	Sedita, 62,324
	Manz, 51,877
	Others (3), 15,704

3. Cincinnati—Walton Bachrach. *Note:* Council *elected* Bachrach mayor.

1961	Bachrach, 68,092; 1st councilor in field of 37
1963	Bachrach, 74,398; 1st councilor in field of 28
1965	Bachrach, 66,192; 1st councilor in field of 20

4. Cleveland—Ralph Locher.

1962	Special election
	Locher, 74, 526

Corrigan, 16,557
McElny, 46,174
1963 Locher ran unopposed, receiving 156,066
1965 Locher, 87,858
Stokes, 85,716
Perk, 41,045
McAllister, 22,650
1967 Democratic primary
Celeste, 8509
Locher, 92,321
Stokes, 110,552

5. Columbus—W. Ralston Westlake.

1959 Westlake, 52,840
Sensenbrenner, 47,606
1963 Westlake, 53,863
Sensenbrenner, 58,688

6. Dallas—Erik Jonsson. *Note:* Council elects mayor.

1965 Jonsson, 59,348; for council seat 9 Jonsson was the #1 vote getter
Blesseny, 21,353
1967 Jonsson unopposed
1969 Jonsson, 33,683; for council seat 11 Jonsson was the #1 vote getter
Green, 8930

7. Fort Worth—Thomas A. McCann. *Note:* Council elects mayor.

1957 McCann, 31,123; only candidate running for place #6
1959 McCann, 23,079; first in field of 3 for place #6
1961 McCann, 21,518; first in field of 3 for place #6

8. Houston—Louis Welch.

1963 Welch, 45,151
Hervey, 28,910

Curtier, 28,365
Baily, 20,516
Others (2), 6486
1965 Welch, 87,569
Curtier, 24,253
1967 Welch, 97,965
Curtier, 41,829
1969 Welch, 98,110
Graves, 58,773
Nesmith, 24,138
Others (3), 3877
1971 Welch, 141,753
Hofheinz, 126,637

9. Indianapolis—Charles Boswell.

1959 Boswell, 70,031
Sharp, 51,994

10. Jersey City—Thomas Whelan.

1965 Whelan, 57,610
Gangeni, 22,798
Connors, 11,335
1967 Whelan, 43,105; runoff, 50,524
Gangeni, 20,996; runoff, 33,881
Maresca, 11,963

11. Kansas City—H. Roe Bartle.

1955 Bartle, 57,421
Berry, 28,558
1959 Bartle, 53,880
Cowan, 40,425
1963 Bartle defeated in primary

12. Louisville—William O. Cowger.

1961 Cowger, 61,651

Milburn, 50,219

13. Minneapolis—Arthur Naftalin.

1961	Naftalin, 62,642
	Peterson, 57,737
1963	Naftalin, 63,406
	Peterson, 56,829
1965	Naftalin, 56,417
	Leslie, 40,492
1967	Naftalin, 56,623
	Carlson, 53,862

14. New Haven—Richard Lee.

1953	Lee, 39,526
	Celentano, 35,944
1955	Lee, 43,847
	Mancini, 23,039
1957	Lee, 41,694
	Cook, 18,363
1959	Lee, 36,694
	Valenti, 22,710
1961	Lee, 30,638
	Townshend, 26,638
1963	Lee, 33,150
	Townshend, 21,805
1965	Lee, 33,392
	Einhorn, 17,094
1967	Lee, 25,525
	Whitney, 16,582

15. New Orleans—Victor H. Schiro.

1962	Schiro, 52,685; runoff, 94,157
	Duplantier, 57,001; runoff, 73,057
	Others (7), 58,000
1966	Schiro, 81,973
	Fitzmorris, 78,654

Others (3), 2805

16. Newark—Hugh Addonizio.

1962	Addonizio, 62,338
	Carlin, 38,115
	Weiner, 1,375
1966	Addonizio, 45,817; runoff, 49,834
	Carlin, 18,740; runoff, 19,629
	Gibson, 16,114
	Others (3), 13,091

17. Norfolk—Roy Martin, Jr. *Note:* mayor elected by council.

1962	Martin, 13,127; second in field of 9 for council
1966	Martin, 13,161; second in field of 12
1970	Martin, 13,574; fourth in field of 20

18. Rochester, New York—Frank Lamb. *Note:* mayor elected by council.

1961	Lamb, 65,176; first in field of 10 for councilman at large
1965	Lamb, 61,237; first in field of 19
1969	Lamb, 42,230; fourth in field of 15, and not elected mayor

19. San Diego—Frank Curran.

1963	Curran, 25,480; runoff, 96,898
	Goodrich, 23,843; runoff, 55,520
	Casey, 23,178
	Cobb, 7662
	Others (6), 15,560
1967	Curran, 52,355; runoff, 96,597
	Hitch, 36,060; runoff, 47,230
	Others (5), 22,595
1971	Primary election
	Wilson, 57,940
	Bulter, 28,870
	Walsh, 25,546

Curran, 16,743
Others (10), 28,433

20. San Francisco—George Christopher.

1955 Christopher, 162,280
Reilly, 77,085
1959 Christopher, 145,009
Wolden, 92,252

EXHIBIT II EXPERTS' RATINGS

		Category			
City	Mayor	1 (Positive)	2 (Neutral)	3 (Negative)	4 (Don't know)
Atlanta	Allen	8	0	0	0
Buffalo	Kowal	0	1	4	3
Cincinnati	Bachrach	0	2	1	5
Cleveland	Locher	0	0	5	3
Columbus	Westlake	0	1	2	5
Dallas	Jonsson	5	1	0	2
Fort Worth	McCann	0	3	1	4
Houston	Welch	5	0	1	2
Indianapolis	Boswell	0	2	1	5
Jersey City	Whelan	0	1	4	2
Kansas City	Bartle	0	2	3	3
Louisville	Cowger	3	0	0	5
Minneapolis	Naftalin	5	3	0	0
New Haven	Lee	6	2	0	0
New Orleans	Shiro	0	0	3	5
Newark	Addonizio	0	0	8	0
Norfolk	Martin	3	0	0	5
Rochester	Lamb	1	3	0	4
San Diego	Curran	2	3	0	3
San Francisco	Christopher	1	5	0	2

BIBLIOGRAPHY

Aldrich, H. "Organizational Boundaries and Interorganizational Conflicts," *Human Relations*, **24**, No. 4, 1971.

Allen, Ivan, Jr. *Mayor: Notes on the Sixties.* New York: Simon & Schuster, 1971.

Argyris, Chris C. *Personality and Organization.* New York: Harper & Row, 1957.

Assael, H. "Constructive Role of Interorganizational Conflict," *Administrative Science Quarterly*, **14**, No. 4, 1969, p. 573.

Banfield, E. C. *Political Influence.* New York: Free Press, 1961.

Banfield, E. C., and J. Q. Wilson. *City Politics.* Cambridge, Massachusetts: Harvard University Press and Massachusetts Institute of Technology Press, 1963.

Barnard, Chester I. *The Functions of the Executive.* Cambridge, Massachusetts: Harvard University Press, 1938.

Bean, Walton. *Boss Ruef's San Francisco.* Berkeley: University of California Press, 1952.

Blau, Peter. *Exchange and Power in Social Life* New York: Wiley, 1964.

Bower, Joseph. *Managing the Resource Allocation Process.* Homewood, Illinois: Irwin, 1970.

Braybrooke, David, and Charles E. Lindblom. *A Strategy of Decision.* New York: Free Press, 1963.

Buckley, Walter. *Sociology and Modern Systems Theory.* Englewood Cliffs, New Jersey: Prentice-Hall, 1967.

Buckley, William F., Jr. *The Unmaking of a Mayor.* New York: Viking, 1966.

Bullock, Alan *Hitler: A Study in Tyranny.* New York: Harper & Row, 1962.

Burns, T., and G. M. Stalker. *The Management of Innovation.* London: Tavistock Institute, 1961.

Carter, Barbara. *The Road to City Hall.* Englewood Cliffs, New Jersey: Prentice-Hall, 1967.

Chandler, Alfred. *Strategy and Structure.* Cambridge: Massachusetts Institute of Technology Press, 1962.

Clark, B. "Interorganizational Patterns in Education," *Administrative Science Quarterly*, **10**, No. 3, 1968, pp. 224–237.

Committee for Economic Development. *Modernizing Local Government.* New York: 1967.

Committee for Economic Development. *Reshaping Governments in Metropolitan Areas.* New York: 1970.

Cunningham, James V. *Urban Leadership in the Sixties.* Cambridge, Massachusetts: Schenkman Publishing Co., 1970.

Curley, James M. *I'd Do It Again.* Englewood Cliffs, New Jersey: Prentice-Hall, 1957.

Cyert, Richard, and James March. *A Behavioral Theory of the Firm.* Englewood Cliffs, New Jersey: Prentice-Hall, 1967.

Dahl, Robert A. *Who Governs?* New Haven, Connecticut: Yale University Press, 1961.

Dorsey, George. *Christopher of San Francisco.* New York: Macmillan, 1962.

Emery, F. I., and E. L. Trist. "The Casual Texture of Organization Environments," *Human Relations,* **18**, 1965, pp. 1–10.

Etzioni, Amitai. *A Comparative Analysis of Complex Organizations.* New York: Free Press, 1961.

Evan, W. "The Organization Set: Toward a Theory of Interorganizational Relationships," *Approaches to Organization Design.* J. D. Thompson, ed. Pittsburgh: University of Pittsburgh Press, 1966.

Fiedler, F. E. *A Theory of Leadership Effectiveness.* New York: McGraw-Hill, 1967.

Flax, Michael J. *A Study in Comparative Urban Indicators.* Washington, D.C. Urban Institute, 1972.

Fowler, Gene. *Beau James.* New York: Viking, 1949.

Garrett, Charles. *The La Guardia Years, Machine and Reform Politics in New York City.* New Brunswick, New Jersey: Rutgers University Press, 1961.

George, Alexander L. and Juliette L. *Woodrow Wilson and Colonel House: A Personality Study.* New York: Dover, 1964.

Gittell, Marilyn. "A Metropolitan Mayor—A Political Dead End?" *Public Administration Review,* **23**, March 1963, pp. 20–24.

Gottfried, Alex. *Boss Cermak of Chicago.* Seattle: University of Washington Press, 1962.

Guetzkow, H. "Relations Among Organizations," *Studies on Behavior in Organization.* Vol. 1. Joseph Bowers, ed. Athens: University of Georgia Press, 1966.

Hall, Calvin, and Gardner Lindzey. *Theories of Personality.* New York: Wiley, 1970.

Hargrove, Irwin C. "Dramatizing Reform," *Political Leadership in American Government.* James D. Barber, ed. Boston: Little, Brown, 1964, pp. 103–112.

Heskett, J., and L. Stern and F. Beier. "Bases and Uses of Power in Interorganizational Relations," *Vertical Marketing Systems.* Louis Bucklin, ed. Glenview, Illinois: Scott, Foresman, 1970.

Hodge, Robert W., and Paul M. Siegel and Peter H. Rossi. "Occupational Prestige in the United States 1925–1963," *Class, Status and Power.* Reinhard Bendix and Seymour M. Lipset, eds. New York: Free Press, 1966.

Hofstadter, Richard. *The Age of Reform.* New York: Knopf, 1959.

Hunter, Floyd. *Community Power Structure.* Chapel Hill: University of North Carolina Press, 1953.

Kast, F. E., and J. E. Rosenzweig. *Contingency Views of Organization of Management.* Chicago: Science Research Associates, 1973.

Keen, Peter, and James McKenney. "The Evolution of an Experimental Design for the

Study of Cognitive Style," Harvard Business School, Working Paper #1687, January 1973.

Kotter, J. P., and P. R. Lawrence. "The Mayor: An Interim Report," Harvard Business School, Working Paper #72-27, 1972.

Kotter, J. P., and C. Allen. "A Model of Organizing a Comprehensive Community Health System," unpublished paper, 1971.

Kotter, J. P. "The Psychological Contract," *California Management Review*, Spring 1973.

Kuhn, Thomas. *Structure of Scientific Revolutions.* Chicago: University of Chicago Press, 1970.

Lawrence, Paul, and Jay Lorsch. *Organization and Environment.* Boston: Division of Research, Harvard Business School, 1967.

Leavitt, Harold. *New Perspectives in Organizational Research.* New York: Wiley, 1964.

Leavitt, Harold. "Unhuman Organizations," *Harvard Business Review*, July–August 1962.

Levine, S., and P. White. "Exchange as a Conceptual Framework for the Study of Interorganizational Relations," *Administrative Science Quarterly*, 5, 1961, pp. 583–601.

Levinson, H., et al. *Men, Management and Mental Health.* Cambridge, Massachusetts: Harvard University Press, 1962.

Likert, Rensis. *New Patterns of Management.* New York: McGraw-Hill, 1961.

Lindsay, John V. *Journey into Politics.* New York: Dodd, Mead, 1967.

Litwak, E., and L. F. Hylton. "Interorganizational Analysis: A Hypothesis on Coordinating Agencies," *Administrative Science Quarterly*, 6, 1962, pp. 395–420.

Litwak, E., and H. Meyer. "A Balance Theory of Coordination Between Bureaucratic Organizations and Community Primary Groups," *Administrative Science Quarterly*, 11, No. 1, 1966, p. 31.

McKean, Dayton D. *The Boss: The Hague Machine in Action.* Boston: Houghton Mifflin, 1940.

McKenney, James. *The Taxonomy of Problem Solving.* Harvard Business School, Working Paper #1689, 1973.

Maddi, Salvatore R. *Personality Theories.* Homewood, Illinois: Dorsey, 1968.

Maier, Henry. *Challenge to the Cities.* New York: Random House, 1966.

Mann, Arthur. *La Guardia Comes to Power: 1933.* Philadelphia and New York: Lippincott, 1965.

March, J. G., and H. A. Simon, *Organizations.* New York: Wiley, 1958.

Paige, G. D., ed. *Political Leadership.* New York: Free Press, 1972.

Parsons, Talcott. *Economy and Society.* New York: Free Press, 1957.

Perrow, Charles. *Organizational Analysis. A Sociological View.* Belmont, California: Wadsworth, 1970.

Pilat, Oliver. *Lindsay's Campaign.* Boston: Beacon Press, 1968.

Report of the National Advisory Commission on Civil Disorders. New York: Bantam Books, 1968.

Ridgeway, V. F. "Administration of Manufacturer-Dealer Relations," *Administrative Science Quarterly*, 1, No. 4, 1957, p. 464.

Rosenbloom, R. S., and R. Marris. *Social Innovation in the City.* Cambridge,

Massachusetts: Harvard University Press, 1969.

Rosenbloom, R. S., and J. R. Russell. *New Tools for Urban Management.* Boston: Harvard Graduate School of Business, 1971.

Ruchleman, Leonard, ed. *Big City Mayors.* Bloomington: Indiana University Press, 1969.

Salisbury, Robert H. "Urban Politics: The New Convergence of Power," *Journal of Politics,* **26,** November 1964, p. 782.

Schumpeter, Joseph A. *Capitalism, Socialism, and Democracy.* New York: Harper & Row, 1947.

Schumpeter, Joseph A. "Economic Theory and Entrepreneurial History," *Explorations in Enterprise.* G. J. Aitken, ed. Cambridge, Massachusetts: Harvard University Press, 1965.

Schein, Edgar. *Organizational Psychology.* Englewood Cliffs, New Jersey: Prentice-Hall, 1965.

Selznick, Philip. *TVA and the Grass Roots.* Berkeley: University of California Press, 1949.

Talbot, Allan R. *The Mayor's Game.* New York: Harper & Row, 1967.

Terreberry, S. "The Evolution of Organizational Environment," *Administrative Science Quarterly,* **12,** 1968, pp. 590–613.

Thompson, James. *Organizations in Action.* New York: McGraw-Hill, 1967.

Thompson, J., and W. McEwen. "Organizational Goals and Environment," *American Sociological Review,* **23,** 1958, pp. 23–31.

Trist, E. L., and G. W. Higgin, H. Murray, and H. B. Pollock. *Organizational Choice.* London: Tavistock Institute, 1963.

Turk, H. "Interorganizational Networks in Urban Society," *Administrative Science Quarterly,* **35,** No. 1, 1970, pp. 1–19.

Udy, Stanley. *Organization of Work: A Comparative Analysis of Production Among Non-Industrial Peoples.* New Haven, Connecticut: HRAF Press, 1959.

von Neumann, John, and Oscar Morgenstern. *Theory of Games and Economic Behavior.* Princeton: Princeton University Press, 1944.

Vroom, Victor. *Some Personality Determinants of the Effects of Participation.* Englewood Cliffs, New Jersey: Prentice-Hall, 1960.

Warren, R. "The Interorganizational Field as a Focus for Investigation," *Administrative Science Quarterly,* **12,** 1967, pp. 396–419.

Wendt, Lloyd, and Herman Kogan. *Big Bill of Chicago.* Indianapolis: Bobbs-Merrill, 1953.

Woodward, Joan. *Industrial Organization: Theory and Practice.* London: Oxford University Press, 1965.

AUTHOR INDEX

SUBJECT INDEX